Cultural Analytics

Cultural Analytics

Lev Manovich

The MIT Press
Cambridge, Massachusetts
London, England

This book was set in ITC Stone Serif Std and ITC Stone Sans Std by New Best-set Typesetters Ltd. Printed and bound in the United States of America.

Library of Congress Cataloging-in-Publication Data

Names: Manovich, Lev, author.
Title: Cultural analytics / Lev Manovich.
Description: Cambridge, Massachusetts : The MIT Press, [2020] | Includes bibliographical
    references and index.
Identifiers: LCCN 2020003045 | ISBN 9780262037105 (hardcover)
Subjects: LCSH: Culture—Research—Statistical methods. | Culture—Research—Data processing.
    | Mass media—Research—Statistical methods. | Mass media—Research—Data processing. |
    Information visualization.
Classification: LCC HM623 .M365 2020 | DDC 306.0285—dc23
LC record available at https://lccn.loc.gov/2020003045

10 9 8 7 6 5 4 3 2

Contents

Acknowledgments

I am very grateful to all the people and institutions that made this book possible:

The MIT Press: Doug Sery, senior acquisitions editor, Noah Springer, assistant acquisitions editor, Kathleen Caruso, manuscript editor, and Melinda Rankin, copyeditor.

Larry Star, director of the California Institute for Telecommunications and Information Technology (Calit2), Ramesh Rao, director of the UCSD Division of Calit2, and all the staff at Calit2, which has been supporting the work of our lab since its start in 2007.

Noah Wardrip-Fruin, who cofounded Software Studies Initiative (later renamed Cultural Analytics Lab) with me in 2007. Sheldon Brown, who invited us to the Center for Research in Computing and the Arts, which became our lab's home from 2008 to 2012. Mathew Gold who supported my work at The Graduate Center, CUNY, after I started teaching there in 2013.

Lab members, 2007–2018: Jeremy Douglass, William Huber, Tara Zepel, Cicero Inacio da Silva, Jay Chow, Everardo Reyes, Mehrdad Yazdani, Damon Crockett, Nadav Hochman, Alise Tifentale, and Agustin Indaco.

Lab collaborators and visiting fellows: Moritz Stefaner, Dominikus Baur, Daniel Goddemeyer, Miriam Redi, Nadav Hochman, Almila Akdag, Jean-François Lucas, Tristan Thielmann, Hijoo Son, Kay O'Halloran, Isabel Galhano Rodrigues, Falko Kuester, Jim Hollan, Matthew Fuller, Brynn Shepherd, and Leah Meisterlin.

Graduate and undergraduate students who worked in the lab: So Yamaoka, Sunsern Cheamanunku, Matias Giachino, Xiangfei Zeng, Cherie Huang, Chanda L. Carey, Daniel Rehn, Laura Hoeger, Rachel Cody, Devon Merill, Jia Gu, Agatha Man, Nichol Bernardo, Bob Li, Kedar Reddy, Christa Lee, Victoria Azurin, Xiaoda Wang, and Nadia Xiangfei Zeng.

The organizers of the UCLA IPAM Culture Analytics Institute (2016): Timothy Tangherlini, Tina Eliassi-Rad, Mauro Maggioni, and Vwani Roychowdhury.

The universities and educational programs where I have been permanent or visiting faculty between 2005 and 2020 (from the moment I first thought of cultural analytics to finishing this book): University of California, San Diego (UCSD); The Graduate Center, City University of New York (CUNY), National University of Singapore (NUS); Strelka Institute for Media, Architecture and Design; the European Graduate School (EGS); and the Institute of Social Sciences and Humanities, Tyumen State University (UTMN).

Illustrations

Examples of projects from our lab are used throughout the book to illustrate the concepts and techniques being presented. In my classes and workshops, I use the same approach because it allows me to show students the concrete steps involved in creating such projects, to discuss the multiple choices each step entails, and to point out what remained outside the analysis. Each of our projects has its own website or a web page where you will find descriptions, high-resolution color visualizations, and in some cases interactive interfaces with the datasets. You can access them from the Projects page of the Cultural Analytics Lab website:

http://lab.culturalanalytics.info/p/projects.html

Note that although some of the visualizations appear in the book as color plates and others as grayscale figures, the originals are all in full color. Most of the visualizations are the result of joint work between lab members, with a few people working on each project—creating the data, analyzing it and interpreting results, and making visualizations.

Introduction: How to See One Billion Images

The impact of the computer in the human sciences, however, is likely proportionally to be more revolutionary in the long run [than in physical and life sciences]. . . . Some of it has to do simply with willingness to take advantage of the opportunity, or predisposition through already extensive use of processes, especially statistical, facilitated by the computer. More, perhaps, has to do with what a computer, in a sense like a telescope or a microscope, can enable us to *see*. In simplest terms, computer processing, properly prepared, can enable us to see relations and patterns in masses of data previously too large to comprehend; and to see the literal consequences of an idea applied to data, if not uniquely, then certainly far more inexorably and quickly.

—Dell H. Hymes, "Introduction," in *The Use of Computers in Anthropology*, 1965[1]

This book is situated at the intersection of data science, media studies, and digital culture studies. It presents selected concepts and methods for computational analysis of cultural data. These methods can be used to explore digitized historical artifacts and contemporary digital media. While we can apply them to a single or a few artifacts, they become especially important if we want to explore millions of artifacts.

In fact, the astonishing scale of digital culture is what motivated me to start exploring these methods in 2005 and eventually write this book. How can we understand contemporary popular photography that grows by billions of images every day? Or contemporary music as represented by hundreds of millions of songs shared by twenty million creators on SoundCloud? Or the content of four billion boards on Pinterest?[2] Or patterns in the intellectual interests of people in 190 countries as represented by 330,000 Meetup groups and 84,000 events per month (as of 2019)?[3] This is also "digital culture" because these physical events are enabled by the Meetup web platform. In my view, the only possible way to study the patterns, trends, and dynamics of contemporary culture at that scale is to use data science methods.

You do not need to have a background in data science, programming, statistics, or math to use this book. My intended audiences are academic researchers and students in art, design, the humanities, social sciences, media studies, data science, and computer science; professionals working in design, photography, film, urban design, architecture, journalism, museum and library fields, curating, and culture management; and everybody who works with social media and the web in any role (creator, blogger, strategist, manager, developer, marketer, etc.).

Even if you have no interest in analyzing cultural datasets yourself, you are encountering such analysis on a daily basis. Maybe you are looking at your Facebook, Instagram, or Weibo analytics, or Google Analytics for your blog or website, or using a social media monitoring dashboard at work. And if you don't pay attention to such data, you are constantly interacting with the results of computational analysis when you do anything digital. For example, every time you capture a photo, the phone camera algorithms automatically choose the exposure and adjust the contrast of the photo and also identify the type of scene and objects in the photo.[4] Computational analysis of media artifacts and user interactions is what enables web search, recommendations, filtering, customization, interactions with digital devices, behavioral advertising, and other operations that form the "vocabulary" of digital culture. For example, web search engines such as Baidu, Bing, Yandex, or Google rely on continuous computational analysis of contents of billions of web pages, online images, and other web content to bring you relevant results.

I think that to be literate in such a society, you need to know the core ideas and principles that make such operations possible. This book is a gentle, nontechnical introduction to some of these ideas. Thus, it teaches you how you can explore cultural datasets yourself and also explains how our society thinks using data and algorithms.

Looking at Culture with Computers

In this book, you will find many examples of computational culture analysis from many researchers and also from my own lab. Right now, I want to describe two examples to illustrate the possibilities and challenges of this analysis.

The first example is the project *Elsewhere* that my collaborators and I have been working on since 2018. The project investigates the growth and diffusion of contemporary culture, taking into account many smaller cities, as opposed to only a handful of global capitals. Today, a small selection of these capitals gets a disproportional amount of attention in media, research studies, and various ratings. Therefore, it is easy to assume that a handful of "top" cities continue to act as the "centers" and the rest of the world is still on the periphery, receiving new ideas after a delay. But what is the real picture? How did globalization and the rise of new communication technologies change the geography of culture? Can we find every contemporary cultural trend today in thousands of smaller cities? Is it possible that some of these cities are more culturally innovative precisely because of their distance from the capital and their smaller size? Are there big parts of the world left today that are not aware of these trends and do not innovate? How has contemporary culture developed and diffused around the world since the beginning of globalization? Was the growth even or uneven, accelerating or slowing down in some periods? Are the growth patterns the same for different cultural fields, or does each of them develop in its own way?

Certainly, no one project can answer all these questions. The goal of *Elsewhere* is to develop and a test a new methodology that uses public data about cultural events and the places that organize these events. The numbers of these places and events in the world today have become so large that we can now to treat them as "big data"—and use data science methods for their analysis. This perspective should allow us to create much more detailed maps and timelines of contemporary culture than what is provided in existing studies of culture industries or lists of cultural institutions. We also run text analytics on all texts that organizers publish about their events: descriptions of millions of exhibitions, lectures, workshops, festivals, meetings of interest groups, and other event types. This will allow us to look for patterns in themes, interests, and "keywords" across geographies and over long time periods.

Figure I.1 shows growth in the numbers of cultural events over time using selected platforms and networks via which such events are promoted or organized. Together, our dataset, assembled from events announcements on six such platforms and networks, contains 4,380,946 events in 21,072 cities in 200 countries on six continents. These platforms and networks are Behance, E-Flux, Arts and Education Network, Meetup, TED Local Events, and TimePad. (In the case of Behance, an *event* is the registration of a new user account.)

As we see in the graphs, the numbers of cultural events on each platform and network have been growing over time. For 2006, our dataset has 11,642 events (adding all sources together); for 2009, it has already 102,211 events; and for 2018, it has 781,697 events. Of course, there is one single global platform that lists all cultural events, and we have to be careful in generalizing the results obtained from our particular sources. This project exemplifies the challenges of using digital phenomena to learn about other phenomena. Does the growth we see in all six data sources over time represent the real growth of cultural events in many countries? Or is it only a sign of diffusion of digital culture itself, showing that more organizations in more countries were gradually

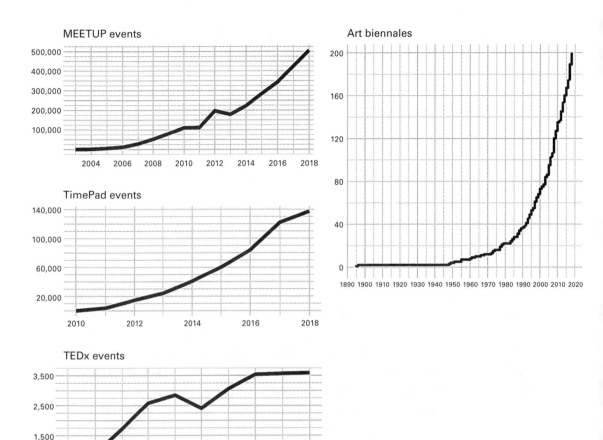

Figure I.1
Growth of numbers of cultural events over time as represented by particular data sources from the *Elsewhere* project.

using the platforms and networks we chose to look at to promote their events? Or do we simply see the winner-takes-all effect, in which certain information platforms become dominant and everybody starts using them? It is likely that all these effects are presented in our data. Some of the growth over time we see is due to the increasing popularity of the platforms themselves. Other growth reflects a real increase in the numbers of cultural places, actors, and events.

Elsewhere uses dates, locations, categories, and text content of the events announcements. In the second example I want to describe, we are looking at actual media artifacts using data science and visualization. The goal is to be able to study various contemporary cultural fields by looking at many more works than media studies examine normally. The project in question is One Million Manga Pages that Jeremy Douglass, Wiliam Huber, and I started to work on in 2009. Figure I.2 shows one of the visualizations we created while exploring a dataset of 1,074,790 unique pages from 883 manga series. The pages come from the most popular fan manga site at that time—OneManga (onemanga.com). The site contained most pages for these series that fans scanned and translated into multiple languages.

The longest running manga series available on OneManga has been published continuously since 1976. The most popular series on this site were *Naruto* (8,835 pages for the 1999–2009 period) and *One Piece* (10,562 pages for the 1997–2009 period). Along with such long manga series, our dataset also contains shorter series that appeared in the 2000s and only ran for one to three years.

We used our own image analysis software to measure each page, converting its selected visual characteristics into numerical features. The visualization maps the pages onto x- and y-axes according to two of these features. The x-axis represents the standard deviation of the pixels' grayscale values, measured per page. The y-axis represents the entropy of all the pixels' grayscale values, also measured per page. What do these measurements mean in practice? The pages in the bottom part of the visualization are the most graphic and have the least amount of detail. The pages in the upper right have lots of detail and texture. The pages with the highest contrast are on the right, while pages with the least contrast are on the left.

In between these four extremes, we find every possible stylistic variation. This suggests to me that our basic concept of "style" may not be appropriate when we consider large cultural datasets. The concept assumes that we can partition a set of cultural artifacts into a small number of discrete categories. In the case of our One Million Manga Pages dataset, we find practically infinite graphical variations. If we try to divide this space into discrete stylistic categories, any such attempt will be arbitrary.

Visualization also shows which graphical choices are more commonly used by manga artists (the central part of the "cloud" of pages) and which appear much more rarely (bottom and left parts). We can ask why manga evolved in particular ways visually, with some choices used very frequently, others less frequently, and others almost never. And if we want to understand the visual originality of a new manga series (as represented by selected visual features we can measure), we can add its pages to such a visualization and—if we like—even quantify this originality. Later in the book, I present another analysis of this dataset, looking at connections between visual styles, gender of manga audiences, and manga genres (see figures 7.1 and 7.2 and plate 9).

Figure I.2
Visualization of 1,074,790 manga pages sorted by two visual characteristics algorithmically computed on every page: standard deviation of grayscale values (x-axis) and entropy of grayscale values (y-axis).

Cultural Analytics: Five Ideas

I first started to think about analyzing and visualizing patterns in contemporary digital culture on a large scale in the fall of 2005. At that time, were there already examples of computational analysis of collections of websites and blogs carried out by researchers in computer science. However, computer science is a huge field with dozens of sub-fields. This research was appearing in journals and conferences of various subfields and did not have its own unique name. In the humanities, the term *digital humanities*, first introduced in 2003, was becoming known. But here as well, computational analysis of cultural datasets was only one part of this emerging larger field, which also included digitization and publication of historical collections, using digital tools in teaching, and other activities. The term "digital humanities" also had another limitation for me: digital humanities scholars were working almost exclusively with datasets of historical literary texts as opposed to other types of media or contemporary digital culture—so this term was both too broad and too narrow. Finally, I already knew of a number of very impressive artistic and design projects that visualized large cultural datasets, but this work was done outside the academic departments and also did not have a single term describing it.

In my mind, the existing work on analyzing and visualizing large-scale cultural data I saw happening across a number of fields was creating a new research paradigm—but it did not have its own name. I felt the need for a term that can refer to computational analysis of patterns and trends in *contemporary digital culture* (as opposed to only his-torical culture) and can cover analysis of all kinds of media (as opposed to only texts). When we were establishing our own lab to do this research in spring 2007,[5] I came up with the term *cultural analytics*.

Our lab pursued two goals. The first was practical: using methods from computer science, data visualization, and media art to explore and analyze different kinds of contemporary media and user interactions with them. The second was theoretical: we asked how the use of such methods and large datasets of cultural media challenges our existing modern ideas about culture and methods to study it. What exactly are the new possibilities they offer, and can they work with any kind of media? What are the limita-tions of computational methods and large-scale analysis?

In practice, our lab focused on analyzing and visualizing patterns in visual data-sets, such as millions of photos shared on Instagram and Twitter, a million pages from manga publications, dozens of feature films, and thousands of magazine covers. This focus led many people who were following our work to associate cultural analytics with the use of computation and visualization for exploration of large visual collections. In the last few years, the term *cultural analytics* (or *culture analytics*) started to be used more broadly by many other academics, as exemplified by two symposiums;[6] a four-month-long research program at UCLA in 2016 that brought together 120 leading researchers from universities and industry labs;[7] an academic peer-review journal, *Journal of Cultural Analytics*, established in 2016;[8] the use of the term in calls for conferences and academic job listings; and a number of academic programs and particular undergraduate and graduate courses.

In September 2019, I looked at these programs and courses: the Cultural Analytics BA course at King's College, London (UK); the cultural analytics concentration in the master of science in informatics and analytics at the University of North Carolina (US); the cultural analytics graduate certificate at Temple University libraries (US); the Center for Cultural Analytics at University College Dublin (Ireland); the Cultural Analytics course at Dartmouth College (US); the MA in data, culture and visualization at ITMO University (Russia); Cultural Analytics: The Computational Study of Culture, a course at McGill University (Canada); the CulturePlex Lab at Western University (Canada), which is doing research on "culture analytics and digital innovation"; the Distant Reading and Cultural Analytics course at the University of California, Los Angeles (US) and Cultural Data Analytics lab at Tallinn University (Estonia). The descriptions of all these programs and courses are using the term "cultural analytics" in a variety of ways related to the institutional context in which they are offered (e.g., a literature department, an information science department, etc.).

Looking at the papers published during its first three years by *Journal of Cultural Analytics*, we similarly see a range of subjects—although analysis of literary texts does dominate over other types of media. These subjects include nineteenth-century and contemporary English-language novels, nineteenth-century illustrated newspapers, late imperial Chinese literature, folklore classifications, menus of restaurants in the United States, and US television series.[9]

The term "cultural analytics" may mean different things to different people, and it can be used in different contexts to do different work. This is fine, and I am not interested in controlling its usage. This book does not try to summarize all cultural analytics research or to cover everything that is relevant to such research (e.g., inferential statistics, experiment design, supervised and unsupervised machine learning, text analysis, geospatial analysis, music data analysis, network analysis, agent-based simulation, and other topics that I do not discuss). Rather than trying to make an encyclopedia covering every relevant topic and technique, I decided instead to focus on a smaller number of topics and explore them in more depth.

The choice of these topics reflects the original motivations that led me to research how computers can help us see contemporary culture; my experience since 2008 of working on over forty practical projects in our lab; teaching practical cultural analytics every year in all my university classes since 2006 to undergraduate and graduate students; conducting many workshops in different countries; and learning from collaborations with other academic researchers and designers. You can see all the topics I included by consulting the table of contents. The topic organization follows a logical progression. Part I gives examples of computational cultural analysis and discusses the shift from "new media" of the 1990s to "more media" of 2000s, which motivated me to start thinking about cultural analytics. In part II, I discuss types of cultural data and techniques for representing cultural processes as computational data. Part III introduces concepts for exploring cultural datasets using data visualization and then focuses on recently developed methods for exploration of image and video collections.

Among all the topics and ideas presented in this book, there are five that I am most passionate about. Taken together, they describe a version of cultural analytics explored in this book—but other versions, visions, uses, and definitions of the term are certainly welcomed. Here are these five ideas:

(1) My original motivation for turning to computational methods and big data came from realization that the scale of culture in the twenty-first century makes it impossible to see it with existing methods. Therefore, in this book *cultural analytics refers to the use of computational and design methods—including data visualization, media and interaction design, statistics, and machine learning—for exploration and analysis of contemporary culture at scale.* One goal of these explorations is to *enable us to see what hundreds of millions of people around the world today create, imagine, and value.* This includes cultural activities of both normal people and professionals and students in creative industry: think of hundreds of design weeks and fashion weeks happening every year, thousands of film festivals, tens of thousands of educational programs, hundreds of thousands of cultural projects and exhibitions that announce themselves on the web and in social media, and so on. Thus, the key practical goal of cultural analytics for me is to work toward a more inclusive and democratic understanding of the cultural present and also of cultural histories. This means making fully visible the "long tail" of cultural life—and placing on our culture maps cities, countries, groups, individual creators, and artifacts that have been left out from both contemporary and historical cultural narratives.

The second goal is to come up with *new theoretical concepts* appropriate for the scale, speed, diversity, and connectedness of contemporary global digital culture. How is this different from twentieth-century culture theory? Our new concepts should be not only theoretical but also *qualitative*; that is, they should allow us to measure dimensions of digital culture and compare styles, taste, imagination, and cultural behaviors in many geographic places, networks, and creative fields. (This means that we may also want to formalize and quantify existing concepts—such as, for example, *style*.) But we also need to be thinking about the limits of such quantification and be sensitive to dimensions and aspects of culture that existing measurements do not capture.

(2) The use of numerical representation and data analysis and visualization methods offers a new language for describing cultural artifacts, experiences, and dynamics. As I argue in chapter 7, the human languages that developed rather recently in human evolution are not good at capturing analog properties of human sensorial and cultural experiences. These limitations become particularly worrying if we want to compare thousands, millions, or billions of artifacts—that is, to study contemporary culture at its new scale. When we instead use numbers and visualization, we can better capture small differences between lots of artifacts and also between groups of artifacts. (Here data science, which has many methods to characterize relations between any number of objects—cluster analysis, dimension reduction, network analysis, and so on—becomes particularly relevant.)

Numbers and visualization also give us a language to represent *gradual and continuous temporal changes*. We can now describe the characteristics of cultural processes that are hard to capture linguistically—for example, gradual historical changes in visual culture over long periods or temporal changes in visual form in the career of an artist.

Given my commitment to analysis of visual culture, I contend that having a better language to describe its *analog dimensions* is invaluable. Digital computers that operate on numerical representations can better capture these dimensions that natural languages cannot describe adequately, such as motion or rhythm.

(3) While many ideas and discussions in the book are relevant for working with all kinds of data, I pay particular attention to *visual media*. I want to demonstrate through many examples how we can use computational and visualization methods to explore visual collections, asking interesting cultural questions. The larger portion of the computational work in the humanities so far has focused on literary texts, historical text records, and spatial data. In contrast, other types of media, such as still and moving images and interactive media, have received relatively little attention. This situation is gradually improving, but as I am writing this, analysis of visual media is still a small part of digital humanities.[10] You can see this yourself by browsing programs of annual conferences organized by the Alliance of Digital Humanities Organizations or by looking at the field journals. The field limitations are well summarized by the title of an

article published in 2017 in the *Digital Scholarship in the Humanities* journal: "Digital Humanities Is Text Heavy, Visualization Light, and Simulation Poor."[11]

This is surprising because computer scientists had already started to develop methods for analysis of images at the end of 1950s. Today they are implemented in numerous digital services and devices, including web image search engines, standalone photo cameras and cameras in mobile phones, image editing software such as Photoshop, image sharing networks, and so on. In computer science fields called computer vision and multimedia computing, researchers for many years have been publishing new algorithms for automatic detection of image content, artistic styles, photographic techniques, genres of TV and video, and applying them to progressively larger datasets.[12] In our lab, we have been using some of these methods to analyze many types of both historical and contemporary visual media—for example, twenty thousand photographs from the collection in the Museum of Modern Art (MoMA) in New York, films by Dziga Vertov from the Austrian Film Museum, sixteen million images shared on Instagram in seventeen global cities, 270 million images shared on Twitter globally, one million manga pages, and one million artworks from popular art network DeviantArt. In this book, I will refer to the details of some of these projects and to papers and work of other researchers (typically in computer science) who analyze visual content using algorithms.

(4) Can we explore and study collections of cultural media and records of cultural behaviors *without systems of categories* that languages impose on reality? Can we *avoid the quantification, measurements, and summarization* that comes with the use of statistics? Can we study big cultural data *without using numbers?*

The seemingly obvious answer to these questions is no. But the answer given by cultural analytics is yes (at least for some types of media, such as images and video). Any numerical measurements, linguistic categories, sets of tags, networks, or other *forms of representation*—regardless of their descriptive power and capacity to make visible similarities and other forms of relations between objects—are also *forms of omission.* For example, computer vision techniques today are able to detect thousands of object types in photographs[13]—but any art student or professional photographer knows that a photo is not simply a collection of objects or human figures in it. Rather than replacing human cultural observers with algorithms, the intention of cultural analytics is to augment our human abilities by *providing new interfaces and techniques for observing massive cultural datasets and flows.* (This is consistent with the vision of computing developed by Douglas C. Engelbart in his famous report from 1962, "Augmenting Human Intellect."[14]) Humans can notice more meaningful dimensions, recognize small details that really matter, and place information in more contexts than any algorithm at this point, and unless the work on "artificial general intelligence" progresses sufficiently, this will remain true for the indefinite future. But can we extend these human capacities to deal with the scale of global cultural production and participation? In short: How can we see (for example) one billion images?

(5) Cultural analytics includes not only the application of currently available computational methods for data analysis to cultural datasets and flows, but also *critical examination of these data science methods and their assumptions*. Today our interactions with digital media, our access to information and each other in social networks, is mediated by software systems. They continuously analyze "big cultural data"—that is, the content of billions of media artifacts we share, our online interactions with these artifacts, and our other online and physical behaviors. In cultural analytics research, we often use similar methods for different purposes—for example, seeing patterns in cultural history, exploring the work of contemporary designers, and examining the content and styles of photos shared by billions of people online. What are the similarities and differences between the use of these methods in industry and in cultural research? Are there some assumptions and goals built into methods that are widely used in industry that we need to question if we adopt them? What historical developments led to the popularity of certain methods today? Addressing such questions is also the key part of the cultural analytics agenda.

Critical examination of data science and algorithms and data use in society in general also takes place in a number of research fields, including science and technology studies, digital humanities, digital culture studies, critical algorithm and data studies,[15] and software studies. Among many academic journals in social science and the humanities that publish articles about these topics, I can highlight *Big Data & Society*. I advise you to look at publications and conferences in these fields and read the papers that look particularly relevant to your interests.

Throughout this book, I will discuss what I personally see as the *most interesting and promising research directions in cultural analytics*. By *interesting*, I mean the analysis that allows us to think of contemporary culture in new ways and helps us to question concepts and methods for studying culture that we take for granted. Some of these directions can be illustrated by existing work, while others have not yet been pursued. So, if you are going to get into cultural analytics, I hope that you will find interesting ideas in this book for new things to try.

Cultural analytics is only one among the paradigms that emerged in the second part of the 2000s to take advantage of the availability of large cultural and social data. These include digital humanities, computational social science, social computing, digital anthropology, digital history, the science of cities, urban informatics, and culturomics.[16] At the same time, big cultural datasets started to be analyzed and used in many areas of computer science, such as machine learning, AI, computer vision, natural language processing, and computer multimedia, as well as in network science and communication studies. In the early 2010s, the "quantitative turn" began in art history, with *International Journal for Digital Art History* starting its publication in 2015. In film studies, the first monograph that uses quantitative methods and data visualization to analyze works of a single film director appeared in 2018.[17]

In the same decade, a number of new research agendas emerged to address the growing use of algorithms, data, and artificial intelligence (AI) systems from the perspectives of social sciences and humanities. These research areas include machine behavior, and the already mentioned algorithm studies and critical data studies. (The 2017 open access anthology *The Datafied Society: Studying Culture through Data* collects a number of articles addressing methodological and ethical questions related to the use of data and algorithms in academic research.[18])

The research we undertook in our lab developed as a dialog with the work by researchers in such fields and all relevant projects I saw, and that research would not have been possible without everything I was learning from them. The goal of this book is not to draw a boundary around the field or to claim that we are the only ones who did research on particular topics. Cultural analytics for me is the instrument to question all categorical boundaries, so certainly it also would not be wise to draw a border around all cultural analytics research taking place across many academic and professional fields.

Cultural Analytics: Twelve Research Challenges

My thinking about cultural analytics and work in our lab has been guided by a list of theoretical and practical challenges that I defined around the time the lab was created. Only some of these questions will be discussed in detail in this book: they are the ones that I ended up spending more energy and time on. But I want to give you the full list because these questions can be also useful to you in your work. I made a list of first eight challenges in 2005–2007 (questions 1–8 below); after years of research, the new challenges become apparent (questions 9–12):

1. How can work with "big cultural data" help us questions our stereotypes, assumptions, concepts, and existing knowledge about cultures?

2. What are the fundamental new ways of understanding and studying visual and media cultures enabled by computational methods and large datasets?

3. How can we explore massive visual collections that may contain billions of images and video?

4. How can we combine computational media analysis with qualitative media studies methods and theories?

5. How do we use computational approaches to analyze interactive media and experiences (e.g., playing a video game, interacting with the Instagram app, experiencing an interactive installation), as opposed to only static media artifacts?

6. What theoretical concepts and models do we need to deal with the mega scale and velocity of user-generated content and user interactions online?

7. How can we analyze and visualize the diversity of contemporary global digital cultures, taking into account the activities of billions of creators and trillions of objects they are creating?

8. What will the "science of culture" driven by massive cultural datasets and computation look like, and what will its limitations be?

9. Can we define general quantitative measures of cultural variability, diversity, temporal change, difference, influence, and uniqueness that will be meaningful for many types of media and different periods and cultures—and in particular our own period?

10. Given that statistical and data science methods are based on data reduction and summarization, how can we also analyze computationally small differences and unique details of individual artifacts and experiences?

11. Can we describe cultures—both objectively and as we perceive them—as statistical distributions and combinations of elements, themes, and strategies? Or is culture about gestalts not reducible to their parts? (If the answer to the second question is yes, this may make cultural analytics impossible.)

12. Let's assume that we can detect a small number of themes, topics, styles, and cultural techniques in billions of cultural artifacts, experiences, and interactions. Let's further assume that we track these culture DNAs across the world, adding new ones when we detect these. What level of reduction is appropriate when we extract small number of topics from billions of cultural "objects," and what is lost at each level? For example, how much information is lost if we extract 10,000 topics, and then aggregate them into 1,000 topics, and then aggregate this data again to have only 100 topics? Is reduction a wrong approach? If contemporary authors want to create unique artifacts and experiences that cannot be duplicated, will we inevitably miss true uniqueness in our quest to track larger trends?

I see this last challenge as the most important. Should we aggregate big cultural data and reduce it to a smaller number of structures—only the most frequently occurring ideas, themes, styles, patterns, and behaviors? This is the paradigm we inherited from the history of statistics, and many quantitative studies of culture in computer science follow it. In this paradigm, we focus on what is common between a number of objects, and we do not include what occurs infrequently. Or should we develop the opposite paradigm—refuse aggregation and reduction, and instead focus on diversity, variability, and differences among numerous artifacts, behaviors, and individuals? In this paradigm, we include all the data, and we pay special attention to the infrequent and rare phenomena.

Together these twelve questions should further clarify in what ways my own cultural analytics motivations and interests that guide this book differ from those of other researchers working in this area. My main motivations in using "big cultural data" is to question what we think we know about cultures (1), as opposed to only making technical progress in already well-established paradigms; to address the challenges of thinking about new forms of digital culture (5); and to understand how its scale, speed, and diversity can be dealt with, both on the level of theoretical concepts and as characteristics we can measure (6, 7, 9). Other challenges arise when we confront the "data cognition" of contemporary society (i.e., data science assumptions and methods) with the types of subjects that these methods were not designed for—cultural life, experiences, and artifacts (2, 3, 4). My original optimism about the seemingly endless possibilities of cultural analytics gradually gave way to a more realistic view when I realized the limitations of statistical and computational approaches—and more generally, the limitations of thinking of cultures as combinations of elements that we can track (10–12).

Thus, this book aims to both convince you that these approaches are very useful and sometimes the only way to start dealing with the scale of culture today—and at the same time clearly explain what at least at present computers cannot see. And this is not because they are born, so to speak, with blindness to the aesthetic domain and cannot be cured. They are not. The problem lies with their teachers—that is, with us. If we ourselves do not understand why, out of hundreds of photographs of the same subject, the magazine editor choses a particular one, even though when a computer measures their many characteristics, they turn out to be practically identical, then how can we hope to teach such aesthetic judgments to a machine? Certainly, we can feed millions of such examples to a neural network and it will learn to predict with a certain precision the "best" photographs—but such probabilistic vision is not the same as understanding.

What Cultural Analytics Is Not

Having defined key ideas and twelve research challenges for cultural analytics as I see it, I also need to clearly state what cultural analytics is not. The rapid growth of many social networks and the availability of their data via application programming interfaces (APIs) between approximately 2007 and 2015 stimulated lots of research activity across a number of fields. In our lab, we have also taken advantage of having access to data from this new cultural universe. Between 2012 and 2015, we and our collaborators worked with datasets of publicly shared images or information about them from Twitter, Instagram, and VK, created a number of visualizations and published our research in a few papers. (Networks' APIs provided usernames of visual posts, but we never used this information in any publications or exhibitions.) Big social media data was also used during the years of open APIs by tens of thousands of scientists. In fact, for a number of years now, downloading data from Twitter and analyzing it is often used as an exercise in many computer science and data science classes.

The global growth of social networks and media sharing sites after 2007 certainly confirmed my ideas about the need for cultural analytics formulated earlier. However, cultural analytics is not "married" to this type of media and data. Social media networks emerged recently in the long history of media, and they may not exist in the same form in the future. In fact, 2005 I was not even thinking about using social media data, because social networks were not yet very popular, and there was no mechanism to download their data. Instead, I was thinking about collecting information from numerous websites belonging to individual designers, cultural centers, publications, art schools, museums, and analyzing the content of culture-related blogs that were already very popular. I imagined accessing content from as many sites as possible around the world and visualizing the changing patterns in real time (see plates 1 and 2).

The free access to content from leading social networks that became available in a few years was important in making visible opportunities and challenges in observing and analyzing cultural data on the scale—but the cultural analytics program does not depend on access to social media, or any particular source. If at some point in the future, websites and social media cease to exist in their present forms, some other forms of collective media publishing and sharing are likely to replace them.

It is almost certain that particular technologies will be changing, but the fundamental new conditions that were already established during the 2000s will remain: the new scale of culture and the growing presence of culture in contemporary societies. This includes both "more culture" (more cultural producers, more objects and events, more areas of society where aesthetics becomes very important, etc.) and "more information" about culture (websites, posts, publications, datasets). The goal of cultural analytics is to address the challenge of seeing and thinking about culture at this new scale.

Cultural Analytics, Media Theory, and Software Studies

Cultural Analytics is a book of *media theory*. I argue that to systematically study global media cultures today, media theory needs to turn to data science. In fact, computational methods are necessary in order not only to analyze and theorize these global cultures, but even simply to *see* them in the first place.

If we rely only on our intuitions based on content we happened to see online, algorithmic recommendations, or intuitions about what is important, it is too easy for us to stay in our cognitive and historical *filter bubbles*, projecting our biases onto the world.[19] The academic fields may have their own filter bubbles, in which established research paradigms can make invisible to academics emerging types of cultural activities they should be attending to. For example, while interaction design has become central to our daily cultural experiences in the forms of apps, websites, and connected devices, it is not yet sufficiently discussed in media studies or humanities.

Of course, computational methods and large datasets do not automatically guarantee more objectivity and inclusion. However, they can help us to *confront our assumptions, biases, and stereotypes*. They allow us to notice what we overwise may not be able to see—the content and its creators that do not make it to the top results of search or recommendation engines, do not appear in top ten or top 100 lists, and thus remain invisible.

How do you go about researching the long tail of digital culture?[20] Many computer researchers have been using random sampling to select millions of text posts, images, and videos shared on Twitter, YouTube, Instagram and other networks and then analyze them. Such large samples capture a snapshot of global activity on such networks, but they may not represent well the substantial differences in content shared in different geographic areas or by different demographic groups. In several projects in our lab, we have followed a different strategy: selecting a small geographic area and then collecting all content shared in this area. For example, for the *On Broadway* and *Inequaligram* projects, we analyzed data on *all* geolocated Instagram images that were shared across all of Manhattan for five months.[21] We did not filter anything out. We did not start with any hashtags that represent a particular topic. We did not only look at images that have more likes. We did not separate "art" from "nonart" or "original" images from copies or "influencers" from regular users. Instead, all posts with location information indicating that they were shared in Manhattan during this period—all 7,442,454 geo-located images, hashtags, and descriptions from 1,890,585 Instagram users—were collected in our lab and considered to be equally valuable for further analysis.

Before we can "theorize" contemporary media, we need to see it, and this is not possible anymore without computers because of its new scale. Thus, rather than only being the *subject of analysis*, as in my book *The Language of New Media*, the computation becomes the *practical tool* for studying media in this new book.

Since 1984, I have been working practically with digital media in different capacities: as computer animator, motion graphics designer, software developer, media artist, and professor of digital art. I have taught hands-on classes in digital art since 1992, data visualization since 2006, and data science since 2013. I also wrote software tools that I and others in our lab used to visualize large visual datasets. This practical experience designing, programming, and teaching digital media, visualization, and data analysis is reflected in this book. Exploring, manipulating, and visualizing datasets for me is a direct continuation of creating art and design with code that I have been doing since 1984.

In a parallel way, I see my cultural analytics research as a direct extension of my new media theory work of the 1990s and 2000s. The difference is the scale of digital culture then and now. In the middle of the 1990s, the number of artists working with algorithms was so small that we could all meet in a single conference. Two such key annual conferences were the *Ars Electronica* festival that began in 1979 and the annual International Symposium on Electronic Art (ISEA) that first took place in 1988. In the 1994 ISEA in Helsinki, approximately 150 participants gathered, and this motivated the international takeoff of new media art.

Today, hundreds of thousands of people identify themselves as digital artists, creative technologists, or creative coders, and a few billion people with camera phones have become digital photographers. A search for the phrase "How do I edit my Instagram" on YouTube (January 15, 2016) returned 150,000 videos with how-to advice by Instagram users. And the same search on October 11, 2017, returned 228,000 videos. The top videos in this genre have millions of views each.[22] This new scale of media production and participation calls for new research methods, concepts, and tools, and this motivates this book. In the world in which digital media is created by a few billion rather than by a few thousand, like it was twenty-five years ago, we need to reinvent what it means to study culture.

Cultural Analytics also incorporates perspectives of the software studies field, which asks how software shapes the world today. In *Software Takes Command*, I wrote: "If we want to understand contemporary techniques of *control, communication, representation, simulation, analysis, decision-making, memory, vision, writing, and interaction,* . . . we [must] consider this software layer."[23] *Software Takes Command* presented theoretical and historical analysis of popular tools for media creation such as Photoshop and After Effects; *Cultural Analytics* looks at some of the core concepts and assumptions of the data-centric world view. It asks *how our society thinks and acts using data and algorithms* and *how the algorithmic analysis of user content and interactions by the industry shapes culture today.*

I believe that all members of the creative class, media researchers, humanists, and social scientists need to have *data science literacy*: knowledge of core principles of data analysis, machine learning, and predictive analytics methods and applications. Why? Because the software and code based on these principles is employed throughout our society, including digital culture industry, businesses, nonprofits, and government. And if data science has not yet started to be used in a particular academic field, it is only a matter of time.

In summary, I see my move from *media* to *data analysis* as a logical progression. *The Language of New Media* (written in 1999) described forms of digital culture that emerged in the 1990s. *Software Takes Command* (2007) covered the history of software programs for media creation and editing and the new visual languages they enabled as they were adopted around the turn of the twenty-first century. *Cultural Analytics* now investigates the new post-2005 stage in which billions of people create digital media and share it online. Also, at this stage, cultural software is given a new role. We delegate more agency to it. It is no longer only a tool, a medium, or an assistant. Instead, it now engages in *cultural behaviors* (e.g., deciding what new social media posts to show, improving quality of our photos, writing news articles, etc.). And while for now we still write posts, take photographs, and perform other cultural actions ourselves, gradually such actions may become fully automated in the future. (For example, in 2018 Google added an autocomplete feature to Gmail that automatically completes your email response as you start writing—you only need to press the Tab key to accept the suggestion.) This is why all cultural and media scholars and students need to acquire a good understanding of the data science and AI fields. Chapter 3 of this book presents an analysis of these new cultural roles of computers; my 2018 book *AI Aesthetics* discusses how the growing use of algorithmic systems may affect cultural diversity.[24]

Using This Book in Classes

The content and the structure of this book reflect my experience teaching hands-on cultural analytics classes to diverse groups of students. They included undergraduates in digital art, media art, computer science, and art history, and graduate students in computer science and humanities and social science fields including art history, literature, musicology, communication, economics, sociology, anthropology, psychology, and digital humanities.[25]

The chapters of this book present a sequence of topics that can be covered in a semester or a quarter-long class (10–14 weeks). The goals are to familiarize students with examples of work with cultural datasets in humanities, computer science, design, and other fields, and explain why we need computational methods for analyzing contemporary culture (part I); to learn the conceptual operations, choices, and constraints involved in creating "cultural data" (part II); and to understand how to explore media datasets using data visualization (part III).

Why did I choose to include these topics and not others? More generally, what is the difference between cultural analytics and data analytics? Why don't I have chapters in the book on data analysis?

Consider the workflow for doing a research, design, or artistic project with data: (1) think of how some subjects can be analyzed or represented quantitatively; (2) research what suitable data is available or how to generate it; (3) assemble the data; (4) use visual methods to explore this data; (5) analyze the data using methods from statistics and data science (i.e., descriptive and inferential statistics, unsupervised and supervised machine learning, time-series analysis, network science, etc.); and optionally (6)—create interactive visualization tools for others to explore this data, or make other design and media outputs.

In my view, for cultural analytics, step 5 is not really different from what you would do with any other data. Because there are lots of good textbooks, online courses, and tutorials available to learn these methods, in addition to courses your university may offer, you should use these resources to learn them. So instead of covering the material that already exists elsewhere, this book deals with other parts of the workflow—1, 2, 3, 4 and 6. In other words, what is unique in cultural analytics is not what you do with data—but how do you get from this elusive thing we call *culture* to its data representation in the first place. That is, *how do you turn cultural experiences, events, actions, and media into data*? What is gained and what is lost in this translation? And once you get it into data form, how can you explore it on multiple scales, seeing both unique and infrequent as well as common and regular patterns?

However, while I am not going to teach you statistics and data analysis in this book, I will talk about the assumptions behind some of their methods, what they can enable us to see, and what they can't, at least at present. Therefore, ideally, you should read this book in parallel to learning data science techniques, or after you have learned some of them.

You can read the book chapters in sequence, or just move to any chapter that interests you. I have tried to make each chapter relatively self-sufficient. Throughout the book, you will find summaries of the already covered material and presentations of new material organized in numbered lists. I hope that this organization is helpful if either the whole book or separate chapters are used in classes.

I Studying Culture at Scale

1 From New Media to More Media

The natural sciences were the first to start quantifying the world, developing systems for measurements, comparison, and analyzing change based on numbers, calculus, and graphs. Starting in the middle of the nineteenth century, the emerging social sciences similarly started to quantify human senses, mental phenomena, and group behaviors. The examples of early quantitative concepts and graphical techniques in psychology and sociology include Gustav Fechner's invention of "the just noticeable difference" to measure psychological sensation in 1850, factor analysis in psychology developed by L. L. Thurstone in the early 1930s, and graphs showing structures of social groups, introduced by Jacob Moreno, also in the early 1930s.[1]

It is only logical that media and digital culture studies and humanities are next to start approaching their subjects using quantification, mathematic models, and data visualization. The key reason in my view that this is both possible and inevitable is the new scale of cultural production, dissemination, and participation. As billions of people create, modify, share, and curate digital artifacts and communicate using apps, social media networks, blogs, and websites, *the scale of culture has approached that of physical or biological phenomena*. With many billions of online interactions with these artifacts happening every day, quantitative analysis may reveal many regularities and patterns that can have the generality of science laws (e.g., the power law and scale-free networks.) This new scale in fact makes possible the idea of the *science of culture*, which I will discuss in more detail in chapter 2.

In 2008, I drafted a first text to present my vision of cultural analytics.[2] I am going to reproduce this text, called "From *New Media* to *More Media*," in the next section without any changes because it captures well the moment of the "explosion" of digital culture in terms of its scale. Today the reality of billions of people creating media, sharing them, and having access to trillions of media objects created by others is taken for granted. Similarly, millions of cultural works created by professionals are also available via free or paid services, such as Spotify for music and Netflix for films, and also language-specific collections, such as the free Russian site Proza.ru (proza.ru), hosting seven million short stories and novels, and another Russian portal Stihi.ru (stihi.ru), hosting forty million poems.

But first I want to contextualize this text historically and point out the ideas that for me remain most important today. The first International AAAI Conference on Web and Social Media (ICWSM) took place in 2007,[3] and it marks the moment when quantitative research of social media started to grow. The conference organizers described their goals as follows: "The conference aims to bring together researchers from different subject areas (e.g., computer science, linguistics, psychology, statistics, sociology, multimedia and semantic web technologies) and foster discussions about ongoing research on weblogs and social media."[4] Note however that big collections of professional media and software have been available via BitTorrent already much earlier. Similarly, people have been posting and discussing topics in Usenet newsgroups since 1981—that is, for twenty-five years before social media networks run by companies took off. Other popular internet communication platforms for posting texts and discussions include BBSes (bulletin board systems, 1978 onward), forums, mailing lists, and blogs. It has been estimated that in 2015 Baidu hosted five hundred thousand groups;[5] the popular site Quora, on which professionals answer questions, had one hundred million active monthly users in 2017;[6] and Academia (academia.edu), a platform for academics to share and read papers, had fifty-five million users.[7]

Forms of sharing, platforms, types of media, search and recommendations, public versus private sharing, privacy expectations and other elements of the digital ecosystem may all change in the future, but the phenomenon of so many people creating media is unlikely to disappear. Given this, it is important to remember the moments in digital culture history when a new paradigm was emerging and that what is normal today was then very new and unprecedented. My text with all its details that I am leaving intact on purpose—such as the numbers of portfolios being shared on professional sites in 2008 and the names of these first sites and website references—is one such document.

The text begins by reflecting on the new scale of digital culture, referring to it as the shift "from new media to more media." But while the growth of social media was widely covered in the news media, another equally important development noted in this text still had not been given proper attention. This development is the rapid growth of *professional culture industries* and *educational programs in creative fields* worldwide after 1990. The new scale of professional cultural and media production and education around the world creates a real challenge: "Before, you could write about culture by following what was going on in a small number of world capitals and schools. But how can we follow the developments in tens of thousands of cities and educational institutions?"

Thus, the rise of user-generated digital content and digitization of large numbers of historical cultural artifacts are not the only conditions motivating looking at culture as data and analyzing it with computational methods. Cultural globalization, which leads to the emergence of hundreds of fashion weeks and art biennales around the world, thousands of new cultural festivals, tens of thousands of new cultural organizations, and a multitude of many other types of cultural events and projects, makes it impossible to explore the world of professional culture without computer tools.

Companies that detect and forecast consumer and professional trends in consumer fields such as lifestyle products, fashion, hospitality, and fitness employ many people and use a combination of diverse methods. For example, according to its website in early 2020, one such leading London-based company, WGSN, was publishing 250 fashion trend reports per month and 150 catwalk analysis reports per season and tracking twelve thousand brands and retailers. Their methods include analysis of data from social media, attending and taking photos at hundreds of fashion shows per year, compiling industry sales figures, identifying and following fashion communities and influencers on social media, and building custom analytics dashboards for their customers.[8] The company was employing "250 trend forecasters and data scientists."[9]

WGSN and similar companies continuously analyze trends across many product categories and consumer industries, geographic regions, and demographic categories. Big retailers such as Urban Outfitters have their own forecasting teams.[10] And, of course, all big consumer companies are doing their own market research using methods ranging from focus groups and surveys to computational analysis of social media and *neuromarketing*, which refers to the use of fMRI, EEG, eye tracking, and other technologies for capturing consumers' emotional and cognitive responses to products and content.[11]

However, these extensive research efforts—which we as individual cultural analytics researchers can't compete with—cover only the selected areas of contemporary culture that have to do with consumer behavior. The universe of ideas, conversations, images, imaginations, and experiences that are not directly relevant to this behavior is of little use to the industry. Luckily for us, today this universe is either reflected in a digital online "mirror" (certainly with many omissions and distortions) or it directly exists as digital "matter": online posts, comments, projects, announcements, links, and other elements. In many cases, this online matter can be accessed on a large scale and explored computationally by individuals or small research teams, as opposed to only big companies.

One very good online source for analyzing trends in creative industry are portfolio sites. My 2008 text refers to early examples of professional portfolio- and project-sharing sites in the fields of architecture, design, motion graphics, and data visualization. Such sites, where professionals and students from practically every country share their projects, exemplify the emergence of a global professional cultural space in the middle of the 2000s. In this space, all actors who also happen to use the same small set of design tools (such as Adobe Creative Cloud apps) can see each other work, compete for the same assignments, attract followers, and post new projects. The numbers of projects and portfolios uploaded to these professional sites in 2008 were small in comparison to today, but the contours of this space were already established. For example, Coroflot (coroflot.com) housed 90,657 portfolios as of May 7, 2008; their number grew to 157,476 portfolios as of October 11, 2009.

Today the leading site used by creative professionals in design, photography, fashion, and dozens of other creative fields to share their portfolios is Behance (behance. net). It was started in 2006; by the end of 2015, it had six million members around the world, with participation from Ukraine and Sao Paulo, Brazil, growing most rapidly that year according to the company report.[12] In our *Elsewhere* project, we explored 82,684 Behance member accounts that publicly shared their locations. The accounts in our sample were created between May 22, 2007, and February 9, 2019. Their locations include 5,567 unique cities and 162 countries. The list of twenty cities with the most accounts by 2019 reveals a new geography of digital culture where the old twentieth-century centers of culture industry coexist with the twenty-first-century newcomers in developing and ex-communist countries. Here is the list of these cities sorted by number of accounts in descending order: London, Moscow, New York, Paris, Barcelona, Los Angeles, Seoul, Buenos Aires, San Francisco, Berlin, Montreal, Saint Petersburg, São Paulo, Kiev, Brooklyn, Warsaw, Istanbul, Milan, Budapest, Toronto.

"From *New Media* to *More Media*" (2008)

We have moved from the stage of "*New Media*" to the stage of "*More Media*" (2004–.)

We are living through an exponential explosion in the amounts of data we are generating, capturing, analyzing, visualizing, and storing—including cultural content. On August 25, 2008, Google's software engineers announced on googleblog.blogspot. com that the index of web pages, which Google is computing several times daily, has reached one trillion unique URLs.[13] During the same month, YouTube.com reported that users had uploaded thirteen hours of new video to the site every minute.[14] And in November 2008, the number of images housed on Flickr reached three billions.[15]

User-generated content is one of the fastest growing parts of the expanding information universe. According to a 2008 study, "Approximately 70% of the digital universe is created by individuals."[16] In other words, the size of media created by users competes well with the amounts of data collected and created by computers (surveillance systems, sensor-based applications, data centers supporting "cloud computing," etc.).

The exponential growth of a number of both non-professional and professional media producers over the last decade has created a fundamentally new cultural situation and a challenge to our normal ways of tracking and studying culture. Hundreds of millions of people are routinely creating and sharing cultural content—blogs, photos, videos, online comments and discussions, and so on. As the number of mobile phones with rich media capabilities is projected to continue growing, this number is only going to increase. In early 2008, there were 2.2 billion mobile phones in the world; it is projected that this number will become four billion by 2010, with the main growth coming from China, India, and Africa.

Think about this: the number of images uploaded to Flickr every week is probably larger than all objects contained in all art museums in the world.

At the same time, the rapid growth of professional educational and cultural institutions in many newly globalized countries along with the instant availability of cultural news over the web and ubiquity of media and design software has also dramatically increased the number of culture professionals who participate in global cultural production and discussions. Hundreds of thousands of students, artists, and designers have now access to the same ideas, information, and tools. It is no longer possible to talk about centers and provinces. (In fact, based on my own experiences, I believe the students, culture professionals, and governments in newly globalized countries are often more ready to embrace latest ideas than their equivalents in "old centers" of world culture.)

If you want to see the effects of cultural and digital globalization in action, visit the popular websites where the professionals and the students working in different areas of media and design share their projects and note the range of countries from which the authors come from. Try Xplsv.tv (motion graphics, animation), Coroflot.com (design portfolios from around the world), Archinect.com (architecture students' projects), and Infosthetics.com (information visualization projects). For example, when I checked on December 24, 2008, the first three projects in the "artists" list on Xplsv.tv came from Cuba, Hungary, and Norway. Similarly, when I visited Coroflot.com (the site where designers from around the world upload their portfolios) on the same day, the set of entries on the first page revealed a similar global cultural geography. Next to the predictable twentieth-century Western cultural capitals—New York and Milan—I also found portfolios from Shanghai, Waterloo (Belgium), Bratislava (Slovakia), and Seoul (South Korea).[17]

Before, cultural theorists and historians could generate theories and histories based on small datasets (for instance, "classical Hollywood cinema," "Italian Renaissance," etc.). But how can we track "global digital cultures" with their billions of cultural objects and hundreds of millions of contributors? Before, you could write about culture by following what was going on in a small number of world capitals and schools. But how can we follow the developments in tens of thousands of cities and educational institutions?

The ubiquity of computers, digital media software, consumer electronics, and computer networks led to the exponential rise in the numbers of cultural agents worldwide and the media they create, making it very difficult, if not impossible, to understand global cultural developments and dynamics in any substantial details using our twentieth-century theoretical tools and methods. But what if can we use the same developments—computers, software, and availability of massive amounts of "born digital" cultural content—to track global cultures in ways impossible with traditional tools?

To investigate these questions—and to understand how the ubiquity of software tools for culture creation and sharing changes what "culture" is—in 2007 we established Software Studies Initiative (softwarestudies.com) at University of California, San Diego (UCSD) and California Institute for Telecommunications and Information (Calit2). Together with the researchers and students working in our lab, we have been developing a new paradigm for the study, teaching, and public presentation of cultural artifacts, dynamics, and flows. We call this paradigm *cultural analytics*.

Today, sciences, businesses, governments, and other agencies rely on computer-based analysis and visualization of large datasets and data flows. They employ statistical data analysis, data mining, information visualization, scientific visualization, visual analytics, and simulation. We propose to begin systematically applying these techniques to contemporary cultural data. Large datasets are already here—the result of the digitization efforts by museums, libraries, and companies over the last ten years (think of book scanning by Google and Amazon) and the explosive growth of newly available cultural content on the web.

We believe that a systematic use of *large-scale computational analysis and interactive visualization of cultural patterns* will become a basic research method in humanities and in cultural criticism. What will happen when humanists start using interactive visualizations as a standard tool in their work, the way many scientists do already? If slides made possible art history, and if a movie projector and video recorder enabled film studies, what new cultural disciplines may emerge out of the use of visualization and data analysis?

In our lab, we have been developing techniques to analyze and visualize the patterns in movies, cartoons, motion graphics, photography, video games, websites, design, architecture, and other types of visual media. The key idea underlying all our projects is to bring together three developments: (1) availability of massive cultural datasets; (2) the techniques of image processing and computer vision to automatically analyze visual media; and (3) techniques from information and science visualization, media design, and digital art to visually represent the results of the analysis.

One of the directions we are now beginning to explore is the development of visual systems that would allow us to follow global cultures in real time. Imagine a real-time traffic display (à la car navigation systems), except that the display is wall-sized, the resolution is thousands of times greater, and the traffic shown is not cars on highways, but *real-time cultural flows* around the world. Imagine the same wall-sized display divided into multiple windows, each showing different real-time and historical data about cultural, social, and economic news and trends, thus providing *a situational awareness for cultural analysts*. Imagine the same wall-sized display playing an animation of what looks like an earthquake *simulation* produced on a supercomputer, except in this case the "earthquake" is the release of a new version of popular software, the announcement of an important architectural project, or any other important cultural event. What we are seeing are the effects of such cultural earthquakes over time and space. Imagine a wall-sized computer graphic showing *the long tail* of cultural production that allows you to zoom in to see each individual product, together with rich data about it (à la a real estate map on zillow.com)—while the graph is constantly updated in real time by pulling data from the web. Imagine a visualization that shows how other people around the word remix new videos created in a fan community or how a new design software gradually affects the kinds of forms being imagined today (the way Alias and Maya led to a new language in architecture). These are the kinds of projects we want to create.

Observing Global Culture in Real Time

The vision presented in the 2008 text reproduced in the previous section started to emerge in my head a few years earlier. I first realized the possibilities to study global culture with computational tools in October 2005. A few weeks later, on November 14, Google launched a free product called Google Analytics.[18] This software collected and analyzed information about all visits to your website or blog. It had a rich interactive visual interface, allowing you to study every imaginable detail of these visits using tables, different kinds of graphs, and maps (see figure 1.1).

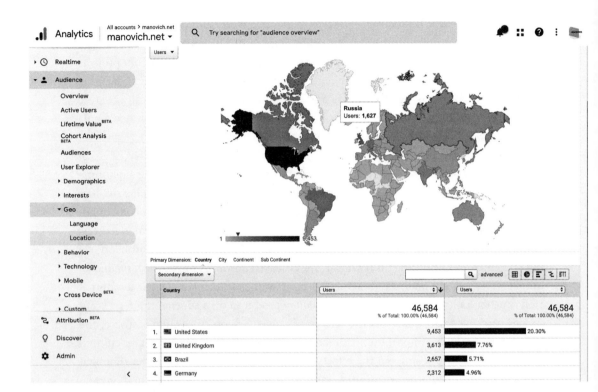

Figure 1.1
Google Analytics screen for manovich.net website showing visitors' geographic information for a selected time period.

I did not yet have the term to refer to the possibilities of large-scale cultural analysis, but when I saw the Google Analytics interface, it was perfect for what I was imagining. What if we had a similar interface for seeing and zooming into global cultural trends? I considered various options for the term to describe what I was imagining, including *computational cultural analysis*. By spring 2007, I settled on a shorter term: *cultural analytics*.

Our lab was launched in May 2007 at the UC San Diego Division of the California Institute for Telecommunication and Information (Calit2). Our very first project was a design prototype called the Cultural Analytics Research Environment. The system interface was inspired by Google Analytics. However, instead of data about user visits to a website that you can look at in Google Analytics, I imagined a system that will allow us one day to explore patterns in *all available digitized and born-digital cultural artifacts and activities.* For the coverage of contemporary culture, the data driving the system would be continuously updated by crawling millions of websites and blogs of cultural organizations such as museums, portfolio sites such as Coroflot and Archinect, and individual creators.

Plate 1 shows three designs for this interface, which we created in Spring 2008. In the photographs in plate 2, we see lab postdoctoral researcher Jeremy Douglass in front of two designs loaded on a visualization supercomputer that was created at Calit2 a bit earlier. The display consisted of seventy thirty-inch Apple computer monitors joined together.[19] At that time, this was one of the biggest visualizations walls constructed by academic researchers, and we intended our future system to use such walls. The size of the wall was 9.7 × 2.3 m, and its combined resolution was 35,640 by 8,000 pixels, or 287 megapixels. It was driven by eighteen computers with one hundred processor cores and thirty-eight graphics processor units (GPUs). To be able to load images of arbitrary resolution onto this seventy-monitor display and support interaction with these images, researchers at Calit2 labs developed custom software.[20]

Being invited to work inside Calit2, where I saw such a visual supercomputer with a combined display size, resolution, processing power, and graphics capacities many times beyond what was available in a normal computer, expanded my research vision and ambitions—metaphorically and literally. A prototype for an interactive interface for exploring global cultural trends on many levels of detail, which we conceptualized and sketched, was the first outcome. In my mind, this interface would allow researchers to zoom in any location in the world and see images of contemporary cultural environments at this location, media being created there, and statistics on other cultural activities in that location. These statistics would be always placed within the numbers for the corresponding activities worldwide. (Besides Google Analytics, my other main inspiration for our interface mockups was the Gapminder World interactive visualization application for economic and social data, launched online in 2006 by Hans Rosling.[21])

We sketched three different interfaces for our imagined Cultural Analytics Research Environment (see plate 1). One interface displays a long tail of cultural production, with works sorted by popularity. Clicking on any point shows images of the related work. The works can be space designs, buildings, fashion items, books, websites, music videos, and so on. In the second view, the interface changes to a global map with superimposed lines indicating how cultural themes and trends travel around the world. In the third design, the interface becomes a network view displaying connections among themes, topics, design patterns, styles, and techniques within some cultural area: cinema, web design, popular music, games, and so on. This network view was inspired by maps of the sciences that started to appear in the early 2000s. They showed connections among scientific fields or research paradigms derived from the analysis of citations in millions of scientific publications or users accessing papers in scientific databases.[22] Our system would similarly show clusters of themes, topics, and techniques derived from computational analysis of millions of cultural artifacts.

The user of the Cultural Analytics Research Environment would switch among all three data views, zooming in and out, seeing trends in a larger context and making comparisons. In the background, the data was to be collected and analyzed in real time. The graphs that appear on the side of each of three interfaces update to show statistics for the geographic area, cultural activity, or cultural genre currently selected.

At that time, the genre of *social media and monitoring dashboards* did not yet exist. These dashboards only became popular a few years later. In retrospect, the speculative interface we prototyped can be said to anticipate this genre. Today, media monitoring dashboards are used by millions of companies, nonprofits (including universities), and individuals to understand what people say about them online, to compare themselves to competitors, and to research global conversations and posts about any keyword, URL, or brand. But you can also use these dashboards as cultural analytics tools in relation to the types of data they capture—activities on social networks (following, sharing, liking, etc.) and text posts of blogs and websites. Although they can't do the key things that we imagined in 2005, they are nevertheless useful for cultural research.

For example, a popular dashboard product from Sprout Social monitors Twitter, Facebook, Instagram, LinkedIn, and Pinterest.[23] A platform called Mention monitors "billions of sources in over forty languages."[24] Yet another platform, Brandwatch, includes "every tweet back to 2006."[25] Google Trends can display the volume of searches for any term since 2004 for an arbitrary geographic area. You can choose to look at searches for web pages, images, news, and YouTube videos. There are also companies like DataSift that aggregate data from dozens of social networks, blogs, news sites, and other sources; enhance this data by detecting topics, languages, sentiments, and mentions of products, companies, and places; categorize it; and make it available to paying customers, who can then do their own analysis.[26]

Social media monitoring dashboards demonstrate that real-time analysis of some types of online cultural activities is possible. Today, the Cultural Analytics Research Environment as we imagined it in 2008—interactive visualizations of themes in global cultural environment—can be built by a small team and deployed on a cloud platform. However, the relative ease of software development would be balanced by a new challenge: in contrast to 2005, the number of cultural posts, projects, programs, and portfolios we would need to scan is much larger, and it continues to increase. But there is also a much bigger challenge that became clear to me only gradually: It is one thing to monitor trends in text data from blogs and social media posts, searching, for example, for all appearances of a particular brand name, a proper name, or another text element. (After advances in computer vision in 2010s, it has also become possible to monitor trends in subjects appearing in massive numbers of photographs and videos.) But this is still very far from being able to monitor a full range of aesthetic and semantic characteristics of cultural media and subtle but crucial differences between numerous cultural artifacts, especially on a global scale. So, while building a real-time map that shows the cultural DNAs currently present in various geographic locations and types of media is in principle possible, this map will not capture everything. In fact, it may miss most unique cultural artifacts. This point is discussed in more detail in the book's conclusion, in the section titled "Is the Goal of Cultural Analytics to Study Patterns? (Yes and No)."

Cultural Analytics in Historical Context

My own interest in the possibilities of algorithmic culture analysis using large data was stimulated by witnessing the cultural globalization that started after the end of the Cold War (1991). Seeing so many new actors and institutions in many so-called developing countries and also post-communist countries starting to participate in a global universe of ideas, images, meanings, and software tools linked by the global web, I felt that the only way to start mapping this expanding universe was by including as many artifacts and as many places as possible. This became possible because globalization and digitization took place in parallel, so this universe was now well represented online. Consequently, in defining my version of cultural analytics for this book, I started with *the use of computational and design methods for exploration and analysis of contemporary global culture at scale.* (Other researchers and readers of this book will have their own interests that lead them to cultural analytics, and they are all equally valuable.)

We can also situate current work with computation and large cultural datasets within a much longer history. This history covers describing and analyzing culture using diagrams, visualization, operationalization, statistics, mathematics, and more recently, analog and digital computers.[27] Importantly, the use of mathematics and visualization for cultural analysis predates computers by many decades. One example is the studies by Russian poet and literary theorist Andrei Bely of rhythms in Russian poetry. A son of a prominent mathematician, Bely used statistics and invented a graphical system to visualize structures in poems. These studies were collected in his 1910 book *Symbolism*.[28] Another example is the influential 1919 article by the leading American anthropologist A. L. Kroeber titled "On the Principle of Order in Civilization as Exemplified by Changes of Fashion." It presented quantitative analysis and interpretation of patterns in nineteenth-century women's fashion.

The introduction to the 1965 collection *The Use of Computers in Anthropology*, which opened this book, shows that by that time, the key advantages of using computers were already well understood by some. In fact, the justification for the use of computers that Dell Hymes formulates in this text is the best one I have ever seen: "In simplest terms, computer processing, properly prepared, can enable us to see relations and patterns in masses of data previously too large to comprehend; and to see the literal consequences of an idea applied to data, if not uniquely, then certainly far more inexorably and quickly."[29]

In the early 2000s, digital artists and designers created imaginative data visualizations of cultural patterns. *The Shape of Song* (Martin Wattenberg, 2001) and *History Flow* (Fernanda Viégas and Martin Wattenberg, 2003) visualized patterns in musical compositions and in Wikipedia pages as they change over time.[30] The *Listening Post* installation (Mark Hansen and Ben Rubin, 2001–2002) was filtering discussions of internet chat rooms in real time and animating extracted text fragments across an array of hundreds of screens.[31] In *The Top Grossing Film of All Time, 1 × 1* (Jason Salavan, 2000), the frames of the movie *Titanic* were reduced to single representative colors, and small squares in these colors were placed in a rectangular grid, making visible visual rhythms in the movie.[32] *Making Visible the Invisible* (George Legrady, 2004–2005) installed in the main Seattle Public Library building, visualized in real time the flow of information (via data on checked-out items) in the library.[33] (I will discuss some of these projects in more detail in part III.)

Digital humanities scholars have published a number of historical accounts of quantitative and computational text analysis. In the US context, the field of humanities computing, in which researchers started to analyze small bodies of literary and other texts in the 1950s, is seen as a precursor to digital humanities.[34] More recently, scholars in different countries started to question and expand these US-centric accounts. This is certainly a good development, but a broader historical perspective that is not limited to humanities may be even better.

As I position it in this book, cultural analytics is not tied to any field and may include work in the humanities, social science, and computer science. It is also not limited to academic research but includes relevant media and data design and art projects. Because the use of mathematics and visualization for cultural analysis also predates computers by many decades, it would be wrong to identify cultural analytics only with computation or big data. For example, many composers in the twentieth century developed original systems of graphical music scores—and these hand-drawn visualizations also belong to cultural analytics understood more broadly. The same goes for hand-drawn diagrams in architecture and urban designs, dance-notation systems, and film visualizations by directors such as Dziga Vertov and Sergei Eisenstein created from the 1920s to the 1940s.

2 The Science of Culture?

While in the physical sciences the investigator will be able to measure what, on the basis of a *prima facie* theory, he thinks important, in the social sciences often that is treated as important which happens to be accessible to measurement. This is sometimes carried to the point where it is demanded that our theories must be formulated in such terms that they refer only to measurable magnitudes.

—Friedrich August von Hayek, Nobel Prize Lecture, December 11, 1974[1]

Analyzing, Visualizing, and Interacting with Cultural Data: Examples

Today, the research that uses computation and large cultural datasets is spread among many academic fields, professional practices, and publication formats. It includes publications in academic journals, conference papers, blog posts, GitHub code and depositories, large long-term institutional projects to assemble the digital records of many separate collections such as Europeana.eu, short-lived art installations in museums and public spaces, and interactive projects by data artists and designers.

Let's look at some examples of this research and the academic publications and conferences in which this work often appears. In computer science, the numbers of relevant publications and conference papers that analyze cultural contents and interactions now number in the hundreds of thousands. Some of this research appears in conferences on "social computing"[2] and "computational social science." Other work is done in various subfields of computer science, including computer multimedia, computer vision, music information retrieval, natural language processing, web science, and machine learning. *Nature* and *Science*, the two most prestigious international science journals, have also published a number of important papers (I will discuss two of them ahead.)[3] Another prestigious journal with many publications that use computational methods to analyze large social media datasets is *PLOS One*.[4] Among annual conferences that feature such work, two very important ones are the International World Wide Web Conference (1994–present) and, as mentioned earlier, the International AAAI Conference On Web And Social Media (2007–present).

Much of such research in computer science relies on large samples of user content shared on social networks and data about people's behaviors on these networks, such as the numbers of views, likes, and shares for a post, lists of followers, and so on. The papers analyze user behavior on most popular social networks and media sharing services such as Weibo, Facebook, Instagram, Flickr, YouTube, Pinterest, and Tumblr. They also analyze computationally the characteristics of image, video, and text posts and propose models that connect user behavior and these characteristics. For example, in one research area called *computational aesthetics*, scientists create mathematical models that predict which images and videos will be popular and how this popularity is affected by their content and by other characteristics such as "memorability," "interestingness," "beauty," or "creativity."[5] (The researchers proposed metrics to measure these characteristics.)

For examples of how scientists analyze cultural behaviors on a media sharing platform, consider work on Instagram. On Google Scholar, my search for "Instagram dataset" conducted on February 3, 2020, returned 17,110 journal articles and conference papers. One publication analyzed the most popular Instagram subjects and types of users in terms of what kinds of subjects frequently appear in photos in their feeds.[6] Another paper used a sample of 4.1 million Instagram photos to quantify the effect of using filters on the numbers of views and comments.[7] In another paper, a group of researchers analyzed temporal and demographic trends in Instagram selfies by using 5.5 million photos with faces they collected from the network. They have also tested three alternative hypotheses about the reasons behind posting selfies in each of 117 countries in their dataset.[8] Yet another paper investigated clothing and fashion styles in forty-four world cities using one hundred million Instagram photos.[9]

These papers illustrate the general characteristics common to a large proportion of cultural research in computer science. This research deals with the present time. It relies on large random samples of user-created content and user activities, such as many millions of posts on social and media sharing networks by millions of people. As a result, what this research looks at and quantifies is *popular culture*—that is, the tastes, interests, and imagination shared by majorities. (Because of privacy issues, scientists can't ask each of these users to identify themselves or submit demographic information.)

There are obvious advantages of such scale (e.g., we can find more reliable statistical patterns), but the desire to model and predict human cultural behavior on that scale can be also blinding. As I will discuss later in more detail, the small "islands" of global culture—groups of unique cultural artifacts, unique cultural behaviors, and unique tastes—can easily become invisible when we aggregate all data together and analyze it as though it is coming from a single population.

Contemporary popular culture as it exists in social media, blogs, forums, and other online platforms receives the most attention in computational research, but we can also find some very interesting quantitative work on media history. A number of scientists published studies of historical visual and audio media that creatively use methods from the fields of image processing, computer vision, and music information retrieval. The examples of such work that I find particularly interesting are "Toward Automated Discovery of Artistic Influence,"[10] "Measuring the Evolution of Contemporary Western Popular Music,"[11] and "Quicker, Faster, Darker: Changes in Hollywood Film over 75 Years."[12] The first paper presents a mathematical model for the automated discovery of influence among artists. The model was tested using 1,710 images of paintings by sixty-six well-known artists. Although some of the discovered influences are the same ones often described by art historians, the model also suggests other visual influences among artists that had not been discussed previously. The second paper investigates changes in popular music using a dataset of 464,411 songs produced between 1955 and 2010. The third paper analyzes gradual changes in the average shot duration across 9,400 English-language narrative films created between 1912 and 2013.

The analysis of mostly historical text cultures has been central to the field of digital humanities as it developed in literary studies departments. The history that this field constructed for itself (especially in English-language countries),[13] starts in 1949 with a project by Italian priest Roberto Busa to make an index of words in the writings of St. Thomas Aquinas that eventually was supported by IBM. (For alternative histories of the field's beginnings, see "A Genealogy of Distant Reading" by Ted Underwood[14] and "Search and Replace: Josephine Miles and the Origins of Distant Reading" by Rachel Sagner Buurma and Laura Heffernan[15]). Important institutional milestones for the field's development in the United States include the founding of *Computers and the Humanities* journal (1996–present), the Association for Computers and the Humanities (1978–present), the NEH Office for Digital Humanities (2008–present) and Annual Digital Humanities Conferences (1989–present) internationally.[16] Any attempt at a summary of the field today will be incomplete given its size and diversity, but for a compact view from 2015, I recommend "Seven Ways Humanists Are Using Computers to Understand Text" by Underwood.[17] I can give lots of interesting examples of digital humanities research, but I will mention just one example here because it illustrates well what I see as the most interesting type of inquiry: using bigger cultural data to question our existing concepts and methods of analysis (this idea appears as the first in my list of twelve research questions for cultural analytics in the book's introduction). The authors of the paper "Mapping Mutable Genres in Structurally Complex Volumes" apply computer methods to analyze texts of 469,200 digitized English language volumes covering a number of centuries.[18] The initial problem of automatically classifying these volumes by genre leads to the discussion of instability of genre categories over time:

> Existing metadata rarely provides unambiguous information about genre. More troublingly, when you dig into the problem, it becomes clear that no amount of manual categorization will ever produce a definitive boundary between fiction and nonfiction in a collection with a significant timespan, because the boundary changes over time. Form and content didn't necessarily align in earlier centuries as they do for us. Nineteenth-century biographies that invent imagined dialogue often read exactly like a novel; eighteenth-century essays like Richard Steele's Tatler use thinly fictionalized characters as a veil for nonfiction journalism.[19]

Among multitudes of papers that analyze cultural data computationally, some of the most interesting are ones that test existing cultural theories and/or propose new ones. One such study is called "Fashion and Art Cycles Are Driven by Counter-Dominance Signals of Elite Competition: Quantitative Evidence from Music Styles."[20] The paper uses data on eight million music albums released between 1952 and 2010 to test two common theories of art and fashion cycles. As the authors of the paper summarize it, "According to 'top down' theories, elite members signal their superior status by introducing new symbols (e.g., fashion styles), which are adopted by low-status groups. In response to this adoption, elite members would need to introduce new symbols to signal their status. According to many 'bottom-up' theories, style cycles evolve from lower classes and follow an essentially random pattern." The quantitative analysis of the historical data leads authors to propose a different theory supported by statistical tests: "changes in art and fashion styles happen whenever a new elite successfully challenges the hegemony of a previous elite." As they note, the sociologists have been interested in mechanisms of style cycles ever since the 1905 book *Philosophy of Fashion* by Georg Simmel. By formulating and testing quantitative models for different mechanisms of change, the paper provides a methodology that can be used to study style cycles in other cultural areas besides popular music.

Work with large cultural datasets includes not only researchers doing analysis in their labs and publishing papers, but also creation of interactive web interfaces that allow the public to explore trends in such datasets. One such prominent project is the Ngram Viewer, created in 2010 by Google scientists Jon Orwant and Will Brockman following the prototype by two PhD students from Harvard University in biology and applied math.[21] A visitor to the Ngram Viewer's website can enter several words or phrases and instantly see plots comparing the frequencies of the appearances of these words across millions of books published over a few centuries.

Among the experiments to create interfaces to large image collections, I want to mention the pioneering projects by the New York Public Library (NYPL) labs. One of these projects created in 2016 allows online visitors to browse 187,000 public domain images from NYPL by century, genre, collection, and color.[22] The interface shows all these 187,000 images at once in small size; clicking on each thumbnail brings up the larger image and the related information. Another project called the Photographers' Identities Catalog supports exploration of data for 128,668 photographers, studios, and dealers covering the history of photography worldwide.[23] The interface includes an interactive map showing detailed locations for records on a city street level. If a photographer lived in a number of places, the map connects all these places, thus giving us a spatial overview of photographer's career.

In our own lab, we created two projects that make it possible for visitors to explore and interact with large collections of social media images and data. *Selfiecity* (2014–2015) enables interactive comparison of patterns in thousands of Instagram self-portraits (selfies) that were shared in six global cities (see plate 5). *On Broadway* (2014) uses a touch screen to present an interface for navigating a "data city"—specifically, the area along 21 km of Broadway in Manhattan (see plate 11). The images and data used in this project include 660,000 geocoded Instagram photos, eight million Four-square check-ins, and twenty-two million taxi pickups and drop-offs for one year. Our lab participants worked on collecting and organizing the data; interface design and programming was done by the team, consisting of one of the world's leading data visualization designers, Moritz Stefaner, an expert in programming interactive applications, Dominicus Baur, and a data products designer, Daniel Goddemeyer.

The previous examples of cultural analytics research and projects may create an impression that this work only serves academic or artistic interests. However, cultural analytics also is often carried out as part of design projects to create new or improve existing digital products and services. These can range from design of new media interfaces for digital collections for museums and libraries to analysis of urban social media for guiding urban design and policy. The large-scale analysis of people's interactions with media content and each other mediated by computer systems can be used to improve these systems. For example, we can propose algorithms to help people discover more types of content or discover content they would normally ignore. In fact, computer scientists that work on improving recommendation systems devote significant energy to figuring out how to deliver more diverse but still relevant recommendations. (In October 2018, Spotify said that its *listening diversity*, defined as the number of artists the average user streams per month, "has risen on Spotify over the past 10 years at an average of about 8 percent per year."[24])

Some computer scientists have been studying the aesthetic preferences and dynamics of attention in visual media among social networks users—asking what images or videos users prefer and how these preferences can be predicted from media content and visual characteristics. For example, consider the 2015 publication titled "An Image is Worth More than a Thousand Favorites."[25] (One of the authors of this work, Miriam Redi, later collaborated with us on analysis of Instagram images.) The paper presents "analysis of ordinary people's aesthetics perception of web images" using nine million Flickr images with Creative Commons licenses. Reviewing the large body of quantitative research that uses large data, the authors note:

> The dynamics of attention in social media tend to obey power laws. Attention concentrates on a relatively small number of popular items and neglecting the vast majority of content produced by the crowd. Although popularity can be an indication of the perceived value of an item within its community, previous research has hinted to the fact that popularity is distinct from intrinsic quality. As a result, content with low visibility but high quality lurks in the tail of the popularity distribution. This phenomenon can be particularly evident in the case of photo-sharing communities, where valuable photographers who are not highly engaged in online social interactions contribute with high-quality pictures that remain unseen.

The authors propose an algorithm that can find "unpopular" images (i.e., images that have been seen by only a small proportion of users) that are equal in aesthetic quality to the popular images. Implementing such algorithm would allow more creators to find audiences for their works. Such research exemplifies how large-scale quantitative analysis of cultural patterns and situations can be further used to offer constructive solutions that can change these situations for the better.

History versus Present, Professionals versus Amateurs

The research that analyzes large cultural datasets using computational methods today can be found in many academic disciplines, including computer science, data science, anthropology, sociology, communication, media studies, game studies, linguistics, geography, folklore studies, history, art history, and literary studies. The examples in the previous section illustrated some of the questions being studied. But rather than providing more examples from each of these disciplines, I want to move from individual examples to a larger question. This question is about assumptions and goals of the larger intellectual paradigms that separate these disciplines—and the possibilities of bringing them together in cultural analytics as equal intellectual contributors.

These three paradigms are humanities and qualitative social sciences, quantitative social sciences, and computer science. Each has different goals, different research methods, and different ways to evaluate the originality of research. When researchers study cultural data, what they do with it and how they do it reflects the assumptions and norms of these paradigms. In fact, if we know these norms, we may expect that research in each paradigm will develop in its own direction. Thus, computer scientists can be expected to be searching for general laws that describe patterns in large cultural data and creating quantitative models that can predict future patterns, particularly in relation to user behaviors online (following recommendations, disseminating information, purchasing, etc.). Quantitative social scientists will be asking social science questions and using particular statistical methods that are accepted in their fields with the data. Given that their focus is on social phenomena, we may also expect them to study group behaviors online. Humanists will be analyzing particular historical datasets and also particular cultural texts, and ideally questioning existing interpretations of cultural histories and offering new interpretations.

But we don't have to select either of these approaches or goals. Cultural analytics does not have to choose between humanistic and scientific goals and methodologies or subordinate one to another. Instead, we may want to put together elements from both humanities and sciences for the study of cultures. The humanities can contribute their strengths—focus on the particular (e.g., single artifacts and authors), the meanings of the artifacts, and orientation toward the past. And the sciences can give us theirs—focus on the general (e.g., large-scale patterns), use of the scientific method and mathematics, and interest in predicting the future.

In this section, I will further look at some of the assumptions and norms of humanities, qualitative social sciences, and computer science and will discuss how cultural analytics can potentially combine them. To get started, let's ask a question: What types of cultural data so far have been analyzed in computer science and the humanities? In other words, what counts as "culture" in each discipline?

In keeping with the historical orientation of the humanities, the researchers in the humanities have been using computers to analyze mostly *historical* artifacts created mostly by *professional authors*, whether this be medieval manuscripts by learned monks or nineteenth-century novels by authors paid for their work by the publishers. This focus on historical data is easy to see if you go through the issues of digital humanities journals such as *Digital Humanities Quarterly* (2007–present), or programs of the annual international Digital Humanities Conference.

In contrast, as I noted earlier, relevant publications in computer science focus almost exclusively on the period after 2005 because they analyze data from social networks, media sharing services, online forums, and blogs. The datasets used in these studies are often much larger than those used in digital humanities. Tens or hundreds of millions of posts, photos, or other items and billions of recorded interactions is not uncommon. And because the great majority of user-generated content is created by regular people rather than professionals, computer scientists have been studying *nonprofessional vernacular culture* by default. Or, as I expressed this idea earlier, what this research looks at and quantifies is *popular culture.*

Thus, we have two research universes that often use the same computational methods but apply them to different "cultures." On the humanities side, we have the past that stretches into hundreds or even thousands of years. On the computer science side, we have the present that starts in the beginning of the twenty-first century. On the humanities side, we have artifacts created by professional elites. On the computer science side, we have artifacts and online behavior by everybody else.

The scale of the research in computer science that uses web and social media datasets may be surprising to humanities and arts practitioners, who may not realize how many scientists are working in this area. I have given a number of research examples thus far but did not made fully clear how much is being published on these topics. Let's again turn to Google Scholar to see this. My recent searches on Google Scholar for "Twitter dataset algorithm," "YouTube dataset dataset," and "Flickr images algorithm" returned hundreds of thousands of journal articles and conference papers. I use words *dataset* and *algorithm* to limit results to papers that use computational methods. Not all these publications directly ask cultural questions, but many do.

Why do computer scientists rarely work with large historical datasets of any kind? Typically, they justify their research by reference to already existing industrial applications—for example, search or recommendation systems for online content. The general assumption is that computer science will create better algorithms and other computer technologies useful to industry, government, NGOs, and other organizations. The analysis of historical artifacts falls outside this goal, and consequently not many computer scientists work on historical data (the field of digital heritage being one exception).

However, looking at many examples of these papers, it is clear that they are actually asking questions typical of humanities or media studies in relation to contemporary media—but using bigger data to answer them. Consider, for example, these papers: "Quantifying Visual Preferences around the World" and "What We Instagram: A First Analysis of Instagram Photo Content and User Types."[26] The first study analyzes worldwide preferences for website design using 2.4 million ratings from forty thousand people in 179 countries. The study of aesthetics and design traditionally was part of the humanities. The second study analyzes the most frequent subjects of Instagram photos—a topic that can be compared to art historical studies of the genres in the seventeenth-century Dutch art.

Another example is an influential paper called "What is Twitter, a Social Network or a News Media?"[27] Published in 2010, it has since been cited 7,480 times.[28] This paper describes the first large-scale analysis of the Twitter social network using 106 million tweets by 41.7 million users. The authors looked at trending topics, exploring "what categories trending topics are classified into, how long they last, and how many users participate." Such analysis can be seen as an update of the classical work in the communication field, going back to the pioneering work of Paul F. Lazarsfeld and his colleagues in the late 1930s when they manually counted the topics of radio broadcasts.[29] The big difference is that in the 1930s such broadcasts were created by a small number of professional stations and belonged to a small number of genres, whereas Twitter may have numerous topics with different levels of generality, time duration, and geographic coverage. At the same time, given that Twitter and other microblogging services represent a new form of media—like oil painting, printed books, and photography before them—understanding the specificity of Twitter as a medium can be also seen as a contribution to the humanities.

The Regular versus the Particular

When humanities were concerned with "small data"—that is, content created by single authors or small groups—the sociological perspective was only one of many options for interpretation—unless you were a Marxist. But when we start studying the online content and activities of millions of people, this perspective becomes almost inevitable. When we look at big cultural data, the cultural and the social closely overlap. Large groups of people from different countries and socioeconomic backgrounds (sociological perspective) create, share, and interact with images, videos, and texts, and they make certain semantic and aesthetic choices when they do this (humanities perspective). Because of this overlap, the kinds of questions investigated in the sociology of culture of the twentieth century, as exemplified by its most influential researcher, Pierre Bourdieu, are directly relevant for cultural analytics.[30]

Given that demographic categories are taken for granted now in our thinking about society, it appears natural today to group people into these categories and compare them in relation to social, economic, or cultural indicators. For example, the Pew Research Center regularly reports the statistics of popular social platform use in the United States, breaking their user sample into demographics such as gender, ethnicity, age, education, income, and place of living (urban, suburban, and rural).[31] So if we are looking at types of social media content and behavior, such as types of images shared and liked, filters used, or selfie poses, it is logical to study the differences in content and activity among people from different cities and countries, ethnicities, socioeconomic backgrounds, levels of technical expertise, education, and so on. The first wave of relevant publications in computer science in the second part of the 2000s often did not do this, treating all social media users as one undifferentiated pool of humanity. However, later some publications started to break users into demographic groups.

Although this is a very good move, we also want to be careful. Humanistic analysis of cultural phenomena and processes using quantitative methods should not be simply reduced to sociology—that is, to considering common characteristics and behaviors of human groups defined using some taken-for-granted criteria, such as age, gender, income, and education. And given that we can now see daily the cultural choices of millions of individuals on social networks, is it still necessary to divide people in socioeconomic groups and look for differences between cultural preferences and behaviors of these groups? The idea that a group or a single person has consistent cultural behaviors and tastes made sense in ancient and modern societies, when taste was governed by prescriptive aesthetic norms. (This was the society of Kant and of Pierre Bourdieu.) But with numerous cultural choices available today, and the ability to "vote" for this or that choice using a single press of a button, we may find that the idea of a stable taste or stable "cultural personality" is an illusion.

Sociological tradition is concerned with finding and describing the general patterns in human behavior, rather than with analyzing or predicting the behaviors of particular individuals. Cultural analytics is also interested in patterns that can be derived from the analysis of large cultural datasets. However, ideally *the analysis of the larger cultural patterns should also lead us to particular individual cases*—that is, individual creators and their particular creations or cultural behaviors. (And as I just suggested, an individual can be further divided into separate personas with many different behaviors and cultural tastes.) For instance, the computational analysis of all photos made by a photographer during her long career may lead us to the outliers—the photos that are most different from all the rest. Similarly, we may analyze millions of Instagram images shared in multiple cities to discover the images unique to each city and the most original local photographers.

In other words, we may combine the concern of social science, and sciences in general, with the *general* and the *regular* and the concern of humanities with *individual* and *particular*. The examples just described of analyzing large cultural datasets to detect unique outliers is one simple way of doing this, but it is not the only one.

The Science of Culture? Deterministic Laws, Statistical Models, Simulation

The goal of science is to explain phenomena and develop compact mathematical models that describe how these phenomena work. The three laws of Newton's physics are a perfect example of how classical science approaches this goal. Since the middle of the nineteenth century, a number of new scientific fields have adopted a different, probabilistic approach to describing physical reality. The first instance of this new approach was the statistical distribution describing likely speeds of gas particles, presented by physicist James Maxwell in 1860 (it is now called the Maxwell-Boltzmann distribution).

And what about the social sciences? Throughout the eighteenth and nineteenth centuries, many thinkers were expecting that, similar to physics, the quantitative laws governing societies also eventually would be found. In his 1785 *Essay on Applications of Analysis to the Probability of Majority*, French mathematician Condorset writes: "All that is necessary to reduce the whole of Nature to laws similar to those which Newton discovered with the aid of calculus, is to have a sufficient number of observations and a mathematics that is complex enough." In the nineteenth century, the founder of sociology August Compte makes a similar statement in *Cours de philosophie positive* (1830–1842): "Now that human mind has grasped celestial and terrestrial physics, mechanical and chemical, organic physics, both vegetable and animal, there remains one science, to fill up the series of sciences of observations—social physics."[32]

However, this never happened in a way similar to classical physics. The closest that nineteenth-century social thought came to postulating objective laws were the theories of Karl Marx. But by the end of the nineteenth century, economists demonstrated that his analysis was mostly wrong, and twentieth-century attempts to create new societies based on his theories all ended in disaster. Instead, when quantitative social sciences started to develop in the late nineteenth and early twentieth centuries, they also adopted a probabilistic approach. Instead of looking for deterministic laws of society, social scientists study correlations among measurable characteristics and model the relations between dependent and independent variables using various statistical techniques.

After deterministic and probabilistic paradigms in science, the next paradigm was computational simulation—running models on computers to simulate the behavior of systems. The first large-scale computer simulation was created in the 1940s by the Manhattan Project to model a nuclear explosion. Subsequently, simulation was adapted in many hard sciences, and in the 1990s it was also taken up in the social sciences.

The twentieth-century humanities stayed away from looking for either physics-like laws of culture or modeling cultural processes probabilistically. Although literary studies, art history, and later film and media studies described various semantic and aesthetic patterns in the cultural corpora they studied, counting how frequently these patterns appeared in these corpora and interpreting the results was not seen as something humanists should be doing. A handful of people who were doing such quantitative analysis were real exceptions (e.g., Boris Jarkho in Russia in the 1930s or Barry Salt in the United States in the 1970s).

The explosion of digital cultural content and online interactions mediated by software and networks in the early twenty-first century has changed how culture functions. The volume of this content and user interactions allow us to think of a possible *science of culture*. For example, by the summer of 2015, Facebook users were sharing four hundred million photos and sending forty-five billion messages daily,[33] and the number of monthly users worldwide reached 2.5 billion by the end of 2019. This scale is still much smaller than that of atoms and molecules; for example, 1 cm^3 of water contains $3.33 * 10^{22}$ molecules. However, the number of weekly Facebook messages is already bigger than the numbers of neurons in the whole nervous system of an average adult brain, estimated at around one hundred billion.

Although the idea of a science of culture may terrify some readers, you should not be scared. As I explained, the concept of science as a set of hard laws is only one among others. Today, science includes at least three different fundamental approaches to studying and understanding phenomena: *deterministic laws*, *statistical models*, and *simulation*. Let's continue our thought experiment and ask which of these approaches will be most useful for a hypothetical science of culture.

Looking at the papers of computer scientists who are studying social media datasets, it is clear that their default approach is statistical. They characterize social media data and user behavior in terms of probabilities. They frequently create *statistical models*—mathematical equations that specify the relations between variables that may be described using probability distributions rather than specific values. Many papers published after 2010 also use supervised machine learning—a paradigm for teaching a computer to classify or predict values of new data using already existing examples. Note that in both cases, a model usually can correctly describe or classify only some of the data and not all of it. This is typical of the statistical approach.

Computer scientists use statistics differently than social scientists. The latter want to *explain* social, economic, or political phenomena—for example, the effect of family background on children's educational performance. Computer scientists are generally not concerned with explaining patterns they discover in social media or other cultural data by referencing external social, economic, or technological factors. Instead, they typically either analyze social media phenomena by themselves or try to predict the outside phenomena using information extracted from social media datasets. Examples of the former include network measurements of connections between friends in a social network, or a statistical model that predicts the effects of filter use on number of views and comments a photo on Instagram may receive. An example of the latter is the Google Flu Trends service that was designed to predict flu activity using a combination of Google search data and US Centers for Disease Control and Prevention (CDC) official flu data.[34]

The difference between deterministic laws and nondeterministic models is that the latter only describe probabilities and not certainties. The laws of classical mechanics apply to any macroscopic objects. In contrast, a probabilistic model for predicting the numbers of views and comments for an Instagram photo as a function of filter use cannot predict exactly these numbers for any particular photo. It only describes the overall trend. So, if we have to choose between deterministic laws and probabilistic models for a hypothetical science of culture, the second approach is better. If instead we start postulating deterministic laws of human cultural activity, what happens to the idea of free will? Even in the case of seemingly almost automatic cultural behavior, such as social media photos of perfect beaches or luxury hotels getting likes, we do not want to reduce humans to mechanical automata always behaving in the same way when presented with an appropriate stimulus.

The current focus on probabilistic models of online activity in computer science studies of social media data leaves out the third scientific paradigm: simulation. In sociology, economics, political theory, and history, simulation has already been in use for a few decades, and recently a few digital humanities scholars have also showed interest in using this paradigm.[35]

In 2009, scientists at the IBM Research Almaden Center simulated the human visual cortex using 1.6 billion virtual neurons with nine trillion synapses.[36] Given this, why can't we begin thinking about how to simulate, for instance, all content shared every month on Instagram? Or all content shared by all users of major social networks? Or, more interestingly, can we simulate the evolution of the types of content being shared and aesthetic strategies over time?

The point of such simulations is not to get everything right or to precisely predict what people will be sharing next year. Instead, we can follow the authors of the influential textbook *Simulation for the Social Scientist*, who state that one of the purposes of simulation is "to obtain a better *understanding* of some features of the social world" and that simulation can be used as "a method of *theory development*."[37] Because computer simulation requires developing an explicit and precise model of a phenomenon being simulated, thinking of how cultural processes can be simulated can help us to develop more explicit and detailed theories of cultural processes.[38]

And what about big data? Does it represent a new paradigm in science that allows us to think about and also study phenomena differently? In natural sciences, the impact of big data depends on a particular field. But if we are talking about research methods and techniques, the developments in computer hardware in the 2000s, including increasing CPU speed and RAM size and the use of GPUs and computing clusters, were likely more important than the availability of larger datasets. And although the use of supervised machine learning with large training datasets has achieved remarkable successes in some cases, as can be seen in industrial applications such as speech recognition and synthesis or image content categorization, its role in the sciences is more ambiguous. If we assume that the goal of science is to provide an explanation and a mathematical model of some natural or biological phenomena, the existence of a successful machine learning system that can correctly classify the new inputs usually does not provide explanations of the phenomena.

However, as I argue in this book, big data is certainly of fundamental importance for the study of culture. (See in particular the section "Why We Need Big Data to Study Cultures" in chapter 5). But the magnitude of this impact also has to do with the fact that humanities and media theory did not use science principles and methods before. So along with big data, the humanities are also discovering how scientific thinking and methodologies can be applied to their subjects. And here the concepts and methods of sampling, feature extraction, and exploratory data analysis are more important than data size (see chapters 5–9).

3   Culture Industry and Media Analytics

Culture today is infecting everything with sameness. Film, radio, and magazines form a system. . . . Interested parties like to explain culture industry in technological terms. Its millions of participants, they argue, demand reproduction processes that inevitably lead to the use of standard processes to meet the same needs at countless locations. . . . In reality, the cycle of manipulation and retroactive need is unifying the system ever more tightly.
—Max Horkheimer and Theodor W. Adorno, *Dialectic of Enlightenment*, 1947[1]

Scuba is Facebook's fast slice-and-dice data store. It stores thousands of tables in about 100 terabytes in memory. It ingests millions of new rows per second and deletes just as many. Throughput peaks around 100 queries per second, scanning 100 billion rows per second, with most response times under 1 second.
—J. Wiener and N. Bronson, "Facebook's Top Open Data Problems," 2014[2]

Our data is literally a *big deal*. Measuring every second of engagement on every single page on most every major website in the globe means a scientifically defined insane amount of data.
—Chartbeat, "About," 2015[3]

When I first thought of cultural analytics in November of 2005, the paradigm of *computing culture*—using algorithms to analyze online digital content and people's online behaviors—was already largely in place. The first web search engines were created in 1993 to 1994, and Google started operating in 1998. In March 2005, Amazon begun to display a few statistics calculated from the texts of all its books in searches, such as the most unique phrases per book and one hundred most common words in a book.[4] Earlier, in 2001, Amazon engineers presented a paper describing an important recommendation algorithm that was later implemented on the Amazon site: item-to-item collaborative filtering.[5] The social network Friendster that launched in 2002 patented a few fundamental techniques of social networking: "A method and apparatus for calculating, displaying and acting upon relationships in a social network," "System and method for managing connections in an online social network," and "Method of inducing content uploads in a social network."[6] However, as of 2005, social networking was not yet a massive phenomenon, the iPhone did not exist, and the term *data science* was not yet popular.

This situation changed dramatically over the next few years. The types of digital cultural data being analyzed, the methods for analysis, the scale of data, and the number of companies involved all grew quickly. By November 2017, Facebook was available in 101 languages; 75 percent of its two billion users were outside the United States and Canada.[7] Instagram reached eight hundred million users by September 2017, while Chinese WeChat, QQ, and Qzone reached 960, 850, and 650 million users, respectively.[8] When the top US social networks limited access to their data, hundreds of academic researchers signed a letter explaining why they need this access, giving examples of numerous social science studies that would be impossible without access to this data.[9] In 2018, Facebook—together with its partners, Harvard University's Institute for Quantitative Social Science and the Social Science Research Council—started a project called Social Science One, with the goal to enable "academics to analyze the increasingly rich troves of information amassed by private industry in responsible and socially beneficial ways."

In this chapter, I will discuss large-scale analysis of online cultural content and users' interactions with this content and each other by companies, NGOs, and other actors. I call these practices *media analytics*. While cultural analytics and media analytics share the same idea—large-scale computational analysis of cultural artifacts and behaviors—their goals and motivations are different. Media analytics always serves practical goals: decide when and what ads to show to users, index billions of web pages as part of a search engine, automatically pick up the best images representing businesses on a recommendation site, and so on. The goals of cultural analytics as I see it are observation and analysis of global culture, and developments of analytical concepts and methods that combine the respective strengths of data science, the humanities, and media theory.

Another key difference is what happens with the results of the analysis. Companies that use media analytics do so to improve their services and almost never make available the detailed results of such analysis (Google Search Trends is one exception). Cultural analytics researchers should not only publish their research findings and datasets, but ideally also create public interactive visualization and exploration tools accessible to everybody.

Cultural analytics research can certainly benefit from learning the details of how industry analyzes digital media artifacts and user activities. In its quest to optimize products, automate decisions, and create personalized experiences, industry often analyzes more dimensions and details of cultural artifacts and interactions than researchers in the humanities or social sciences were ever able to do or even imagine. Another fundamental aspect of media analytics is its scale. In the humanities, scholars of literature, cinema, music, digital media, and other art forms often think about the effects of artistic works on readers, viewers, and listeners using only their own experience with particular works. In social sciences, the sociology of culture and communication studies have been using surveys and interviews to learn about cultural behaviors of larger groups—but this approach does not scale well. In contrast, industry is capturing aspects of cultural experiences of billions of people.

Digital humanities has mostly ignored opportunities to study vernacular digital culture because, as I explained earlier, it follows the traditional humanities paradigm of studying professional and high cultures. But social scientists concerned with society at large have welcomed opportunities to analyze social phenomena via digital networks in the process of developing new research methods such as the design of online experiments. As the organizers of the MIT Conference on Digital Experimentation (2017) point out:

> The newly emerging capability to rapidly deploy and iterate micro-level, in-vivo, randomized experiments in complex social and economic settings at population scale is, in our view, one of the most significant innovations in modern social science. As more and more social interactions, behaviors, decisions, opinions and transactions are digitized and mediated by online platforms, our ability to quickly answer nuanced causal questions about the role of social behavior in population-level outcomes such as health, voting, political mobilization, consumer demand, information sharing, product rating and opinion aggregation is becoming unprecedented.[10]

The use of digital experiments in social science suggests that researchers of culture should be also analyzing data about cultural reception and interaction on a large scale and conducting large digital experiments. So far, such culture experiments are done by the industry itself; think, for instance, of A/B testing in web design or automatic selection of friends' posts in social networks such as Facebook. These are *digital humanities experiments*, so to speak, performed by industry. Of course, the data collected from these experiments is not publicly available, and the experiments are aimed at only a few pragmatic goals: to increase engagement (such as time spent on the site) or to increase brand awareness or to lead people to purchase goods or services. This is why we need to make our own experiments and ask alternative questions.

A New Stage in Media Technology History

The history of technological media can be imagined as a series of many overlapping stages. At each stage, new technologies and new practices for creating, storing, distributing, and using content become prominent. But these practices do not replace each other in a linear fashion. Instead, the older ones continue to coexist along with the new ones. For example, consider mass reproduction of print (1500–), broadcasting (1920–), use of personal computers for media creation (1981–), the web as a publishing and distribution platform (1993–), and social networks and media sharing sites (2003–), to name just a few of these practices. All of them are active today, although over long periods of time, the earlier practices may become less important or be transformed in significant ways.

Media analytics is the newest stage in the development of modern technological media. Unlike other stages, it is not at its core about creation, publishing, or distribution, although it also affects these operations. The focus of this new stage is automatic computational analysis of the content of all media available online, as well as online personal and group behaviors and communication.

The motivations and uses of media analytics are multiple, but they all are related to the scale of digital culture in the early twenty-first century. This scale is the volume of digital content: in 2017 the Web had 14 billion web pages, and 2 billion photos were shared daily on Facebook alone. It is also the numbers of people active online. As of early 2020, there were 3.8 billion active social network users and 4.5 billion internet users, and these numbers continue to grow. Therefore, to say that media analytics and the rise of the big data paradigm are related is an understatement. In fact, Google and Facebook developed the next generation of technologies to store, retrieve, and analyze big data, and these are now also used in other fields because of the volumes of data they are dealing with.

Media Analytics Examples

Companies that sell cultural goods and services via websites or apps (e.g., Amazon, Apple, Spotify, Netflix); organize and make searchable information and knowledge (Google, Baidu, Yandex); provide recommendations (Yelp, TripAdvisor); and enable social communication, information sharing (Facebook, QQ, WeChat, WhatsApp, Twitter), and media sharing (Instagram, Pinterest, YouTube, iQiyi) all rely on computational analysis of massive media datasets and data streams. These datasets include the following:

- Records of users' online behavior (i.e., digital footprints): visiting websites, following links, sharing posts and "liking," viewing and clicking on ads
- Records of physical behavior: geographical location, date and time when user posts to social networks, location of a user phone or computer connected to the internet
- Media content created by companies: songs, video, books, and movies
- Media content created by users of social networks: posts, conversations, images, and videos

The term *dataset* is often used in industry to refer to static or historical data organized in databases. The term *historical* in industrial data analytics applications means everything that is more than a few seconds, or sometimes even fractions of a second, in the past. *Data streams* refers to the data that arrives in real time and is analyzed continuously using platforms such as Spark Streaming and Apache Storm.[11] So far, digital humanities and computational social sciences have only been analyzing historical, static datasets; meanwhile, the industry has been increasingly using real-time analysis of data streams that are larger and require the special technologies such as Hadoop, Apache Cassandra, Apache HBase, and MongoDB.

Let's look at one example of the industry computational analysis of media content and the use of this analysis. Spotify extracts many characteristics of each music track in its collection of over forty million tracks. These characteristics, or *features*, are also made available to external developers via the Get Audio Features for a Track Spotify API method. The current specification for this method lists thirteen audio features.[12] Many of them are built on top of more low-level features extracted by algorithms from the track audio file. These features are "acousticness," "danceability," duration in milliseconds, "energy," "instrumentalness," key, "liveness," loudness, mode, "speechiness," tempo, time signature, and valence. (Feature extraction is a key part of contemporary data analysis in general, and I will discuss it in chapter 6.)

Spotify and other music streaming services use such extracted features to automatically create custom playlists for users by starting with a song, album, artist, or genre. You can start with a single song, and the app's algorithms select and stream songs that are close to it in a *feature space*. The advantage of this method is that the new songs do not have to belong to the same album or artist—they only need to share some musical features with the previous songs.

There are numerous other applications of media analytics. For example, to make its search service possible, Google continuously analyzes the full content and markup of billions of web pages. It looks at *every* page on the web that its spiders can reach— its text, layout, fonts used, images, and so on, extracting over two hundred signals in total.[13] Email spam detection relies on the analysis of the texts of numerous emails. Amazon analyzes the purchases of millions of its customers to recommend books. Netflix analyzes the choices of millions of subscribers to recommend films and TV shows. It also analyzes information on all its offerings to create more than seventy thousand genre categories.[14] Contextual advertising systems such as Google AdSense analyze the content of web pages and automatically select the relevant ads to show. Video game companies capture the gaming actions of millions of players and use this to optimize game design. Facebook's algorithm analyzes all updates by all friends of every user to automatically select which ones to show in a user's feed if that user is using the default Top Stories option.[15] And it does this for all the posts of its 2.5 billion (as of early 2020) users. Other uses of media analytics in the industry include automatic translation (Google, Skype) and recommendations for people to follow or to add to your friends list (Twitter, Facebook). Using the voice interface in Google Search, Google Voice transcriptions,[16] Microsoft's Cortana, Siri, Amazon Alexa, or the Yandex browser also relies on computational analysis of millions of hours of previous voice interactions.

The development of algorithms and software that make this data collection and analyslis and subsequent actions possible is carried out by researchers in a number of academic fields, including machine learning, computer vision, music information retrieval, computational linguistics, and natural language processing. Many of these fields started to develop in the 1950s, with the key concept of *information retrieval* appearing in 1950 (discussed ahead). The newest term is *data science*, which became popular after 2010. It refers to professionals who know contemporary algorithms and methods for data analysis—described today by the overlapping terms of *machine learning*, *data mining*, and *AI*—as well as classical statistics, and can implement gathering, analysis, reporting, and storage of big data using current technologies.

People outside the industry may be surprised to learn that many key parts of media analytics technologies are open-sourced. To speed up the progress of research, most top companies regularly share many parts of their code. For example, on November 9, 2015, Google open-sourced TensorFlow, its data and media analysis system that powers many of its services.[17] Other companies, such as Facebook and Microsoft, also open-sourced their software systems for organizing massive datasets. Cassandra and Hive are two popular systems developed by Facebook, and they are now used by numerous commercial and nonprofit organizations. The reverse is also true: The data from community mapping project OpenStreetMap (openstreetmap.org), with its more than two million members, is used by many commercial companies, including Microsoft and Craigslist, in their applications.[18] The most popular programming languages used for media analytics research today are open source: R and Python.

If we want to date the establishment of the practices of the massive analysis of content and interaction data across the industry, we may pick 1995 as the starting date (early web search engines) and 2010 (when Facebook reached five hundred million users) as the date these practices fully matured. Today, media analytics is taken for granted, with every large company selling services or products online or physically doing this analytics daily and increasingly in real time. The same analysis is performed by hundreds of companies that offer *social media dashboards*—web tools for monitoring and analyzing user activity and posting content—and perform custom analysis for numerous clients, both profit and nonprofit, including private and public universities.

The Two Parts of Media Analytics

Media analytics is the new stage of media technology that impacts everyday *cultural* experiences of significant percentages of populations in most countries. One part of media analytics—the practices of gathering and algorithmic analysis of user interaction data (i.e., *digital traces*)—has received significant attention. However, most discussions of these practices are focused on political and social issues such as privacy, surveillance, access rights, discrimination, fairness, and biases, as opposed to the history and theory of technological media.

The second part of media analytics—the practices of algorithmic analysis of all types of online media content by the industry, including images, videos, and music—has received less attention in comparison. However, only if we consider the two parts of media analytics together—analysis of user interaction data and analysis of media content—does the magnitude of the shift that gradually took place between 1995 and 2010 become fully apparent. Although articles in popular media have discussed details of computational analysis of cultural content and data in some cases, such as Google Search, Netflix's recommendation system, or US presidential election campaigns starting with Obama's in 2008, they have not explained that media analytics is now used throughout the culture industry.[19]

Media analytics practices and technologies are employed in platforms and services via which people share, purchase, and interact with cultural products and with each other. They are used by companies to automatically select *what* will be shown on these platforms to each user, including updates from friends and recommended content, and *how* and *when*. And they also are used by millions of individuals who participate in the culture industry not only as consumers but also as content and opinion creators; George Ritzer and Nathan Jurgenson called this combination of consumption and production *prosumer capitalism*.[20] For example, Google Analytics for websites and blogs, and analytics dashboards provided by Facebook, Twitter, and other major social networks are used by millions to fine-tune their content and posting strategies.

Both parts of media analytics are historically new. At the time when Max Hork-heimer and Theodor Adorno were writing their book that introduced the term *culture industry* (see the quote at the start of this chapter), interpersonal and group interactions were not part of the culture industry. But today, they have now also become *industrialized*—influenced in part by algorithms deciding what content, updates, and information from people in your networks to show you. These interactions are also industrialized in a different sense: interfaces and tools of social networks and messaging apps are designed with input from user interaction (UI) scientists and designers, who test endless possibilities to ensure that every UI element, such as buttons and menus, is optimized and engineered to achieve maximum results.

The second part of media analytics—computational analysis of media content—also did not exist until recently. The first computer technologies that could retrieve computer-encoded text in response to a query were introduced in the 1940s. In a conference held in in 1948, participants learned about the UNIVAC computer, which was "capable of searching for text references associated with a subject code."[21] Calvin Moo-ers coined the term *information retrieval* in his master's thesis at MIT and published the definition of the term in 1950. According to this definition, information retrieval is "finding information whose location or very existence is a priori unknown."[22] While the earliest systems only used subject and author codes, in the late 1950s IBM computer scientist Hans Peter Luhn introduced full-text processing. I identify this moment as the beginning of the media analytics paradigm.

In the 1980s, the first search engines applied information retrieval technology to files on the internet. After the World Wide Web started to grow, new search engines for websites were created. The first well-known engine that searched the text of websites was WebCrawler, released in 1994. In the second part of the 1990s, many other search engines, including Yahoo!, Magellan, Lycos, Infoseek, Excite, and AltaVista, were analyzing website texts. And in the 2000s, massive analysis of other types of online media, including images, videos, and songs, began. Google introduced Image Search in July 2001, indexing 1 billion images by 2005 and 10 billion by 2010. Another image search service TinEye indexed forty billion web images by early 2020. Music streaming services analyze the characteristics of millions of songs and use this analysis for recommendation. YouTube analyzes the content of posted videos to see if a new video matches an already existing item in the database of millions of copyrighted videos.

Automation: Media Analysis

If we look at the cultural analytics stage of media history in terms of automation, it follows the earlier stage when software tools and computers were adapted for authoring individual media products. [23] The important moments in this history include the introduction of Quantel Paintbox for video effects (1981), Microsoft Word for writing (1983), PageMaker for desktop publishing (1985), Illustrator for vector drawing (1987), Photoshop for image editing (1990), and Video Toaster for video editing (1990). These software tools made possible faster workflows, exchanging and sharing projects' digital files and assets, creation of modular content (e.g., layers in Photoshop), and the ability to easily change parts of the created content in the future. Later, these tools were joined by other technologies that support computational media authoring, such as render farms and media workflow management software.

The tools of media analytics are different: they automate the analysis of (1) billions of pieces of media content shared and published online and (2) data from trillions of interactions between users and software services and apps. For example, in 2018, an Instagram algorithm that creates recommendations for each user utilized these main factors (in addition to many others):

Interest: How much Instagram predicts you'll care about a post, with a higher ranking for what matters to you, determined by past behavior toward similar content and potentially machine vision analyzing the actual content of the post

Recency: How recently the post was shared, with prioritization for timely posts over weeks-old ones

Relationship: How close you are to the person who shared it, with a higher ranking for people you've interacted with a lot in the past on Instagram, such as by commenting on their posts or being tagged together in photos[24]

What is now being automated is no longer a creation of individual media items but other media operations. This includes selection and filtering (what to show), content placement (behavioral advertising), and discovery (search, recommendations). Another application is *how to show*; for example, news portal Mashable automatically adjusts the placement of stories based on real-time analysis of users' interactions with this content. Yet another application of media analytics is *what to create*; for example, in 2015, *New York Times* writers started to use an in-house application that recommends topics to cover.[25]

Just as the adoption of computers for media authoring gradually democratized this process, the development of concepts, techniques, software, and hardware for media analytics also democratizes its use. Today, every creator of web content has free tools that until recently were only available to big advertising agencies or marketers. Every person who runs a blog site or posts content on their social media networks can now act as a media company, studying data about clicks, reshares, and likes; paying to promote any post; and systematically planning what and where they share. All popular media sharing and networking platforms show people detailed graphs and statistics about interactions network users have with their content.

As another example, consider Mailchimp, a popular service for sending and tracking mass emails. When I use Mailchimp to send an email to my own mailing list (Mailchimp is currently free for up to two thousand email addresses and twelve thousand emails per month), I use its Send Time Optimization option. Mailchimp then analyzes data from my previous email campaigns and "determines the best sending time for the subscribers you're sending to and distributes it at the optimal time."[26] To create my posts for Facebook and Twitter, I use the Buffer app, which also calculates the best time for me to post to each network. If I want to promote my Facebook page or Twitter posts, I can use free advertising features that can create a custom audience for my campaign by selecting users on these networks based on hundreds of settings, including country, age, gender, interests, and behaviors. Category-based market segmentation was already in use earlier in marketing and advertising, but Twitter also allows you to "target users who are similar to the people who already follow you" for your account.[27] In this new situation, I no longer have to start with explicit categories or terms; instead, I can let Twitter's media analytics build a custom audience for me.

For web giants such as Google, Baidu, Yandex, and Facebook, their technical and talent resources for data analysis and access to data about the use of their services by billions of people daily give them significant advantages. These resources allow these companies to analyze user interactions and act on them in ways that are quantitatively different from an individual user or a business using Google Analytics or Facebook analytics on their own accounts, or using any of the social media dashboards—but qualitatively, in terms of concepts and most of the technologies, it is exactly the same. One key difference between the largest companies and smaller companies is that the former have top scientists developing their machine learning systems (a modern form of AI), which analyze and make decisions based on billions of data points captured in near real time. Another difference is the fact that Google and Facebook dominate online search and advertising in many countries and therefore have a disproportional effect on the discovery of new content and information by hundreds of millions of people.

Media analytics is big, and it is used throughout the culture industry. But still, why do I call it a *stage*, as opposed to just one among other trends of the contemporary culture industry? Because in some industries, media analytics is used to algorithmically process *every* cultural artifact. For example, digital music services that use media analytics accounted for 70 percent of music revenue in the United States in 2014.[28] This is the new logic of how media work internally and how they function in society. In short, it is crucial both practically and theoretically. Any future discussion of media theory or communication has to start with this new situation.

(Of course, I am not saying that nothing else has happened after 1993 in media technologies. I can list many other important developments, such as the move from hierarchical organization of information to search, the rise of social media, the integration of geolocation information, mobile computing, the integration of cameras and web browsing into phones, and the adoption of supervised machine learning across media analytics applications and other areas of data analysis after 2010.)

Companies that are key players in big media data processing—Google, Baidu, VK, Amazon, eBay, Facebook, Instagram, and the like—are very young. They developed in a web era, as opposed to older, twentieth-century cultural industry players, such as movie studios or book publishers. These older players were, and continue to be, the main producers of "professional" content. The newer players act as interfaces between people and this professional content, as well as user-generated content. The older players are gradually moving toward adoption of analytics, but key decisions (e.g., publishing a book) are still made by individuals following their instincts. In contrast, the new players have built their business on computational media analytics from the beginning.

On the one hand, companies use media analytics to optimize distribution, marketing, advertising, discovery, and recommendations—that is, the part of the culture industry in which customers find and purchase cultural products. On the other hand, the users of social networks and web platforms become "products" to each other. Thus, Amazon algorithms analyze data about what goods people look at and what they purchase and use this analysis to provide personal recommendations to each of its users. Facebook algorithms analyze what people do on Facebook to select what content appears in each person's news feed.[29]

Although the word *algorithms* and the term *algorithmic culture* are convenient, they can be also misleading—and that is why I use *analytics* instead. The most frequently used technology for big data analysis and prediction is supervised machine learning that uses neural networks, and it is quite different from our common understanding of an algorithm as a finite sequence of steps executed to accomplish some task. Some machine learning applications are *interpretable*, but many are not. The process of creating such a system often results in a black box, which has good practical performance but is not interpretable; that is, we do not know how it generates results.[30] For these reasons, I prefer to avoid using the terms *algorithms* and *algorithmic* when referring to the real-world systems deployed by companies to analyze data, make predictions, or execute automatic actions based on this analysis. My preferred term is *software*, which is more general; it does not assume that the system uses traditional algorithms, nor that these algorithms are interpretable.[31]

Media analytics is the key aspect of "materiality" of media today. Fifteen years ago, this concept may have been used in discussions of computer hardware, programming languages, databases, network protocols, and media authoring, publishing, and sharing software.[32] Today, media materiality includes big data storage and processing technologies such as Hadoop and Storm, paradigms such as supervised machine learning and deep learning, and popular machine learning algorithms such as k-means clustering, decision trees, support vector machines, and k-NN (k-nearest neighbors). Materiality is Facebook "scanning 100 billion rows per second,"[33] and Google processing 100+ TB of data per day (2014 estimate)[34] and automatically creating "multiple [predictive] models for every person based on the time of the day."[35]

Automation: Media Actions

So far, our discussion has focused on automatic analysis of media content and user interactions with the content. I now want to talk about another novel aspect of media culture enabled by media analytics: automation of *media actions* based on the results of earlier and/or real-time analysis. These actions can be divided into two types: (1) automatic actions partly controlled by explicit user inputs or chosen settings and (2) automatic actions not controlled by explicit user inputs.

Examples of automatic actions partly controlled by explicit user inputs or chosen settings include search results returned in response to a text search query, image search results produced in response to the user choosing an image type to find, and music tracks recommended by a music streaming service in response to the user's initial selection of a musician or tracks. For example, Google image search options currently have a choice of face, photo, clip art, line drawing, or animation; and full color, a dominant color, or black and white. Examples of settings that can be changed by users are ads chosen by the system to show in response to the user's ad preferences and types of images shown in response to "safe search" settings.

These users' inputs and settings are combined with the results of content and interactions analysis to determine the actions taken by the software. The choice of actions may combine previous data from the particular user and data for all other users—such as the purchasing history of all Amazon customers. Other information also can be used to determine actions. For instance, real-time algorithmic actions that involve thousands of ads determine which ads will be shown be on the user's page at a given moment.

Automatic actions not controlled by explicit user inputs depend on the analysis of user interaction activity but do not require the user to choose anything explicitly. In other words, a user "votes" with all of their previous actions. The automatic filtering of emails in Gmail into Important and Everything categories is a good example of this type of action. Most of the automatic actions we encounter in our interactions with web services and apps today can be partly controlled by us via settings; however, not every user is willing to spend the time to understand and change the default settings for every service (e.g., those at https://www.facebook.com/settings).

We can also divide automatic actions into two types, depending on whether they are arrived at in a deterministic or nondeterministic way:

1. *Deterministic actions* are produced by computation that always generates the same outputs given the same inputs.

2. *Nondeterministic actions* are produced by computation that may generate many different outputs given the same inputs. Today, most algorithmic decision-making that uses big data relies on probability theory, statistics, and machine learning. This includes automatic decision-making in web services and apps of the culture industry. For example, a recommendation system may generate different results every time by adding a random parameter to vary these results. But even when a computational system uses deterministic methods, it can still generate different actions every time if the data used as input have changed—as typically is the case with constantly evolving web or social networks.

The overall result is another new condition of media: what we are shown and recommended every time is not completely determined by us or by system designers. This *shift from strictly deterministic technologies and practices of the culture industry in the twentieth century to nondeterministic technologies in the the twenty-first century* is another important aspect of the new stage of media culture. What was strictly the realm of experimental arts—the use of indeterminacy by John Cage or stochastic processes by Iannis Xenakis to create or perform compositions—has been adopted by the culture industry as a method to deal with the new massive scale of available content. But of course, the industry goal is different: not to create a possibly uncomfortable and shocking aesthetic experience, but to expose a person to more existing content that fits with that person's existing taste, as manifested in their previous choices. However, we should keep in mind that industry recommendation systems can be also used to expand one's taste and knowledge, if one gradually keeps moving further from one's initial selections—and certainly web hyperlinking structures, Wikipedia, and open-access publications also can be used to do this.

In addition to the examples of automatic actions based on media analytics I already mentioned, there are many other types of such actions that also make contemporary media different from media of the past. For example, the data on users' interaction with a web service, app, or device also often is used to make automatic design adjust-ments in that web service, app, or device. The data also is used to create more cognitive automation, allowing the system to "anticipate" what users may need at any given location and time and deliver the information best tailored to this location, moment, user profile, and type of activity. The term *context-aware* is often used to describe com-puter systems that can react to a location, time, identity, and activity.[36] The Google Now assistant introduced in 2012 is one example of such context-aware computing (since 2016, its functions have been incorporated into Google Assistant).

Twentieth-century industrial and software designers and advertisers used user test-ing, focus groups, and other techniques to test new products and to refine them. But in the media analytics stage, a service or a product can automatically adjust its behavior for each individual user based on that user's interaction history, as well as analysis of interactions of every other user with the service or product. Following the model popu-larized by Google, every web and app user has become a beta tester of many constantly changing systems that learn from every interaction.

Large-scale media analytics is often used in making decisions about what cultural products to create, their contents and aesthetics, and how they should be marketed and to what groups. For example, when you create a post that you want to promote and let Facebook, Twitter, or another social network automatically create a particular audience segment that is, for example, similar to your current followers, you are using media analytics. Here the system automatically decides what audience will be most interested in your content. But media industry is already going further, sometimes using analytics to decide what to create in the first place. Here Netflix has been a pioneer, using data to decide on elements of a new show that became very successful (*House of Cards* in 2013).[37] Netflix also systematically analyzes all kinds of data about what its viewers watch and also the content of the films and TV shows it offers. As the director of engineering at Netflix, Xavier Amatriain, explained in an interview in 2013: "We know what you played, searched for, or rated, as well as the time, date, and device. We even track user interactions such as browsing or scrolling behavior. All that data is fed into several algorithms, each optimized for a different purpose. In a broad sense, most of our algorithms are based on the assumption that similar viewing patterns represent similar user tastes. We can use the behavior of similar users to infer your preferences."[38]

Netflix is even analyzing the colors of the cover images for its programs. On its technical blog, the company published examples of visualizations it created to compare the color palettes of its shows. Describing one such visualization from 2013 that compares the palettes of two covers that are hard to tell apart, Phil Simon points out that it shows that "subtle differences exist—and Netflix can precisely quantify those differences. What's more, Netflix can see if they have any discernible impact on subscriber viewing habits, recommendations, ratings, and the like."[39] In yet another application of media analytics, the blog describes how Netflix uses computer vision algorithms to automatically find images from its films and TV series that would best represent this content on smaller mobile screens.[40] And these are only a few examples of how a company like Netflix uses media analytics to drive all kinds of decisions.

In another example, Yelp is using media analytics to automatically select the best photos to represent businesses on its review site. As explained on its engineering blog (2016):

> In order to provide a great experience for Yelp users, the Photo Understanding team had the challenging task of determining what qualities make photos appealing, and developing an algorithm that can reliably assess photos using these characteristics. . . . At Yelp, each business's page showcases a few of its best photos, which we call cover photos. For many years we have chosen these photos purely by calculating a function based on likes, votes, upload date, and image caption. However, this approach suffered from a few drawbacks. . . . Now, as a result of our scoring algorithm, we believe that the quality of cover photos for restaurants has significantly improved.[41]

Media Analytics and Cultural Analytics

Many of the cultural effects—as opposed to economic, social, and political ones—of the new computational organization of media culture have not been systematically studied empirically by either industry or academic researchers. For example, we know many things about the language of conservative and liberal Twitter users in the United States or the political polarization on the same platform.[42] But we do not know anything about the evolution in topics of hundreds of millions of blogs over last fifteen years or the changes in characteristics of billions of Flickr photos during the same period or the differences in types of content shared on Instagram in thousands of cities worldwide. Nor do we know anything quantitatively about how exposure to algorithmically selected images recommended by Instagram changes users' tastes and affects the new images they create themselves.

The datasets to research such questions exist or can be created. In 2014, Flickr released an open dataset of one hundred million photos with Creative Commons licenses shared between 2004 and 2014 to all interested researchers.[43] Such datasets can be used to study both evolution of global photo culture over time and the differences between local photo cultures. In our own work, we have analyzed one hundred thousand Instagram images shared in five global cities in one week in December 2013 and found significant differences in content, visual styles, and photo techniques between cities.[44] In another project from 2013, we compared temporal rhythms of image sharing in thirteen global cities using a sample of 2.3 million Instagram images.[45]

The industry does extract numerous patterns from professional and user-generated content online, but often the only ones "looking" at these patterns are algorithms and neural networks. Companies use this information for search, recommendation, design, marketing, advertising, and other applications, but they usually do not publish results of the analysis. The business clients of media analytics services are also typically interested in only particular content (e.g., all social media mentions of a particular brand or the activity of competing companies) and particular user behaviors or user activities (e.g., likes for this brand).

Often the same analytical methods used in the culture industry to rationalize and refine content and communications also can be used to research, map, and quantify and interpret cultural effects of industrial media analytics. For example, if the industry uses cluster analysis to study audiences for particular songs or movies, we can use cluster analysis to understand relations among thousands of movies being offered. But as this example demonstrates, there is a crucial asymmetry between what industry is doing and what independent researchers can do. I can assemble large datasets of user-generated content from some social networks, and also some types of professional content, such as music videos or motion graphics shared by designers and companies on Vimeo or design projects shared on Behance. If a given social network API provides this data, I can also access data on how users interact with a particular post, such as the number of likes, comments, and so on. However, I cannot access all such data for all professional media created today, nor can I get the kinds of details Netflix has access to: who is watching every program, at that time, in what locations, what else they searched for, their previous interaction histories, their mouse clicks, and so on. The same goes for data available to Spotify, the iTunes Store, Google Play, Amazon, Etsy, AliExpress, and so on.

One free system that provides a wealth of data, an easy-to-use interface with graphs, and the ability to download results is Google Trends. It can be used to ask interesting cultural questions, and in fact many researchers use its results in their papers. It is also possible to become a paying client for social media monitoring software (Hootsuite, Sprout Social, Brandwatch, Critical Mention, Crimson Hexagon [now part of Brandwatch], etc.) and monitor social media, blogs, reviews, news, forums, and other sources for certain keywords, hashtags, and topics, seeing their relative popularity over time and geography (similar to how Google Trends shows patterns for search terms). However, the main purpose of this software is to enable a business or organization to plan its social media activity, to see what people say about it, and to compare it with its competitors. Therefore, it can't be used as a general cultural analytics tool. To ask many research questions or to be able to analyze large cultural datasets directly instead of relying on algorithms built into social media monitoring software, you have to learn programming and data science, then acquire data (download data via an API, scrape it from websites, or purchase it from data providers such as DataSift or Webhose.io), and then you can start the analysis. If we are interested in fine-grained historical or large-scale cross-cultural analysis, this is often the only way.

The term *culture industry*, which already appeared in this book a number of times, has a precise origin. As I already mentioned, it was developed by German culture theorists Horkheimer and Adorno in their 1947 book *Dialectic of Enlightenment*. They wrote this book in Los Angeles when the Hollywood studio system was in its classical—that is, most integrated—period. There were eight major film conglomerates, and five of them (20th Century Fox, Paramount, RKO Pictures, Warner Brothers, and Loews) had their own production studios, distribution divisions, theater chains, directors, and actors. According to some film theorists, the films produced by these studios during this period also had a very consistent style and narrative construction.[46] Regardless of whether Horkheimer and Adorno had already fully formed their ideas before arriving in Los Angeles as emigrants from Germany, the tone of the book and its statements, such as the famous quote, "Culture today is infecting everything with sameness,"[47] seem to fit the Hollywood classical era—although even during this era, films by different directors were different from each other.

How does the new "computational base" (i.e., media analytics) affect both the products that the culture industry creates and what consumers get to see and choose? For example, do computational recommendation systems used today by many companies help people choose apps, books, videos, movies, or songs more widely (i.e., long tail effect), or do they, on the contrary, guide them toward "top lists"? What about systems used by Twitter and Facebook to recommend to us whom to follow and which groups to join? (For an example of the industry publication that presents details of its recommendation system, see the 2013 paper "Location Based Personalized Restaurant Recommendation System for Mobile Environments";[48] for the quantitative analysis of the effects of an industry recommendation system on media consumption, see the 2010 paper "The Impact of YouTube Recommendation System on Video Views."[49])

Or consider the interfaces and tools of popular media capture and sharing apps, such as Instagram, with its standard set of filters and adjustment controls appearing in a certain order on the user's phone. Does this lead to homogenization of image styles, with the same few filters dominating the rest? Such questions about the effect of digital tools and services on cultural diversity can now be studied quantitatively using large-scale cultural data from the web and data science methods. For example, when we compared the use of Instagram filters in 2.3 million photos shared in thirteen global cities during the spring of 2012, we found remarkable consistency between the cities.[50] The relative frequencies of different filters were very similar across the cities, and their popularity was almost perfectly correlated with the order of their appearance in the Instagram app interface.

Digitization of historical cultural media also makes it possible to quantitatively analyze changes in diversity and homogeneity over time. In the paper "Measuring the Evolution of Contemporary Western Popular Music" (2012), researchers applied computational methods to a dataset of 464,411 distinct music recordings for the 1955–2010 period. They found that many sound parameters of popular music did not change during this period, but some changed significantly. The researchers highlight three changes: "the restriction of pitch transitions, the homogenization of the timbral palette, and the growing loudness levels."[51] The first two findings suggest that on these dimensions, popular Western music became less diverse during the fifty-five-year period being studied.

Another publication, "The Evolution of Popular Music: USA 1960–2010," analyzed 17,094 songs that appeared in the charts for this period. The authors analyzed sound properties "to produce an audio-based classification of musical styles and study the evolution of musical diversity and disparity, testing, and rejecting, several classical theories of cultural change." They also investigated "whether pop musical evolution has been gradual or punctuated" and found that while some periods had gradual changes, there were also three stylistic "revolutions" around 1964, 1983, and 1991.[52]

In this chapter, we looked at media analytics—computational analysis of digital cultural content and user activities that have become the foundation of contemporary digital culture. However, though large-scale computational analysis of content and interaction data by companies such as Google, Facebook, Instagram, Amazon, and their counterparts in other countries gives them lots of power, they are not simply new iterations of the tightly integrated Hollywood conglomerates from the 1940s. The web, social media, and the use of media analytics create a new type of culture industry that coexists and interacts with the older one established in the 1910s–1940s. This earlier culture industry was focused on *creating, distributing, and marketing content*, such as movies, radio shows, songs, books, and TV programs. The new cultural industry of our time is focusing on *organizing, presenting, and recommending content created by various actors, as well as capturing and analyzing individuals' interactions with this content*. In other words, these companies are usually not content creators themselves.

The actors creating content include professional producers of different sizes (e.g., big movie studios, television production companies, book publishers, and music labels—the "old" culture industry) and billions of ordinary casual users, as well millions of people who are situated on many points in between these two extremes. Examples include minicelebrities and "influencers" on social media; freelancers such as photographers, designers, yoga instructors, hairstylists, or interior decorators, along with small shops or individual sellers that promote themselves using social media; creators of online videos in numerous genres, such as anime music videos, YouTube reaction videos, Russian schools' graduation videos, Chinese minimovies, and so on; thirty-five million artists sharing their works on DeviantArt (deviantart.com); one hundred and thirteen million academics who have accounts on academia.edu;[53] and more.[54]

And the content itself is also qualitatively different from what was produced at the time that Horkheimer and Adorno wrote their book (early 1940s): it is not only songs, films, books, and TV shows, but also our individual posts, messages, images, videos shared on Twitter, Facebook, Vine, Instagram, YouTube, and Vimeo, academic papers, code, and so on. All content published by the entire culture industry in the 1940s in the United States probably was under a few million items per year; today, all content shared on social networks adds up to many billions of items every day.

Surfacing the variability of this content so we can understand and interpret it can only be done using computational methods. As I am writing this, the academic fields that aim to understand media and digital phenomena—media theory, digital culture studies, and new media studies—have not yet adopted cultural analytics methods. But just as researchers in the recently emerged fields of digital history, digital humanities, and digital art history have started to apply these methods in their own areas, it is only a matter of time before media theory will start doing the same. This new area may be called *computational media studies*—or perhaps, by the time this adoption fully happens, it would be seen simply as another set of tools and methods that media and new media theory can use, and it would not need its own special name.

II   Representing Culture as Data

4 Types of Cultural Data

What does it mean to represent a cultural object, process, or experience as *data* that can be then analyzed computationally? What elements of these objects, processes, and experiences can be captured, and what remains outside? How can we represent people interactions with computational cultural artifacts and systems that can react to human behaviors, communicate with them (e.g., as AI interfaces can), and act in seemingly intelligent ways? These are all fundamental questions for cultural analytics.

In this chapter, I will look at four categories of "things" in global digital culture that we can analyze computationally on a large scale. Note that "digital" here refers to both the phenomena that are native to computer devices and networks (making posts, sharing media, commenting, participating in online groups and forums, using apps) and the physical phenomena that are represented in digital universe (e.g., webpages for organizations and events). The four categories we will examine are media, behaviors, interactions, and events.

Media here refers to digital artifacts created by professional creatives and users of social networks. *Behaviors* include both online activities that leave digital traces and physical behaviors that can be captured using other methods. *Interactions* refers to the activity of using interactive, algorithm-driven media such as video games, virtual earth software such as Google Earth, or virtual reality and augmented reality applications. Finally, *events* are cultural happenings that have duration in time and involve multiple people: a music performance, an exhibition opening, a fashion show, a workshop, a weekend urban festival, a demonstration by a master coffee maker. These events usually take place in specific *places* and are presented by *organizations*, so this category also includes these entities.

These four categories are not meant to include every phenomenon in digital culture. As an example of other equally important phenomena, consider *networks*. There is an academic field called network science devoted to the study of complex networks and development of theories and ways to measure networks. The network paradigm—that is, seeing a phenomenon as a network—also has been central to other fields since the 1990s. This paradigm assumes that the structure and characteristics of the networks are more important than any individual nodes and links. Adopting this paradigm for the study of digital culture means focusing on a network and the movement of media objects, topics, people, and other objects and actions within it—away from singular media artifacts, behaviors, or events. For example, the authors of the 2018 paper "Quantifying Reputation and Success in Art" performed network analysis of the art world. The authors analyzed data on "497,796 exhibitions in 16,002 galleries, 289,677 exhibitions in 7568 museums, and 127,208 auctions in 1239 auction houses, spanning 143 countries and 36 years (1980 to 2016)."[1] The analysis reveals important patterns in how artists move over time through the network of all these galleries and museums; for example, the artists that had their first five exhibitions in high-prestige institutions were likely to continue exhibiting in such institutions. In contrast, among artists who had their first five exhibitions in institutions ranked in the bottom 40 percent, only 14 percent continued to be active ten years later. The initial exhibition history of an artist was also predictive of other measures of success: "High–initial reputation artists had twice as many exhibitions as low–initial reputation artists; 49% of the exhibitions of high–initial reputation artists occurred outside of their home country, compared to 37% for low–initial reputation artists, and high–initial reputation artists showed more stability in institutional prestige." These and other patterns were revealed by considering the art world as a big network, with artists and artworks moving in it—without having to take into account the styles and content of the artworks themselves or biographic details of the artists.

There are also other ways to look at the digital universe in terms of things that we can select for analysis. For example, we can distinguish among cultural data, cultural information, and cultural discourse:

- *Cultural data:* Photos, music, designs, architecture, films, motion graphics, games, websites, apps, artworks—that is, cultural artifacts and systems that either are born digital or are represented through digital media (e.g., photos of architecture).

- *Cultural information:* Names of artists in an exhibition, addresses of cultural venues, numbers of downloads for an app, and other kinds of information all published online. This can be thought of as metadata about the artifacts in the first category.

- *Cultural discourse:* Reviews, ratings, posts in which people describe their experiences from attending an exhibition, and photos and videos of these experiences, posts, and videos that detail the creation process—that is, a kind of "extended metadata" about these artifacts.

Another important distinction is between the original cultural artifact/activity and its digital representations:

- *Born digital artifacts:* Since they are already in digital form, we are always dealing with the originals.
- *Digitized artifacts that originated in other media:* Their representation in digital form may not contain all the original information. For example, digital images of paintings available in online repositories and museum databases normally do not fully show their 3-D textures. (This information can be captured with 3-D scanning technologies, but this is not commonly done.)
- *Cultural experiences:* For example, experiencing theatre, dance, performance, architecture and space design; interacting with products; playing video games; or interacting with locative media applications on a GPS-enabled mobile device. Here, the properties of material/media objects that we can record and analyze are only one part of an experience. For example, in the case of spatial experiences, architectural plans will only tell us a part of a story; we may also want to use video and motion capture of people interacting with the spaces and their spatial trajectories.

Last but not least, we can also approach digital universe through the lenses of three categories that have been standard in humanities and media studies: *authors*, *texts* (or *messages*), and *audiences*. We can collect and analyze large data on authors, messages, and audiences using many methods—for example, network analysis of the connections between a group of authors, computer vision analysis of content of visual media they created, spatial analysis of people movements in a museum in relation to the exhibits, and so on. (Texts or messages in this scheme correspond to "media" as used in this chapter.)

Media: Social Networks and Professional Networks

Since the middle of the 2000s, large-scale global social and media sharing networks and messaging services such as Facebook, Twitter, Baidu, VK, Flickr, Instagram, Tumblr, Snapchat, WhatsApp, WeChat, Weibo, and LINE have aggregated massive amounts of posts, images, videos, comments, and discussions contributed by billions of people. User-generated content and interactions on some of these networks have been extensively analyzed by researchers in computer science, computational social science, and other fields.

However, it is crucial to remember that "social media" is not limited to content shared on these networks. The following list of types of social media with examples comes from the call for papers for the 11th Annual International Conference on Web and Social Media (2017):

- Social networking sites (e.g., Facebook, LinkedIn)
- Microblogs (e.g., Twitter, Tumblr)
- Wiki-based knowledge sharing sites (e.g., Wikipedia)
- Social news sites and websites of news media (e.g., Huffington Post)
- Forums, mailing lists, newsgroups
- Community media sites (e.g., YouTube, Flickr, Instagram)
- Social Q & A sites (e.g., Quora, Yahoo Answers)
- User reviews (e.g., Yelp, Amazon.com)
- Social curation sites (e.g., Reddit, Pinterest)
- Location-based social networks (e.g., Foursquare, Pokémon Go)
- Online dating sites (e.g., Match, Tinder, Grindr)
- Messaging platforms (e.g., Snapchat, Messenger, WhatsApp)[2]

The rise of online marketplaces such as Amazon, social media networks, and blogs in the 2000s created a new environment in which people voluntarily reveal their cultural choices and preferences: rating books, movies, software, images, videos, and songs; assigning likes and favorites; sharing cultural posts by others; and more. People explain, defend, and debate their cultural preferences, ideas, and perceptions. They comment on Instagram photographs, post their opinions about books on Amazon, critique movies on Rotten Tomatoes (rottentomatoes.com), and enthusiastically debate, argue, and agree and disagree with each other on numerous social media sites, fan sites, forums, groups, and mailing lists.

APIs, web scraping, and social media monitoring software give us access to large samples of content and user activities on these sites and networks. Conversations, discussions, and opinions can be analyzed computationally to find out what cultural topics are important to people in dozens of countries and how they *see* culture.

We can also find out which characteristics of cultural forms and genres people discuss in online forums. These characteristics then can be compared to the vocabularies used by professionals who create these forms and to the languages of academic researchers who write about them. (We are likely to find that fans pay attention to different things than casual viewers and academics.)

One social media type that does not appear in the earlier list but is particularly important for cultural analytics is networks and media sharing sites for *culture professionals*, aspiring creators, and students in creative fields. I described early examples of such sites, such as Coroflot, in chapter 1. In the first part of the 2000s, social networks were mass phenomena only in Japan and Korea, not yet anywhere else. At the time we set up our lab, Flickr was the only visible media sharing site in the United States, having reached two million users by October 2007. And though it was already possible to add images and videos to blogs, the process was not very simple, and not many blogs had visual media.[3] But portfolio sites such as Coroflot for professionals and students in creative fields were already fully operational.

Today, prominent examples of English-language professional portfolio and project sites include Behance (2006–) and dribble (2009–) for all types of design and visual communication, Archinect for architecture (1997–), 500px for photography (2009–), and DeviantArt for user-generated art (2000–). For data scientists, the equivalent of online portfolios is participation in competitions on kaggle.com. For professional writers and journalists, there are Clippings.me, Muck Rack (muckrack.com), and others. For music creators, there is SoundCloud (2007–). Video, motion graphics, and animation professionals use Vimeo (2004–). And all members of the "creative class" can also advertise themselves and look for jobs on freelance sites such as Upwork, Guru, Freelancer, and many others. There are also many similar sites in other languages, and many such sites have APIs.

Professional networks such as Behance are particularly good sources of data for analyzing global professional culture because their users share important information in addition to the examples of work projects: CVs, descriptions of projects, lists of clients, and personal statements. Housing projects and portfolios by millions of artists, media designers, freelance writers, coders, and other culture professionals, such websites provide *live snapshots of contemporary global cultural production, sensibilities, and emerging areas*. They also make possible analyzing changes in content, styles, techniques, and use of various media over time.

One of the earliest media sharing networks aimed at aspiring creatives rather than everybody was DeviantArt (deviantart.com; 2000–). By August 2008, it had eight million members, more than sixty-two million submissions, and was receiving eighty thousand submissions per day.[4] By 2016, DeviantArt had thirty-eight million registered users who were uploading 160,000 original artworks every day.[5] In our lab, we investigated changes in subjects, techniques, sizes, proportions, and selected visual characteristics of images in one million visual artworks shared on DeviantArt during the ten-year period from 2001 to 2010 (see chapter 7 for more details about this project).

Another interesting source for professional content is specialized groups on media sharing sites. For example, the group for motion graphics on Vimeo called Motion Graphics Artists had approximately 110,000 videos shared by thirty thousand members in March 2017.[6] Vimeo also has groups created by artists from various countries and cities, such as Look at Russia, @Mograph Spain, and Motion Graphics New York. We can use works shared by members of these groups to compare design trends between different countries. In one study, we have compared 170,000 images from the Graphic Design Flickr group with the same number of images from the Art Now Flickr group. As our paper explains, one of the purposes of this analysis was to learn "how services such as Flickr influences artists to pool their work together. We speculate that artists often decide to join a particular group by browsing its content and doing the mental computation to understand patterns in this content, the process that we aim at imitating with our algorithms."[7]

In addition to the obligatory presence on general social networks and professional networks such as Behance, today a serious creative professional maintains their dedicated site with a unique URL. A dedicated website is also the default medium to present a large or ongoing project or event in most cultural fields, in addition to a page on Facebook. How many such websites for cultural professionals, projects, and organizations are created or updated every year? As far as I know, nobody has ever bothered to ask such question. And this is a telling example of how little we know about contemporary global culture. The rapid expansion of the digital cultural universe is like an expansion of our physical universe after a big bang a billion years ago (according to the dominant cosmological paradigm). Manually browsing the web or using recommendations provided by social networks and sharing sites, we can see only tiniest corners of the continuously expanding cultural universe. But if we used proper sampling methods to collect big datasets and analyze them with data science methods, what we would be able to see would no longer be limited by lists of automatically generated "trending topics" or inaccessible algorithms underlying recommendation systems or lists of "top" or "most important" items created by some experts and geared to the interests of certain audiences. Such data collection methods include using APIs when they are available and downloading data via web crawling or web scraping when APIs do not exist. Using the latter methods, we can access and then analyze all kinds of cultural content outside social networks. (Of course, we also need to follow accepted guidelines to protect user privacy when using data from websites, social media networks and other online sources. I will discuss this later in this chapter.)

This data potentially can be used to do something that previously was unimaginable: to create dynamic, interactive, detailed maps of global cultural developments that reflect the activities, aspirations, and visions of millions of creators. Such dynamic maps will have a sufficient temporal and geographic resolution to show how trends emerge, travel in space and time, change in popularity, are combined with other trends, and so on (see plate 2).

But we also should not underestimate the challenges. For instance, though digitization and networking of culture gave us a massive volume of artifacts, it also led to the proliferation of new media forms and genres. And if humanities and media studies did not keep up with this proliferation, neither did computer sciences. Here older media popular by the end of the twentieth century—photographs, videos, songs, spatial data and text (including websites, blogs, and social media posts)—received the most attention. Automatic recognition and detection of objects, types of scenes, and higher-level concepts in photos has been a key focus of research in computer vision, and significant progress was made in the 2010s. Good progress has also been achieved for particular types of content, such as fashion photography. Significant accuracy has been achieved in automatic analysis of professional and nonprofessional fashion photos, including detecting types of clothes, poses, brands, and styles (hipster, bohemian, preppy, etc.).[8] Another research area where we see promising results is detection of illustration styles.[9] But at least so far, automatic analysis of styles, techniques, and forms in graphics, products, interfaces, and UI of games has not been posed as a research problem; the first paper on automatic classification of styles in architecture was only published in 2019.[10] (The adoption of neural networks that perform well for classification of new types of cultural data is a good start, but we certainly don't have anything yet that is similar in depth and breadth to the methods in natural language processing for other media.)

In fact, the global use of networked computers and devices for creating and sharing content and communication led not only to the quantitative explosion of cultural artifacts since the middle of the 2000s, but also to growth in number of media genres and their combinations: HDR photos, photos with filters, photos with superimposed stickers and drawings, 360-degree video, vertical video, virtual globes, emoji, screen icons, adaptive web designs, and more.[11] These genres, types, and combinations often change and evolve quickly. This is possible because they all "live" within a strictly software environment, so on a material level nothing needs to change; everything continues to be made from the same pixels, vectors, and text characters.[12] These dynamics and this mutability present a significant challenge for any type of media analysis today, be it nonquantitative media theory or quantitative studies that rely on algorithmic analysis of large samples. In other words, as algorithms to analyze some genres achieve better performance and researchers finally start paying attention to new forms, new genres and new forms keep emerging, and the older ones keep changing.

Behavior: Digital and Physical Traces

It is possible to argue that cultural things in our first category—user-generated and professionally created digital artifacts—are not different from historical artifacts we have from the past, despite their much greater volume, variety, and velocity. Both today and in the past, we have cultural objects created by individuals or groups: builders of a temple, cathedral, or a church eight hundred years ago, a movie studio fifty years ago, or a game design or software company today.

Similarly, you can argue that although reviews are now being created on a massive scale (e.g., Yelp, TripAdvisor, IMDB), they also existed in the past, written by professionals or educated elites. The same can be said about millions of creatives' CVs now shared on job-hunting and portfolio sites. We also have biographies for some professional artists, writers, scientists, and other members of professional and knowledge classes and other creatives who worked in earlier centuries. An article by Maximilian Schich and his coauthors titled "A Network Framework of Cultural History" demonstrates how a new vision of cultural history can emerge by following locations of birth and death of 150,000 notable individuals over two thousand years.[13]

What we certainly don't have from the past are *detailed and large-scale automatic recordings of cultural behaviors in large numbers*: discussing, reading, listening, viewing, gaming, navigating, searching, exploring, collaborating. But once these activities involve computers, the situation changes. Quantitative large-scale studies of what cultural theory refers to as *reception* become possible. Any activity that passes through a computer or a computer-based media device—surfing the web, playing a game, participating in a chat, sharing a post, writing a comment, editing a photo—automatically leaves traces: keystroke presses, cursor movements, controller positions, selected items on a menu, commands typed, and so on. The Undo command and History window present in many applications illustrate this well. Web servers log which pages users visited, how much time they spent on each page, which links they clicked on, and so on. Apps developers use special software services (e.g., Google's Firebase) to record and analyze detailed actions taken by users of their apps.

Thus, it is our second category of cultural things—behaviors—that turns out to be most different in terms of data available for cultural research. Between 2007 and 2018, an unprecedented amount of data on online behaviors was available via social network APIs. (As of 2018, US-based networks have limited third-party access to their data to comply with the EU General Data Protection Regulation and also in response to the news that their data was used to manipulate voters' opinions in the 2016 US presidential election and the 2016 Brexit vote in the United Kingdom.) In some of these years,

APIs from some of the most popular networks allowed access to detailed information for all public posts, including geographic location, the date and time when the post was made, numbers of likes, username of a person who made the post, its text, hashtags, shared images or videos if present, and more. The APIs also made available many types of data about each user. For example, in 2017 the Twitter API provided over forty different pieces of such data, such as self-declared account location and interface language, image used for the profile, IDs and counts of friends, and others.[14] The availability of all this data played a key role in the development of computational social science in the second part of the 2000s.

If we use social media data accessible via APIs for research purposes, we have to follow rules carefully to ensure user privacy. This was not obvious at first, but eventually researchers in computer science and computational social science started to do this, and in 2013 national bodies such as the US Department of Health and Human Services created detailed guidelines.[15] Companies such as Facebook also created guidelines and review boards for data use by their own researchers after the topic of access to user data started to be widely discussed.[16] Research and publication guidelines by national bodies and academic journals state that any personal data can be used only with explicit user consent. According to one such set of guidelines, in situations where "it is not possible to guarantee that personal data will not be collected," the researchers should delete such data after collection.[17] I have already mentioned industry projects such as Facebook's Social Science One that aim to provide big data to researchers without comprising privacy, but this is only one possible solution. As digital culture researchers Tommaso Venturini and Richard Rogers pointed out in 2019: "The closure of APIs . . . can have positive effects, if it encourages researchers to reduce their dependence on mainstream platforms and explore new sources and ways to collect online records that are closer to the digital fieldwork."[18]

Of course, not all cultural activities and behaviors are mediated by computers. People attend concerts and go museums, read books, spend time in their favorite cafes, travel, and go clubbing. When friends meet, they may browse a magazine together, discuss fashion or food trends, and show each other photos on their mobile photos and comment on them. These are physical activities, even though they probably first used the web to find information about these places and to make reservations to eat together and took photos with their camera phones.

During the twentieth century, social scientists developed various methods for *qualitative research*, including participant observation; field notes; structured, semi-structured, and unstructured interviews; case studies; thick description; and a number of others. These methods are certainly appropriate for the study of cultural behaviors—especially if they are taking place in a physical space like in my earlier examples. Observation, interviews, and participation in activities allow a researcher to understand the motivations of actors and the meanings of an activity.

Interestingly, though recently humanities scholars have shown a strong interest in quantitative approaches, the universe of qualitative methods and the nuanced theoretical discussions about them in the social sciences remain practically unknown in humanities. The reasons for this are likely to do with the historical orientation of the humanities; you can't interview nineteenth-century novel readers or run a focus group with the public that attended the first movie screenings in 1895. But if we are concerned with contemporary culture, qualitative methods should be among our tools. (See work in the field of *digital ethnography*, which uses qualitative methods for study of online communities.)

Although directly observing or participating in a cultural activity, doing interviews, or embedding yourself in a group for a significant period of time are powerful methods, we may not observe everything. Capturing records of human behavior with technology is often helpful—not only because of the possible scale of such observations but also because we can capture dimensions of experiences that participants may not be able to report verbally or evaluate correctly. Combined with a video camera, microphone, GPS device, and other sensors, computer devices can capture many aspects of human physical behaviors and physiological states, such as speech, eye movements, geographic locations, positions of body parts, pulse, electrical and blood and brain activity (using EEG and fMRI), and others.

Such recordings are widely used in the culture industry and IT industry. For example, eye movement recordings are employed in testing advertising and for evaluation of computer and product interfaces and website designs. The production of numerous video games and movies relies on *motion capture*, in which movements of actors' bodies and faces are recorded and then used to animate computer-generated characters.

Capturing aspects of participants' and performers' behaviors has been also an important strategy in interactive art, dance, performance, and music. Artists, dancers, and musicians have been using video capture and sensors to capture body positions and movements for many decades. The prominent early examples include a series of interactive works created by Myron Krueger since 1969, such as *Videoplace*, as well as *Very Nervous System* by David Rockeby (1981–). Artists Joachim Sauter and Dirk Lüsebrink used eye movement capture in their work *Zerseher* (1992) in a very simple but conceptually powerful way. A viewer was presented with a monitor showing a painting. Using eye tracking, the viewer's gaze was captured: "As the viewer looks at the painting, the painting begins to change in the exact places where the gaze of the viewer is pointed."[19]

One of the pioneers of eye movement research was Russian psychologist Alfred Yarbus. In his influential book *Eye Movements and Vision* (1962), translated into English in 1967, he analyzed a series of recordings of eye movements of human subjects viewing a well-known nineteenth-century realistic painting by Ilya Repin. This classical study anticipated the wide use of eye movement recordings in advertising and design, and it has been replicated many times by other researchers in different countries.[20] Yarbus used this painting to show that a task given to a person dramatically affects their eye movements. He wrote: "Eye movement reflects the human thought processes; so the observer's thought may be followed to some extent from records of eye movement (the thought accompanying the examination of the particular object). It is easy to determine from these records which elements attract the observer's eye (and, consequently, his thought), in what order, and how often."[21]

Today, people's geographic locations and body movements are captured on a large scale by mobile phones, fitness trackers, and other wearables. This is, for example, how Google creates the graphs for many businesses that show their popularity for every hour and day of the week: it collects location data captured from phones of users who agreed to share that data. Fitness apps and trackers capture data about types of exercise, speed and intensity, and the duration and density of sleep. And don't forget the many millions of video cameras in our cities and taxi cars, road sensors, GPS devices on bicycles: a giant portrait of humanity engaged in walking, sleeping, driving, bicycling, sitting, lifting, running—a portrait of the human species on Earth as physiological organisms, distributed between multiple systems, file formats, servers, locations, and organizations.

Some parts of this mega portrait have been accessible to researchers. Aggregated anonymized location data has been used in thousands of quantitative studies of tourists' and locals' mobility patterns around the world and inside cities. These studies appear in academic journals in geography, urban studies, tourism studies, environmental science, transportation, and new fields that developed in the second part of the 2000s at the intersection of urban research and computation—urban informatics, urban computing, and the science of cities. For example, in a 2015 study, researchers from the Sensible City Lab at MIT combined location data from 3.5 million Flickr photos, twenty-four million tweets, and anonymized bank transactions from three hundred thousand ATMs in Spain to investigate the relationship between visitor activity and city size.[22] In our work, we have been collaborating with two urban data analysis groups—Habidatum and SPIN Unit. One of SPIN Unit's projects was an analysis of seventy monotowns in Russia using locations and time stamps from millions of posts on VK, the largest social network in Russia. (A *monotown* is a city in which most people work or used to work in one big enterprise. In many such cities in Russia, these enterprises have closed, and how to sustain and improve people's lives in these cities is a big issue.) SPIN Unit determined which areas of cities have more people making posts and at what time, and also made some predictions of types of activities. This project was commissioned by the leading Russian urban design agency Strelka KB to develop guidelines for improving life in these cities via urban interventions.

Sensible City Lab, SPIN Unit, Habidatum, and other groups and labs are frequently commissioned by city agencies around the world to run similar projects, using data from many sources, including vehicles.[23] For example, the New York City bike-sharing program publishes data about bike rides, and its website has a section featuring many artistic visualizations and other creative projects created with this data. For a good example that shows what we can learn from data released by the city bike share system, see "A Tale of Twenty-Two Million Citi Bike Rides."[24] In the future, we are likely also to see visualizations and installations that use data generated by self-driving cars; each car is expected to generate 4 TB of data per day.[25] And of course there will also be data created by all the future robots.

As more and more cities around the world implement "smart city" strategies, massive collections of data about people, vehicles, and devices and their behaviors become more commonplace. This brings out many political and social issues—privacy, access to collected data (such as whether this data can be used by citizens or only by city agencies or private companies), and whether efficiency and economy of resources should be the main goal of a smart city. So far, the old modernist efficiency goal has dominated smart city discussions, at the expense of other potential uses of urban data such as increasing diversity and variability of urban planning and design, and supporting more spontaneous behaviors.

Today location and movement data are utilized by urban planners, engineers, city agencies, and policymakers, while companies such as Uber and Waze share some of their car trip data with researchers.[26] But though such data may look massive and fine-grained today, it is only the beginning. In the future, records of human physiological states and the brain activity of hundreds of millions of people may also become widely available—and widely used. Will millions of people living in megacities agree to make their real-time brain activity and eye movement recordings available to urban planners and architects so they can improve cities? Or will such data collection be required for citizens to have the rights to use basic city services? Or . . . add your own scenario.

To conclude this section, I want to highlight my main point. Analyzing culture at scale computationally means more than only using large collections of media artifacts or records of users' digital behaviors in social networks. The concept of culture also includes physical behaviors, experiences, moods, feelings, and emotional states. Depending on our goals, we may want to analyze these other dimensions. For example, in the case of spatial experiences, architectural plans and photos will only tell us a part of a story; we may also want to use video and motion capture of people interacting with the spaces. Or we may simply spend time and observe what people do, using a notebook and a camera as our only tools.

The systematic observation and capture of people's behavior and interactions for further analysis is nothing new for ethnography, anthropology, urban studies, sport, medicine, and other fields. For instance, French scientist Étienne-Jules Marey invented many devices for capturing movements of humans and animals starting in the 1860s; in the 1910s, Lillian and Frank Gilbreth started to use film recording for motion studies of work processes. In 1969, urbanist William H. Whyte started to use notebooks and cameras to observe people behaviors in New York City streets and public spaces, eventually publishing influential books based on this research such as *Social Life of Small Urban Places* (1980).[27]

In the early twenty-first century, the new digital cultural universe made massive numbers of media artifacts and people's online interactions easily available, and this attracted the attention of many researchers. But we have to remember that people have physical bodies that physical behaviors and cognitive and emotional processes are equally important parts of culture—even if their observation and analysis at scale may take more energy than observing the digital universe.

Representing Interaction

Among all types of cultural behaviors, one category is so important that we need to discuss it separately. In fact, this category is what separates our contemporary culture from earlier periods even more critically then scale. Surprisingly, it has been almost completely ignored in quantitative studies of culture carried out across many academic fields. This category is human-computer *interaction*.

The theoretical understanding of interaction and the choice of appropriate methods for its analysis go hand in hand. Before we rush to capture data, we need to ask: What is interaction, how it is created by particular interfaces, and how can it be represented as "data"?[28] One of the twelve research challenges for cultural analytics formulated in the introduction presents this question: How do we use computational approaches to analyze interactive media and experiences (e.g., playing a video game, interacting with the Instagram app, experiencing an interactive installation), as opposed to only dealing with static media artifacts?

Consider the twentieth-century "atom" of cultural creation: a "document" or a "program"—that is, content stored in a physical form delivered to consumers via physical copies (books, films, audio records) or electronic transmission (television). In software culture, we no longer have documents. Instead, we have software performances. I use the word *performance* because what we are experiencing is constructed by software in real time. Whether we are exploring a website, playing a video game, or using an app on a mobile phone to locate nearby friends or a place to eat, we are engaging with the dynamic outputs of computation.

Although static documents and datasets may be involved in this interaction, you can't simply consult a single PDF or JPEG file the way twentieth-century critics examined a novel, movie, or TV program. Software often has no finite boundaries. For instance, a user of Google Earth is likely to experience a different "earth" every time they use the application. Google could have updated some satellite photographs or added new street views and 3-D buildings. At any time, a user of the application can also load more geospatial data created by other users and companies.

Google Earth is not just an application. It is a *platform* for users to build on. And while we can find some continuity here with users' creative reworkings of commercial media in the twentieth century—pop art and appropriation, music remixes, slash fiction and videos, and so on—the differences are larger than the similarities.

Even when a user is working only with a single local media file stored in their computer, the experience is still only partly defined by the file's content and organization. The user is free to navigate the document, choosing both what information to see and the sequence in which to see it. For instance, in Google Earth, I can zoom in and out, switching between a bird's-eye view of the area and its details; I can also switch between different kinds of maps.

Most important, software is not hardwired to any document or machine. New tools can be easily added without changing the documents themselves. With a single click, I can add sharing buttons to my blog, thus enabling new ways to circulate its content. When I open a text document in the macOS Preview media viewer, I can highlight, add comments and links, and draw and add thought bubbles. Photoshop allows me to save my edits in separate "adjustment layers" without modifying the original image. And so on.

All that requires a new way to analyze media and culture. What is interactive media "data"? Software code as it executes, records of user interactions (e.g., clicks and cursor movements), the video recording of a user's screen, a user's brain activity as captured by an EEG or fMRI? All of the above, or something else? To use terms from linguistics, rather than thinking of code as language, we may want to study it as speech.

Over the past fifteen years, a growing number of scholars in the digital humanities have started to use computational tools to analyze large sets of static digitized cultural artifacts, such as nineteenth-century novels or the letters of Enlightenment thinkers. Often they follow traditional humanities approaches—looking at the cultural objects, rather than peoples' interactions with these objects. What has changed is the scale, not the method.

In my view, the study of software culture calls for a fundamentally different methodology. We need to be able to record and analyze interactive experiences, following individual users as they navigate a website or play a video game; to study different players, as opposed to using only our own game play as the basis for analysis; to watch visitors of an interactive installation as they explore the possibilities defined by the designer—possibilities that become actual events only when the visitors act on them.

In other words, we need to figure out how to adequately represent software performances as data. Some answers can come from the field of *human-computer interaction* (HCI), in which researchers in the academy and in industry study how people engage with computer interfaces. The goals of that research, however, are usually practical: to identify the problems in new interfaces and to fix them. Designers working in interaction design and game design study interaction as well—along with inventing new interfaces and interaction techniques.

The goals of cultural analytics for interactive media include not only quantitative but also theoretical analysis—understanding how people construct meanings from their interactions and how their social and cultural experiences are mediated by software. Therefore, though we can use methods of transcribing, analyzing, and visualizing interactive experiences that have been developed in HCI, interactive design, and game design, we may also need to invent our own.

Events, Places, Organizations

The fourth category of cultural things that we can analyze algorithmically on large scale are *cultural events, places and organizations*. Because so many of them have some online presence or are organized via online services such as Meetup, we can collect, visualize, and analyze data about them.

Let's look at some examples of sources of data in this category. Organizers of endless events around the world—discussions, festivals, concerts, exhibitions, competitions, conferences—create pages for their events on Facebook. Cultural organizations and projects also have their own dedicated websites. You can also start with particular cultural genres and check if there are sites listing large numbers of events worldwide for them.

Examples include electronic music festivals, art biennales, design weeks, and fashion weeks. For instance, for the *Elsewhere* project, we assembled a list of art biennales by merging and checking information from a number of online sources (see figure I.1.)

Many cities have listings of their local cultural events and places. The most comprehensive such listing that I know of is Russian site Afisha (afisha.ru). It presents daily updated information about movie screenings, exhibitions, concerts, music performances, and theater events in almost two hundred cities in Russia. The site also lists cultural facilities (i.e., what I call *places*) and the programs of events there.

People around the world use dedicated online services to organize meetings, workshops, conferences, parties, and other gatherings. Examples of such services include Meetup (meetup.com), Eventbrite (eventbrite.com), and Timepad (timepad.ru). In March 2017, there were 272,000 Meetup groups in 182 countries, 608,036 monthly meetings, and thirty million members, and these numbers continued to grow.[29] In the same year, Eventbrite was used to organize over two million events, with two million event registrations every week.[30] Both platforms have APIs, so information about meetings and events, including group names, descriptions, categories, dates, and geographic locations, can be used in research. For example, browsing the list of groups organized by topic on Meetup for September 21, 2019, I find 935 Alternative Energy groups (288,273 members), 3,640 Environment groups (1,467,963 members), and 22,766 Meditation groups (8,656,762 members). Exploring the data for 2,635,724 Meetup group meetings from 2004 to 2019 we collected for the *Elsewhere* project showed the geographic reach of such platforms: these meetings took place in 17,360 cities in 146 countries.

Of course, we have to remember that such services are not equally popular in every country, and this has to be taken into account in conceptualizing projects and analyzing data. The services available only in English may have more listings from English-language countries. Some services are only used in their countries. For instance, earlier I evoked Behance as an example of broad geographic participation in cultural portals. But although our sample of 81,684 Behance accounts created from 2007 to 2019 collected for *Elsewhere* includes cities in 162 countries, predictably, the two countries with the most accounts were the United States (16.6 percent) and the United Kingdom (6.7 percent).

Meetup, Eventbrite, and Behance have a higher proportion of participants from the United States and/or other English-language countries, but the opposite is true for Facebook. It better represents cultural and intellectual life in the rest of the world rather than in the United States and Western Europe. Many academics, artists, and intellectuals in the West started to leave Facebook after 2016. The reasons for this are multiple: they may not like companies perceived as monopolies; they may believe that by participating, they are doing free labor for Facebook; they may not like that their data is used for personalized ads; they may have been influenced by many negative media stories, such as coverage of Cambridge Analytica's work on the US presidential campaign and the Brexit vote.

Meanwhile, the number of global active users on Facebook has increased every year, reaching 2.5 billion monthly active users by end of 2019. The countries with the most active monthly users at that time were India (260 million), the United States (180 million), Indonesia (130 million), Brazil (120 million), Mexico (84 million).[31] US users only accounted for 7.2 percent of active users worldwide. While people in the United States and Western Europe have access to a variety of older communication and publication platforms, in many other countries Facebook is the only viable and free platform for intellectual and cultural communication and is used by the majority of intellectuals, academics, artists, NGOs, and cultural groups. In some countries, all video and media artists only have YouTube and Vimeo as their exhibition platforms.

One reason for this is the existence of censorship and government surveillance (real, imagined, or both) that pushes cultural and intellectual life and communication to global social networks and messaging apps. For example, in 2019, intellectuals in Russia were publishing whole journals on Telegram (an instant messaging service), while posts of Russian users on Instagram often included long reflective texts.

Another reason is that people and organizations in developing countries are more open to new technologies because their populations are younger or because these countries started to grow economically in the web era. For example, I am often contacted by cultural organizations, museums, festivals, and universities from many countries—and these contacts and all subsequent correspondence would take place over Facebook Messenger (or WeChat in the case of China) for developing countries, while similar organizations in the United States and Europe would contact me via the older technology of email. (And I even still get some invitations though regular mail from Europe.) Trends in the general use of social networks around the world show similar differences. In the *Visual Earth* project, we used a unique dataset of 270 million geotagged images shared on Twitter around the world between September 2011 and June 2014. We looked at correlations between the growth of image sharing on Twitter and a few economic and demographic indicators—and the strongest correlation was with the median age of a country's citizens (-0.73). In other words, the younger the average age of a country, the faster the growth of image sharing from 2011 to 2014. This correlation was even stronger than between growth rate and economic development (-0.52).

As we learned, there are many online sources for data about cultural events, organizations, and professionals. They include millions of dedicated sites for academic conferences, educational programs, and cultural centers; large platforms such as as LinkedIn and Behance; and general social networks in which most cultural events are advertised (e.g., Facebook pages). What all these data sources have in common is that their data is in formats that are relatively easy to analyze—dates, geographical locations, and categories (e.g., the number of artworks a museum has for a given century, in a particular medium, or from a particular country). These are all instances of *structured data*, which can be easily visualized and also explored using well-known descriptive statistics methods. In addition to structured data, such sites have *text data*—names of events and organizations and their descriptions. The methods for text analysis are also well developed, and there are many tutorials and free textbooks online explaining how to perform such analysis using various programming languages. (The field of computer science that develops and tests these methods is called natural language processing. For examples of using this approach for literary and historical texts, look at textbooks and publications in the digital humanities and digital history.)

5 Cultural Sampling

The whole scope of the essay is to recommend culture as the great help out of our present difficulties; culture being a pursuit of our total perfection by means of getting to know, on all the matters which most concern us, the best which has been thought and said in the world, and, through this knowledge, turning a stream of fresh and free thought upon our stock notions and habits, which we now follow staunchly but mechanically, vainly imagining that there is a virtue in following them staunchly which makes up for the mischief of following them mechanically.

—Matthew Arnold, preface to *Culture and Anarchy*, 1875[1]

What does it mean, studying world literature? How do we do it? I work on West European narrative between 1790 and 1930, and already feel like a charlatan outside of Britain or France . . . "I work on West European narrative, etc. . . . ." Not really, I work on its canonical fraction, which is not even one per cent of published literature. And again, some people have read more, but the point is that there are thirty thousand nineteenth-century British novels out there, forty, fifty, sixty thousand—no one really knows, no one has read them, no one ever will. And then there are French novels, Chinese, Argentinian, American . . .

—Franco Moretti, *Conjectures on World Literature*, 2000[2]

In the last chapter, we looked at four types of digital "things" we can use to observe digital culture on multiple levels. These things are media artifacts, behaviors, interactions, and physical events, places and organizations. To analyze cultural activities, we can create large datasets of such things—but how do we choose which items to include and what to leave out? For example, let's say an art museum X has published a dataset containing information and images for some works in its collection. (Many museums have done this.) What works have they included in this dataset, and how was this decided? And what is contained in this museum's collection anyway? How well does it represent the cultural area(s) the museum aims to represent, and what is *not* there?

When we observe, think about, research, write about, and exhibit culture, we almost always *sample*. We select what to include, and we leave the rest in the background. When some humanists recently started to adopt data science methods, the term *sample* and theory of sampling started to become known in the humanities. Outside digital humanities, the choice of objects for exhibition, research, publication, and teaching is often based on ideologies, "common sense," personal opinion, tradition, and established canon, or an attempt to correct it. A key benefit of using the concept of sampling and sampling techniques developed in statistics in the early twentieth century and then adopted in the social sciences is that we can think about selection of objects for study systematically, rather than being guided by ideologies, traditions, or intuitions.

In this chapter, I will discuss the concept and challenges of *cultural sampling*. In statistics and survey methodology, a sample is a small part of the whole data. Natural and social sciences use techniques of sampling developed in statistics to quantitatively study various phenomena, to plan experiments, and to analyze collected data. Because it is often not practical to study a complete phenomenon, process, or population, sampling is used to select a part of the whole using a defined procedure. For example, to find people's opinions about some topics in a given country, an organization may conduct a survey using a sample of a few thousand people. How does this apply to culture? If we are satisfied with seeing a small selection chosen by experts according to their taste (e.g., best books of the year chosen by a prestigious publication), by the market, or by popularity (e.g., photographers with the most followers on Instagram), we don't need to be concerned with sampling. But if we want to see patterns in a cultural field as a whole, we need to learn and use sampling methods.

The "most popular" or "most important" part of any field exposed in ratings, the popular press, or industry awards may not be representative of the field as a whole. This applies to universities, music groups, fashion designers, movies, and so on. Certainly, we can ask experts and judges of competitions what they think is happening in the field, where it is going, are what are the emerging trends, but what they will tell us is not sufficient. They may be also biased in their choices because they only know what is happening in a small number of world cities or in their country. Collecting much larger samples using sampling paradigms can help us see beyond our biases and stereotypes and help to make our knowledge of culture today more global and inclusive.

The Islands and the Ocean

Before born-digital content, media creators used physical and later electronic media (video and audio). Starting in the middle of the 1990s, gradually more and more of this content was digitized. We can call such content *born-analog*.

The very first project to digitize and make freely available literary texts is Project Gutenberg, which began in 1970. Today the largest sites for digitized content in English include Europeana ("58,245,976 artworks, artefacts, books, films and music from European museums, galleries, libraries and archives" as of the middle of 2018),[3] Digital Public Library of America (DPLA; "36,476,461 images, texts, videos, and sounds from across the United States" as of early 2020), HathiTrust (17,255,687 digitized books as of early 2020), the digital collections at the Library of Congress, and the Internet Archive, which has archived 334 billion web pages from 1996 until now.[4]

Such sites typically offer a number of useful ways to navigate these massive collections. For example, the DPLA supports direct search, view by timeline, a map view, and thematic exhibitions. Both DPLA and Europeana also encourage and help developers to create experimental interfaces and apps that expand how their artifacts can be viewed and used. But in terms of their usefulness for cultural analytics research, they do have one limitation: though the digitized works in these and other collections can always be viewed online, not all of them can be downloaded for analysis because of the restrictions imposed by owners of the original works.

Among all numerous digitized collections presented via websites, the site I find most interesting is Google Arts & Culture.[5] It has a fluid and satisfying interface. This site grew from the original Google Art Project (2011–), which worked with many museums to scan artworks and present them online in its virtual museum interface. Today, the Google Arts & Culture site offers virtual tours of many museums, millions of historical digitized artworks and photographs, contemporary art and media projects, and "stories" it produces. The interfaces include zoom, timeline, search by color, thematic exhibitions, and view by categories (artists, mediums, art movements, partners, names of objects, and places). Exploring the site in July 2016, I found three thousand thematic exhibitions on all kinds of cultural topics.

When we started our lab in 2007, it was a gamble. While contemporary culture was already well represented on the web, the large-scale online digital collections with multiple navigation functions and APIs such as Europeana and DPLA did not yet exist. But I assumed that within the next few years, millions of digital images of historical art, photography, graphic design, and works in other media would become available. However, what was not clear to me at that time was how inclusive or exclusive they would be.

In the second article I wrote about cultural analytics in March 2009, I described my experience of trying to use the existing digital image collections available at that time.[6] I was interested in the following question: What did people paint around the world in 1930—aside from a small number of modernist movements that encompassed at best two hundred artists (working in Paris, Amsterdam, Berlin, and a few other cities) who are now included in the Western art historical canon? Ideally, I would love to have images of paintings in tens of thousands of small art museums in small cities worldwide, but such data did not exist then and it does not exist now. But I thought that at least I could easily find online a few thousand images of paintings by nationally "important" artists that have entered art history canons in their countries, although they were not part of modernism canon recognized by the Western art historical narrative.

Together with my students, we did a search on Artstor (artstor.org), a leading commercial service for digital images of art used in most art history classes in the United States and in a number of other countries. In 2009, it already contained close to one million digital images of art, architecture, and design. These images came from many important US museums, art collections, and university libraries.[7]

To collect the images of artworks that are outside the usual Western art historical canon on Artstor, we excluded from the search Western Europe and North America. This left the rest of the world: Eastern Europe, Southeast Asia, East Asia, West Asia, Oceania, Central America, South America, and Africa. But when we searched Artstor for images of paintings done in these parts of the world in 1930, we only found a few dozen images. So, though Artstor held very large numbers of images of paintings by canonical artists from Europe and the United States made in that year, there were only a few images of paintings for a whole continent like Africa.

This highly uneven distribution of digitized cultural artifacts was not due to Artstor's own decisions. Artstor did not digitize images itself; instead, it made available digital images submitted to it by museums and other cultural institutions. The results of our search reflected what participating museums collect and what they think should be digitized first. In other words, a number of major US museum collections and a slide library of a major research university (at which Asian students made up 45 percent of the student body by 2007) together contained only a few dozen paintings from 1930 created outside North America and Europe that had been digitized. In contrast, searching for Picasso at that time returned around seven hundred images.

Describing this example in 2009, I wrote:

> If this example is any indication, digital art depositories may be amplifying the already existed biases and filters of modern cultural canons. Instead of transforming the "top forty" into "the long tail," digitization can be producing the opposite effect. What remains outside of the digitized collections is all the rest: provincial nineteenth-century newspapers sitting in some library somewhere; millions of paintings in tens of thousands of small museums in small cities around the world; millions of thousands of specialized magazines in all kinds of fields and areas which no longer even exist; millions of home movies and photographs . . .

> This creates a problem for cultural analytics. For me one of its important uses is to map everything that remains outside the canons—and to begin writing a more inclusive cultural history without "great names" or biases towards some geographic areas. We want to understand not only the exceptional but also the typical; not only the few "cultural sentences" spoken by a few "great" men and women but the patterns in all cultural sentences spoken by everybody; to bring together what is outside a few great museums, instead of only what is inside them and what has been already extensively discussed too many times.[8]

I worried that what is being digitized is only an *island* and that the massive cultural *ocean* would remain inaccessible for quantitative analysis. Luckily, such amplification of biases and assumptions about "what is important" did not happen. Exploring the online libraries of digitized cultural artifacts ten years later, I am amazed at their richness and variety. (This does not mean that they offer "representative samples" of cultural histories, however, as I discuss ahead.)

The reason for this variety is that Europeana, the DPLA, the Library of Congress, the New York Public Library, the Internet Archive, Google Arts & Cultures, and other many digital collections in other countries do not just offer us images of high art like art museums. Instead, they are extensions of traditional *libraries* (or created on the model of a library), and libraries in modern times have an important function beyond offering readers books and periodicals: they are places to which numerous people and organizations donate their archives. As these archives have started to be digitized, an amazingly rich and varied historical cultural landscape has begun to emerge online.

For example, here are three examples of digital image collections among hundreds of others at the New York Public Library:

"Photographs of the Catskill Water Supply System in Process of Construction." Fifty-five albumen print photographs created between 1906 and 1915.[9]

"Buttolph Collection of Menus." A collection of Miss Frank E. Buttolph (1850–1924), a "somewhat mysterious and passionate figure, whose mission in life was to collect menus," donated to NYPL in 1899; 18,964 digitized items.[10]

"Catalog of the Chiroptera, by G. E. Dobson." Thirty-one digitized prints from an 1878 book.[11]

And here are examples listed in a blog post from Europeana, referred to as "highlights of the new datasets ingested in the last months": "Almost 100 objects (drawings, paintings, photographs) from Telegraph Museum in UK. . . . Over 3,000 photographs, nineteenth and twentieth century, mostly buildings from Culture Centre in Helsingborg. . . . Collection of 620 botanical drawings by Georg Schweinfurth from Botanic Garden and Botanical Museum Berlin-Dahlem."[12]

Museums versus Libraries

Comparing these collections with those of the digital image offerings of the largest art museums, we find that they are complete opposites of each other. Although modern art museum collections, like those of libraries, were also developed through both their purchasing programs and private donations, what was donated to them—or what museums chose to accept—was quite different. Libraries ended up housing millions of all kinds of heterogeneous items, most of them not financially valuable. In contrast, modern art museums only included what has been recognized as already valuable.

Early European collections that evolved into museums included estates of very rich people, parts of royal palaces, or treasures of cathedrals and churches. For example, the Vatican Museums originated in 1506 when Pope Julius II purchased the ancient sculpture of *Laocoön and his Sons* and put it on public display. (Note, however, that digitized collections of *design and crafts* museums such as the Victoria and Albert Museum in London or Cooper-Hewitt in New York are closer to those of libraries; their holdings are more varied and also organized in more categories than those of art museums.)

But the history of a modern museum also contains another trajectory. Some of the original European museums contained not art but "curiosities." One such famous museum is the Kunstkamera, established in St. Petersburg in 1716 by Peter the Great to present "natural and human curiosities and rarities." Another is the British Museum, which opened in London in 1759, showing initially a private collection of the physician and scientist Hans Sloane.

Modern art history and art museums created a highly controlled system that divides our visual heritage into two binary categories: art, and everything else. It organizes the former by artists' names, artists' national origin, time periods, and a work's medium and style. Consequently, the digital online collections of art museums today also look ordered and systematic because they use the same small number of categories.

We are used to their ordered classifications. In comparison, the metacollections of digitized visual artifacts from Europeana, DPLA, and others may remind us of cabinets of curiosities. Instead of military-like "parades" of art history played out in physical museums or on their websites and apps, with everything in perfect order, we find trivia and ephemera. (The latter word comes from Greek and New Latin, in which it referred to insects or flowers that were alive only briefly, sometimes for less than a day.)

Browsing through page after page describing endless items in these large digitized collections that descended from libraries, I often feel uncanny. In such websites, the past looks unperiodic and unsystematized. Endless deposits of human material cultures have been washed onto the shores of the numerous libraries, and they don't always neatly fit into categorical systems. Many of them have been now digitized and connected by common metadata standards, web protocols, Javascript or Python code, databases, APIs, and other computer technologies. We are not used to this experience of the past because modern institutions, textbooks, and thinkers (Hegel, Marx, Foucault, etc.) have trained us to see history as a progression of stages.

Labyrinth, kaleidoscope, Kunstkamera, Memex hypertext, random access memory, relational database—none of these models describe my experience of navigating such digital cultural collections. For instance, consider again Europeana with its dozens of millions of items. The idea behind this massive multiyear project is to connect together digitized artifacts from thousands of European museums and regional archives. So rather than having to search many individual sites, you can use the Europeana platform as a single point of access. The platform provides a common interface to all the objects, but it does not store them; they are located at individual museums and archives. European Film Gateway, one of Europeana's projects, does the same for dozens of European film archives.

Technically and conceptually, this works brilliantly. But experientially, the result has some unintended effects in my experience. Instead of creating a kind of united Europe—a single pan-European space for cultural heritage—the Europeana interface may be fragmenting it. As I browse through endless separate collections or individual items from these collections that fit my search terms, countries, geographic relations, and time periods are dissolved. Instead of a European continent, it feels that I am looking at random surviving files of many alien civilizations that have all been mixed together. I am reminded of a famous two-minute shot in Andrei Tarkovksy's film *Stalker* (1979) in which the camera pans very slowly over a shallow pool of water with random cultural debris visible underneath. But in this shot, the items were all submerged under water intentionally, and this, together with the choices made by the cinematographer, gave them an overall magical and poetic quality and unified them visually; browsing pages of cultural portals in which each item appears by itself, instead I feel dissonance.

This feeling is created by both very heterogeneous topics and the equally heterogeneous styles and media formats of the artifacts. Photographs in all kinds of techniques, engravings, etchings, newspaper illustrations, covers of cigarette cases, early hand-colored photos, paintings; images in rectangle formats, round frames, part of a text page, a drawing in a corner of a handwritten letter; texts typed, typeset, hand-written, printed on early dot matrix printers, drawn with brushes: every possible subject and form of visual inscription is here. (If Instagram in 2010–2015 can be thought of as an extreme example of strong visual constraints, with all images having the same size and proportions, then digital historical collections exemplify the exact opposite.[13])

But though this heterogeneity, richness, and multiplicity of textures, marks, and formats sometimes may make us feels uncomfortable, it is actually a good thing. It makes us aware of how rigid and limited our concepts of an "image" are today—a few mediums that are supposed to contain all of them, rectangular formats, separation between images and texts, and questionable categories such as "art" or "works on paper." So, though the abundance of communication "species" in digital libraries at first look disorientating—and it certainly is a challenge for large-scale computational analysis using computer vision systems trained on contemporary photos—in the long run it is best for us. It forces us to face the human visual culture as it really exists historically: thousands of variations and their combinations, rather then a neat set of a small number of categories.

Creating Representative Samples

The islands of digitized historical artifacts are constantly growing. But will they ever be big enough to let us understand the ocean—that is, to construct a sufficiently detailed map of the human visual history of at least the last few centuries, or the last hundred years? Or even that of a single medium, like global photography, over a single decade? Richness and variety do not mean comprehensiveness. In other words: while digitization and organization of digitized items by Europeana, the Internet Archive, the DPLA, and similar initiatives continues,[14] the fundamental question for any quantitative study of cultural history remains unaddressed. This question is *how to create representative samples* that systematically cover what has been created in a particular period, geographic area, and media—or in many such periods and areas together.

In data science and social science, a data sample is selected using a well-defined procedure. (There are many different sampling methods used today depending on the research needs.[15]) A sample is called *representative* if it accurately represents the characteristics of the whole data.

Let's look at one example that illustrates the application of these concepts to a cultural sphere—and the accompanying challenges. Let's say we want to create a representative sample of Instagram posts worldwide for a given month in a particular year. We can create a *random sample* that contains (for instance) 1/1000 of all posts—chosen randomly. Assuming that Instagram users were sharing eighty million images every day in the selected year, this is 2.4 billion images per month. Choosing one image randomly for every one thousand, we get a sample containing 2.4 million images. This sounds like a reasonable representation of Instagram.

But what does such a random sample actually represent? It contains a disproportional number of posts made in countries where Instagram is used the most widely
(United States, Russia, Brazil)—and it also will be biased toward the largest cities. So,
if we want all different countries and also smaller cities to be represented equally well
in our sample, we need to collect the same number of images from all these countries
and cities. The same questions will come up about subjects of photos, length of image
descriptions, angles of phone camera, and so on. But let's assume that we put in the
time and effort and now have a balanced Instagram sample—with images representing
different subjects, different styles, many geographic locations, and so on. This method
is called *stratified sampling*. We divide the dataset using categories we are interested in,
draw a sample from members of each such category, and combine them.

Such an Instagram sample is more representative, but it still has another problem.
We turned Instagram—a dynamic and evolving social network—into a fixed museum
collection to be viewed by an outside researcher. However, none of Instagram's hundreds of millions of users see anything like this static sample. So, if we want to represent the Instagram universe as seen by the users, we need first to understand the
patterns of who different users follow, what these people share, and what the Instagram
app's recommendation screen shows them. Some users such as celebrities have lots of
followers, whereas most users have far fewer, so now we also need to think of how to
address this issue—for example, we can divide users into categories by number of followers and sample from each category. In short, a seemingly simple question—how to
construct a representative sample—leads us to the world of many opposing points of
view, a kind of mirror-land of reflecting positions that seem to generate endless "yes,
but . . ." points. (There are about a dozen other sampling methods besides the random
and stratified methods I illustrated.)

The first take-home point of this example is that we need to study and understand
a given cultural universe reasonably well before we can construct a representative sample. The second point is that it would not be meaningful to declare that one particular
representative sample represents it correctly because there are multiple ways to define
representativeness. We may therefore agree on two, three, or more such methods and use
them in our investigations.

Constructing samples and estimating the validity of predictions based on these
samples is an important area of statistics. These statistical methods are a part of modern scientific methodology used in the natural sciences, life sciences, and quantitative social sciences. For the latter, including sociology, demographics, psychology, and
political science—as well as health sciences and medical research—the use of sampling
techniques is particularly crucial. These disciplines and professional fields often use

small human groups for surveys, observation, or experiments. Sampling methods are also crucial for marketing research, human-computer interaction research, and other applied fields in which researchers want to find people's attitudes about existing products, interest in new products and new product features, their lifestyle aspirations, and the like.

The availability of large-scale social media data in the second part of the 2000s has opened up the possibilities of using much larger samples than was possible before. Businesses took advantage of this by following millions of individuals online, tracking what pages they visit, what they click on, which ads they look at, and what they purchase, and also performing A/B testing and other online experiments to test many possibilities. As I already mentioned, after 2016 the biggest US-based networks started to limit unrestricted access to this information. But even without these restrictions, there are big advantages in using small groups of human subjects in research. You can ask people who agreed to participate all kinds of questions or place them in situations and see what they choose—something that is not always possible online. And if you know the demographic characteristics of a given human population, you can select participants who have the same range of characteristics.

In contrast, when social science researchers download or purchase social media data, they are expected to strip personal demographic information away if it is present or not try to infer it if is not. So, though such datasets may represent activities of many more people than small human groups, it often is not clear how representative they are of the whole population.

Computer scientists published many algorithms that predict users' age, gender, race, education, and other details from their social media posts and profiles. These techniques are widely used in marketing and advertising—but they also offer benefits for other fields, such as public health research. As a 2017 paper that surveyed this work notes, "Although the endeavor to predict user' demographics is plagued with ethical questions regarding privacy and data ownership, knowing the demographics in a data sample can aid in addressing issues of bias and population representation, so that existing societal inequalities are not exacerbated."[16]

How to See the Invisible

To construct more democratic samples of contemporary culture not governed by our cultural hierarchies and oppositions (such as high/low, art/design, etc.), we may be able to learn from archeologists, who study the material remains of ancient civilizations. But there is a basic question that is more difficult to address: Because the kinds and quantities of artifacts that remain from various ancient civilizations vary significantly, do they together add up to a *representative sample of human cultural history*? As excavations of sites and analysis of new artifacts continue, this sample is being gradually expanded. Still, the further back in time we move, the smaller the number of remaining artifacts.

In my work, I have been dealing with the history of modern visual media of the last two hundred years, and I can confidently say that for this period we do not have any truly representative sample of visual culture—even though the arrival of photography in the 1840s has dramatically widened our visual record. And it was widened once again in the middle of the 1990s (the growth of the World Wide Web) and then again at the end of the 2000s (ubiquity of mobile phones with cameras, media sharing sites, and social networks). And this stage is still unfolding today because in many developing countries visual sharing in social networks only became substantial after 2012–2013, as we discovered in *Visual Earth* project. After the image-sharing feature was added to Twitter in August 2011, sharing of images quickly took off in many high-income countries. By December 2011, the five cities with the largest number of shared images were London, Tokyo, Moscow, Paris, and Mexico City. The number of these visual tweets in developing countries was at first very low, but during 2012–2013 it quickly started to grow. By June 2014, the ten cities with most visual tweets were London, Tokyo, Jakarta, Istanbul, Paris, Mexico City, Manila, Bangkok, Barcelona, and Bogota. (See visual-earth .net for more details.) However, even within the biggest cities in most developed countries, the geographic footprint of visual social media is highly uneven. For the Inequaligram project, we used all 7,442,454 geocoded images shared publicly on Instagram in Manhattan during five months in 2014. We found very large differences in the numbers of Instagram images shared in more affluent areas that are popular with tourists versus less affluent and less touristy areas.[17] Half of all the images shared by tourists were within 12 percent of the Manhattan area. In other words, some areas were represented very well on Instagram and others very poorly. We also observed a big inequality in image coverage for the local residents: half of all their images were shared within 21 percent of the Manhattan area.

If the billions of images and videos now shared daily worldwide still don't amount to a comprehensive representation of human life on Earth, the situation for earlier historical periods before the arrival of photography in the nineteenth century is much worse. So, while the islands of digitized artifacts available for computational analysis are getting bigger and more multiple due to digitization efforts, reconstructing the whole ocean still may be impossible. (But maybe we can use data science, existing artifacts, and our cultural theories to predict what has existed but did not survive, and then simulate these lost artifacts to make our research datasets more representative?)

Many countries and institutions have been investing in numerous digitization projects. But these efforts are not organized around any systematic theory of cultural sampling (i.e., how to define representative cultural samples, methods to construct such a sample, statistical estimates of what can be learned with it and with what certainty, etc.). What has been preserved today was driven by certain cultural values and existing cultural hierarchies, not by the idea of comprehensive sampling of all layers and areas of cultural life. Because we can choose what to digitize in the future, we can try to correct this problem. However, certainly both development and adoption of a *general theory and a methodology of representative cultural sampling* will not be an easy task.

As of today, we do not have systematic samples of even recent modern culture. Instead we have numerous separate collections and archives that are being digitized—tens of thousands of islands of different sizes and shapes that are rather dense in some parts of the culture's ocean and nonexistent in other parts. Therefore, the kind of question I asked in 2009—What did people paint around the world in 1930?—is still unanswerable. For many other questions about cultural history, the situation is even worse. For example, I mentioned that with the entrance of photography in the 1840s and its growing ubiquity in following decades, human life begun to be visually recorded on a massive scale (similar to what happened again at the end of the 2000s when hundreds of millions of people started capturing photos with their mobile phones and sharing them in social networks). But how accessible are these analog photographs today? What do histories of photography and collections in museums and archives make visible, and what remains opaque, out of focus, outside institutional frames?

To start answering this, let me first use an example that illustrates the accessibility of user-created digital photographs today. Between 2013 and 2016, our lab created a number of projects where we assembled and analyzed sixteen million Instagram photos shared in seventeen global cities from 2012 to 2015.[18] Note that these are not only photos with particular tags. Instead of searching by tags, we always collected all geocoded photos publicly shared in large city areas (10 km × 10 km) during particular periods ranging from one week to five months. (The collection was done via the Instagram API or third-party services.) According to a computer science publication that assembled a random global sample of 5,659,795 photos shared on Instagram in 2014, 18.8 percent of these photos had GPS location data.[19] Although these rates may vary from location to location, it is reasonable to assume that our datasets represent a similar proportion of all Instagram photos shared in a given area in that period. From a sampling perspective, 18.8 percent is a very large sample—one-fifth of the whole data.

I wanted to compare the range of topics in Instagram photos and in vernacular twentieth-century analog photography. I certainly did not expect to find anything close to 20 percent of all vernacular photography in that century. But I assumed that after digitization work of the last twenty years by so many museums and archives, I could easily find at least a few thousand digitized photographs for each decade, and maybe even for particular countries. But it turns out that nothing like this exists today in any online collection.

What has been digitized are not random samples, but collections of vernacular photography assembled by particular individuals. They added certain photos to their collections because each photo was interesting to them for some reason. Museum exhibitions of vernacular photography I consulted were similarly nonobjective; they were organized by curators who had their particular curatorial ideas. I did discover groups on Flickr with "found photographs" contributed by group members, but here also the choice was not guided by any sampling principle. Thus, every existing collection or exhibition catalog was the result of individual or group tastes and notions about what should be included. Often collectors and curators were only interested in more "artistic" and "avant-garde" examples of vernacular photography, rather than the more ordinary images.

Nobody thought to assemble and digitize large representative samples that exhibit characteristics and trends of personal vernacular photography as a whole for particular historical periods, geographic areas, or types of cameras and printing. For example, it would be great to have big samples of photos made with the Kodak Brownie camera of 1900, the first portable 35 mm Leica in 1925, prints using Kodak color film after 1942, or Polaroid prints from 1972. Now that we have learned from computer science studies of massive samples of user content and records of interactions in social networks that we can look at any culture as a statistical population by asking about distributions, averages, variance, clusters, and so on, we want similar historical samples. But they do not yet exist. While large institutional photo collections may contain enough historical photos to create such samples, this work has not been done yet. And the idea of systematic cultural sampling—obvious for computer and social scientists but not for the humanities—has not yet entered the world of collections and exhibitions.

For example, in 2007, the National Gallery of Art in Washington, DC, presented an exhibition called *The Art of the American Snapshot, 1888–1978: From the Collection of Robert E. Jackson*. According to the curators, "Organized chronologically, the exhibition focuses on the changes in culture and technology that enabled and determined the look of snapshots. It examines the influence of popular imagery, as well as the use of recurring poses, viewpoints, framing, camera tricks, and subject matter, noting how they shift over time."[20] The online exhibition catalog shows that curators did a wonderful job. However, because the exhibition only had two hundred photographs for a ninety-year period, that means that the historical map the exhibition constructs has a very low resolution (to use a spatial metaphor). Two hundred samples are not enough to represent a ninety-year period. If we want to understand differences in snapshot photography created in different countries or see gradual changes in style or subjects that are not related only to the introduction of new photography technologies, we cannot do it with two hundred photos.

Now consider the Gallup US Poll that run from 2008 to 2017.[21] Gallup interviewed five hundred people across the United States every day over the phone. For a country of three hundred million people, this looks like a tiny sample. But because Gallup selected people at random and conducts these interviews every day, it accumulates fifteen thousand responses per month and 175,000 per year. We learn that "Gallup also weights its final samples to match the U.S. population according to gender, age, race, ethnicity, education, region, population density, and phone status."[22] This weighting was done using data from a number of other surveys. For example, to weight by population density, Gallup used the US Census reports. This systematic approach to sampling is typical of all natural and social sciences and all practical fields, such as public administration, public health, demographics, marketing research, and so on. In fact, the only area where it is absent is the humanities.

Humanists do address the question of selection from a larger population of cultural artifacts, but they approach it using the concept of canon, rather than representative samples. In the humanities, *canon* refers to a body of works in literature, music, art, or other arts considered to be the most important for a particular period or place. Using canons made sense to this point because the works in the canon were the ones written about, taught to students, and analyzed in class discussions. The big question in the humanities over the last few decades was how to make canons in their respective fields more representative, moving away from the situation in which canons in the West often contained only works created by white male authors in the Western world.[23] So canons have been progressively revised to include works by women, people of color, non-Western authors, and others.

We can see a parallel here with the kind of weighting that Gallup and other organizations do when they use demographic information to construct representative samples. However, sometimes in an attempt to compensate for a lack of representativeness in older canons, the new humanities canons are *weighted* (to use a statistical term) toward groups that previously were not represented. For example, if previously canons excluded works by minorities, now they may include disproportionally more works by such authors—but of course the definition of minorities also changes historically and from country to country. Aa a result, we once again get collections driven by ideologies, rather than balanced cultural samples.

I am certainly in support of the changes to have more representative humanities canons. If we read and discuss in detail only a number of works in a semester-long class, it really matters what they are, and including more works from the authors we think are important that were previously not included is a good idea. And we should also think of these issues when we use existing collections of digitized historical works for cultural analytics because often, they are unrepresentative.

From this perspective, working with the web and social networks data is much easier because in many countries today the proportions of users with different genders, ethnicities, education levels, and incomes are similar. For example, according to 2012 Pew Research Center data, in the United States the proportions of female and male users of social networks were 72 percent and 76 percent; the proportions of users in the "high school grad or less" category and college graduate categories were 72 percent and 73 percent.[24] To use a different country as an example, in Russia the proportions of female and male authors of Facebook posts were 58.3 percent and 41.7 percent as of August 2016. (During that month, users in Russia made 292.3 million Facebook posts, 294 million Twitter posts, and 159.6 million Instagram posts.[25] In a rating of the proportion of Instagram users from different countries in the spring of 2016, Russia was the second after the United States, followed by Brazil and Turkey.[26])

A more balanced cultural sample can be created in multiple ways that can complement each other. For example, we can include a proportion of all works produced in a particular medium, period, and place. Or we can focus instead not on what has been produced, but on what audiences actually read, watched, or listened to. We may decide to select only works that achieved a certain recognition or popularity (defined by numbers of social media followers and likes or numbers of reviews in professional publications or the length of entries in an encyclopedia for historical figures, for example)—or disregard this information and instead create a random sample, similar to how many computer and social scientists sample social networks to analyze users' behaviors and the characteristics of content they share.

But whatever we do, we need a systematic procedure, not simply a taste-based judgment. Working over many decades, statisticians refined many sampling methods, and because these methods are used today in all sciences, they should be adopted for analysis of historical cultural artifacts if we want to understand culture as a kind of ecological or geological system in which all participants and artifacts are important, as opposed to only as a canon of "masterpieces."

There is one academic field in which researchers do think about cultural sampling and use statistical methods to create and analyze these samples. This field is the *sociology of culture*. The most well-known book in this field remains *Distinction: A Social*

Critique of the Judgement of Taste by French sociologist Pierre Bourdieu.[27] Published in 1979, it has been recognized as one of the ten most important books of sociology in the twentieth century. Bourdieu developed theories that connect people's cultural taste and their socioeconomic status. These theories were grounded in the statistical analysis of two large surveys of tastes of the French public conducted in the 1960s. Bourdieu collaborated with French statisticians who developed a new analytical and visualization method to represent relations between many elements. This method came to be known as *correspondence analysis,* and Bourdieu used this method in all his later studies, including *Distinction.*[28]

Today sociologists of culture continue to use surveys of groups of people, but they also obtain cultural samples in other ways—such as analyzing publications. One example of survey use is a study in which the researchers "asked 1,544 German-speaking research participants to list adjectives that they use to label aesthetic dimensions of literature in general and of individual literary forms and genres in particular (novels, short stories, poems, plays, comedies)."[29] An example of publications analysis can be found in the article titled "Institutional Recognition in the Transnational Literary Field, 1955–2005." It uses "a sample of articles from 1955, 1975, 1995, and 2005 in French, German, Dutch, and U.S. elite papers (N = 2,419)."[30] Here is another example: an analysis of fashion discourse from 1949 to 2010 that uses 1,301 fashion reviews from the *New York Times* and the *International Herald Tribune.*[31] Although such samples are rather small in comparison to the scale of social media data, they are sufficient to answer particular questions the researchers asked in these studies. (However, the three examples above also illustrate a big problem that remains: in developed Western countries, organizations and companies have had more resources to digitize their cultural heritage and publications. This creates a bias because researchers who need larger data for their studies are more likely to use archives from these countries.)

The Limitations of Random Samples

The idea of creating systematic and representative samples of cultural processes is interesting in itself because it leads to other productive questions about what it means to study these processes quantitatively. And because our textbooks, museums, cultural portals, classes, and documentaries so far have been representing human arts and cultures using a small set of manually chosen works, the questions about cultural sampling are important in general, even if we are not doing any quantitative analysis. They relate to how we understand, represent, and teach human cultural history—and also how we think about our cultural present, with its new scale of billions of online participants.

For example, imagine a hypothetical scenario in which we want to construct a sample of paintings created in France in the nineteenth century. Let's further imagine that every painting that remained has already been digitized, so we can include any of them. We want to create a representative sample, so we randomly select 5 percent of all paintings. Such a sample will include lots of academic salon paintings, genre scenes, portraits, and realistic works in other genres. But it would miss the nineteenth-century art movement that we now recognize as the most important for the history of art—works by impressionists. Why? It has been estimated that French impressionists together created approximately thirteen thousand paintings and pastels during their lifetime.[32] But this is a very small number in comparison to all paintings created by all artists living in France during the nineteenth century, so a small random sample would likely miss all works by impressionists.

I see exactly the same problem in many quantitative studies of social media in computer science. The authors of these studies construct large random data samples drawn from all users of Pinterest, Instagram, Twitter, or other social networks. Using such samples, they then develop statistical models that predict some characteristics of users' behavior or characteristics of the posts' content. This research is valuable because we learn about how these networks function, what content people share, and how they are different from each other. However, using a single global sample of a network that has hundreds of millions of active users from dozens of countries has serious limitations. With such a sample, we can only see the "typical." Such samples cannot reveal small but important differences between user behavior in different geographic locations or characteristics of posts of many small groups of users. In other words, if any of these networks have their own "impressionists," they are not visible in the studies that use single random samples from these networks.

For example, a 2016 paper titled "Teens Engage More with Fewer Photos: Temporal and Comparative Analysis on Behaviors in Instagram"[33] uses a random sample containing 26,885 teen and adult Instagram users to study the differences in posting behavior between these two groups. The sample does not include geographic locations, gender, or any other demographic differences besides age (13–19 for teens, 25–39 for adults). Because 28,885 users was only a tiny percentage of Instagram's five hundred million total user population at that time, there are likely to be lots of other patterns in user behavior that the analysis did not uncover. It is also likely that there are many teens and adults who use exactly the opposite strategies from the ones the authors found.

Sometimes, sampling aimed at constructing a representative sample ends up only including certain types of users. For example, in the 2014 paper "Analyzing User Activities, Demographics, Social Network Structure and User-Generated Content on

Instagram," the researchers state: "To the best of our knowledge, we believe this is the first paper to conduct an extensive and deep analysis of Instagram's social network, user activities, demographics, and the content posted by users on Instagram."[34] They describe the process to create a sample of users for their study as follows:

> First, we retrieved the unique IDs of users who had pictures that appeared on Instagram's public timeline by using Instagram API, which displays a subset of Instagram media that was most popular at the moment. This process resulted in a sample of unique users. However, after careful examination of each user in this sample, we found that these users were mostly celebrities (which explains why their posts were so popular). To avoid the sampling bias, for each user in this sample, we crawled the IDs of both their followers and friends, and later merged two lists to form one unified seed user list which contained 1 million unique users.[35]

The final dataset contains 5,659,795 images for 369,828 users (the rest had private accounts). Out of these images, 1,064,041 have geolocations. This is a much bigger sample than the one used in the other paper I described earlier. But how well do these 369,828 users represent general Instagram's population? People who friends of celebrities represent a unique user type. People who follow celebrities belong to another particular type. I follow over a hundred people on Instagram, and most of them do not follow any celebrities.

Social networks such as Facebook and Instagram are used today in most countries around the world (though they are banned in China, which has more Internet users than Europe and the United States combined). But the numbers of network users can vary significantly from country to country. For example, I already mentioned earlier spring 2016 data on Instagram activity—the three most active countries were the United States, Russia, and Brazil, accounting for 19.97 percent, 7.65 percent, and 6.55 percent of traffic, respectively. Therefore, a single random sample of a network taken as a whole may better represent some countries than others, and the same is true of the results of a study that uses this sample.

These considerations do not invalidate the results in the papers that use a single large sample from a massive global social network. Their findings are valid for particular populations of users that their samples represent well. They just may not apply to every type of user or every type of post on such networks. (Thus, the studies done in the early years of US-based social networks that used single random samples were more likely to describe mostly the behaviors and characteristics of the US users who were then dominating these networks.)

If we want to analyze contemporary global culture quantitatively and capture the diversity of human cultural behaviors, imaginations, motivations, and artifacts, we need to use sampling methods that represent this diversity sufficiently well and draw sufficiently large samples. Stratified sampling or other methods thus are better than single random samples. The finer resolution of analysis is also crucial if we want to discover today's impressionists and not only salon painters.

Statistics as Reduction

We also need to recall the most fundamental Achilles' heel of statistics. The goal of descriptive statistics is to create a description of any data that is smaller in size than this data. A sample containing fewer items than the full population is one such representation. But statistics also uses representations that summarize some properties of a dataset regardless of its size using even fewer numbers. One type of such summary representations is measures of central tendency, such as mean, medium, and mode. Another type is measures of spread of data, such as standard deviation and variance.

So rather than dealing with datasets containing thousands or millions of data points, we can use only a few numbers to represent them. Such compact summaries are very convenient because we can use them to compare any number of datasets or see how phenomena change over time or how they are affected by different conditions. For example, the analysis of global climate change may represent all temperature measurements from every day as a single average per year. In many cases, without such statistics we cannot notice patterns in data.

Descriptive statistics involves reduction of given data or information. (Another term that captures this is "comprehension.") But we pay a big price for such reduction. I described earlier how a single sample drawn from a large population may miss many local and small-scale patterns. But even if we calculate descriptive statistics on a full dataset, the results often may not represent patterns in the data accurately.

The popular measures of the central tendency of quantitative data, such as mean, may not correspond to any existing number in the dataset. For example, let's take a set of numbers: 1, 1, 2, 3, 2, 9, 9, 10, 11, 11, 11. The mean value of this set is 6.36. But we do not have any actual numbers close to this mean in the set! In the case of cultural data, this may also mean that the "average" we discovered does not exist in reality. The average in fact only makes real sense in particular distributions, such as ones having a bell shape, in which most values do lie around the center. The mean gives us the value of this center. But in other distributions in which most values lie somewhere else, the average is not informative.

Such measures of central tendency also may not capture the possible presence of groups in the data. In our set, there are two groups: 1–3 and 9–11. (This is an example of a *bimodal distribution*.) But none of the common measures of central tendency will tell us this. Common measures of the spread of the data (statistics calls this *variability*) also do not detect such patterns. A measure of variability such as *variance* will only inform us how much or little the values are dispersed around the average. It does not capture the presence of groups of values.

In summary, commonly used statistical measures can easily miss the presence of various groups in a population and also may not capture the real shape of its distribution. This also applies to statistical measures of any cultural data. Let's say that we want to summarize patterns in some cultural population: nineteenth-century French paintings, twentieth-century cinema, Instagram content shared from 2010 to 2015, or the global music video production. If we only use a random sample and employ the usual statistical measures, we will miss all kinds of groups. Each group may contain artifacts with similar content, styles, themes, or creators with particular aesthetics, or users who have similar cultural behaviors. In data science, a group whose objects are more similar on some dimensions to each other than to all other objects in the dataset is called a *cluster*. In the cultural datasets in our examples, such clusters include impressionists and Barbizon school painters; Hong Kong New Wave cinema of the 1980s or the 1960s Left Bank French film directors or the 1920s Soviet montage theory in cinema history; and contemporary music videos from Korea and Vietnam (strong visual design and use of special sets) versus videos from Thailand, Kazakhstan, and other Asian countries (contemporary but less stylized) versus videos from India and Japan (the most traditional among music videos from all other Asian countries).

As we also now understand, analyzing cultural samples using basic descriptive statistics may produce cultural averages that often never exist in reality. And rather than capturing the presence of multiple distinct groups, these averages can hide them from view. Why do the fundamental measures of descriptive statistics only work well for some data distributions and not capture well the properties of other distributions? Consider the history of statistics. In the eighteenth century, an important motivation for the development of statistics was predicting the true value of a phenomenon based on its many measurements. For example, if we make many measurements of the shape of the earth, and each is slightly different, what is the true value? In 1809–1810, mathematicians Gauss and Laplace proved that observational errors have a bell-shaped distribution, and therefore a measure of the average of this distribution gives the correct answer. In the 1830s, Adolphe Quetelet also found that single physical characteristics in population samples such as height and weight have a bell-shaped distribution—and in this distribution, measures of central tendency (i.e., mean, median, mode) indeed capture well their characteristics. At the end of the nineteenth century, this distribution often started to be referred as *normal* because it was found in so many phenomena.

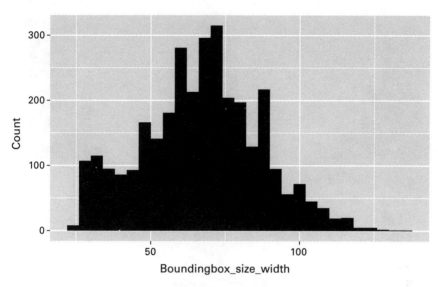

Figure 5.1
Distribution of face sizes in 3,200 Instagram selfie photos in the *Selfiecity* dataset.

But we cannot make any assumption about a distribution of values in a cultural sample. For instance, figure 5.1 shows distributions of head sizes in 3,200 selfie photos we collected for the *Selfiecity* project. (The "head size" here refers to the height of a rectangle drawn around the head automatically by the computer vision software that processed all the photos.) I expected that this distribution would be normal, but it is not. If it was normal, we would have a smooth symmetrical curve. And to the right of the mean, we indeed see a smooth fall off in the number of selfies with bigger head sizes. But to the left of the mean we see a different pattern. The number of selfies with smaller heads is decreasing, then goes up, and then starts decreasing again. If we plot the data separately for each city instead, we find that each distribution is different—but again, none of them look like a normal distribution (see figure 5.2).

This data reveals a number of interesting things about Instagram selfie genre. First, no particular head size dominates. In contrast to cinema and TV cinematography with their established shot types (extreme close-up, close-up, medium close-up, medium shot, etc.), contemporary amateur photographs feel free to frame a selfie shot in any way. But the distribution is not flat either. Some framings are more common than others. Evoking the basic concept of sociology—Émile Durkheim's "social fact" (1895)[36]—we can say that here we discovered the presence of visual social fact, namely, the cultural pressure to represent oneself in particular ways. However, is it a "soft" pressure that does

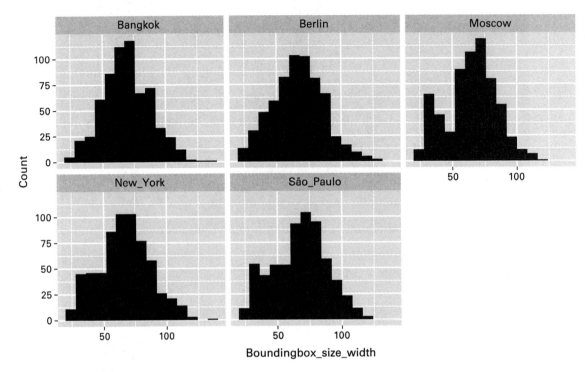

Figure 5.2
Distribution of face sizes by city in the *Selfiecity* dataset. The cities are Bangkok, Berlin, Moscow, New York, and São Paolo.

not completely determine the outcomes, and this is why in our distribution the values are widely spread out around the two peaks. Finally, we see that the representational norms in selfie genre are not universal. The distributions vary in certain ways from city to city, pointing to the existence of cultural differences and different conventions.

Why We Need Big Data to Study Cultures

Often a cultural dataset contains discrete categories. Thus, for the *Selfiecity* project we collected an equal number of selfies from five cities. We can also add our own categories to the data. *Selfiecity* examples of such categories are age and gender values estimated by computer vision software. Now let's say we want to compare patterns in photo compositions between cities and genders or among cities, genders, and age groups.

This is where the issue of data size becomes crucial. If we start separating a dataset into more and more groups, either using existing categories or by dividing continuous distributions of characteristics into parts, the size of each group will be getting smaller. If the groups are still sufficiently large, comparing their statistical measurements is meaningful. But if they are very small, the differences and similarities we may find may be due to chance. They do not represent characteristics of larger cultural fields and processes we want to study. In other words, such samples are not representative. (This is especially true if the distributions of characteristics in a cultural sample do not fit some well-known statistical distribution such as the normal distribution.)

If we are interested in cultural diversity and want to explore potentially small but crucial differences among groups of artifacts, people, and their cultural behaviors, we can never have too much data. Asking for big cultural data is not a luxury but a necessity if we want to study cultural diversity in relation to geography, time, authorship, communication medium, and other characteristics.

But measuring diversity is not the only reason that we really need big data. Rather than only treating culture as data points that together create interesting patterns we want to discover and then disregard these points afterward, cultural analytics should pay equal attention to both patterns and the individual artifacts, experiences, and interactions that give rise to these patterns. After all, we as cultural creators and as audiences engage with and enjoy concrete artifacts and experiences, not patterns.

As I pointed out in chapter 2, in the modern period the sciences and humanities have viewed phenomena in opposite ways. The sciences wanted to arrive at general regularities and laws. The humanities were concerned with particular and unique cultural objects and authors. In being attentive to both regular and particular, the cultural analytics paradigm aims to combine these complementary perspectives. This is why rather than trying to force computational large-scale cultural research on the side of either sciences or the humanities, we should welcome this opportunity to move beyond their opposition.

A particularly successful cultural creation is often described as unique. Computationally this may mean that it cannot be reduced to already known patterns. (This does not mean that an artifact needs to be unique on every possible dimension. Instead, it can be unique just on a few or even one dimension—or mix elements that have not been combined before. As remixing has become a major aesthetic strategy of modern culture since the 1980s, this is a particular common way to create new unique artifacts and experiences today.) As aesthetic subjects, we search for and enjoy such uniqueness. Given the scale of digital culture now being created, computational methods may be the only way to discover unique artifacts in many cases. Flickr's "interestingness" (2005–) and Spotify's personalized Discover Weekly playlists (2015–)[37] are examples of how some companies use algorithms for content discovery.

Discovery of uniqueness is another example of why using all data rather than samples is a better practice. The unique artifacts may lie outside the sample. Here we can learn from web search engines because they don't sample the web. Instead they try to find and index every web page—because in principle any page can be relevant to somebody. Here, "uniqueness" means "relevance": an object is unique to somebody because it's the most relevant object to them out of all possibilities. This practice of using ideally all objects in a giant and expanding universe of cultural content is for me an example of new computational thinking that moves beyond sampling. Although our research datasets are often much smaller, the idea of *looking at everything* as opposed to selecting only a part is relevant to any cultural research project.

Is Sampling Necessary?

I began this chapter with a quote from Franco Moretti's article published in 2000, where he points out how little humanities scholars know about their subjects: "I work on its [West European narrative between 1790 and 1930] canonical fraction, which is not even one per cent of published literature. And again, some people have read more, but the point is that there are thirty thousand nineteenth-century British novels out there, forty, fifty, sixty thousand—no one really knows, no one has read them, no one ever will."[38] And though digitization gradually makes the islands of cultural heritage available for computational analysis larger, the "no one really knows" situation doesn't really change. Even for a single and super canonical artist like van Gogh, we don't know exactly how many paintings he created; the current estimate is that it is around 860. And it is already impossible to "read" the nineteenth century—so what about our own time? It is logical to assume that the new scale of cultural production makes it utterly impossible to see it or simply to know its size.

And yet, this assumption does not apply to the large-scale cultural and educational platforms that define the early twenty-first century—Behance, Knuggets, Meetup, ResearchGate, Tumblr, Twitter, Pinterest, Spotify, Amazon, Scribd, Shutterstock, and so on. The architecture of these platforms and availability of their data questions our assumptions about representation of culture—that we can only study it by looking at the canon (i.e., what experts determine to be most important) or small samples. In principle, I can include in my analysis every project shared on Behance, every board on Pinterest, every meeting on Meetup, every event on Eventbrite, and so on. (Whether in practice this data is available to outside researchers or only to data scientists inside a company is a different question. Also, certainly none of these platforms includes all design projects in the world, or all group meetings about all topics, and so on. However, because of their scale and global reach, they provide us with much wider windows into contemporary world culture than what we could access before.)

As we have discussed, modern quantitative research methods are based on sampling. They assume that for practical reasons we cannot have access to the complete *population*, and therefore can only work with its samples. (In statistics, "population" refers to full data, be it all people living in a given city, all nineteenth-century novels, or all active websites.) Accordingly, modern statistics is divided into two areas. *Inferential statistics* is a set of methods for estimating characteristics of the full population based on its sample(s). These estimations are calculated using samples of the population. *Descriptive statistics* only describes the properties of the data without assuming that this data represents a larger population.

For historical culture, we also sometimes have complete or nearly complete data—but this is more of an exception than the rule. The most important (according to art history and market evaluations) artists have catalogues raisonnés—publications containing information about all known works by an artist. It can take many years to complete one catalog because it is expected to also list which collector or museum holds each work. The *New York Times* offers digital access to over thirteen million articles it has published since 1851—but how many newspapers have the resources of the *New York Times* to create and make available such datasets? The Museum of Modern Art (MoMA) in New York City has compiled and published data about curators, artists, and organizers of all 1,788 exhibitions it has held from 1929 to 1989—and this also took years, with funding coming from a private foundation.[39] Most art museums in the world will never have the resources to do this or even to publish the listings of their collections.

The conceptual importance of born-digital networks and services such as Behance or Meetup for our discussion is that everything there is already in digital form. Because these digital platforms are global by design, they offer unique opportunities to people in developing countries or smaller cities. And because they are not limited physically like a museum space or a conference of only a few days, they don't have to select who to invite, who to include or to exclude. Still, they do not represent cultural and intellectual activities in all countries and cities equally well, so they are not ideal samples. For instance, our Behance dataset from the *Elsewhere* project includes 82,684 users that chose to share their locations. They represent 162 countries and 5,567 cities. However, for most cities only one user indicated their location; only 141 cities have more than one hundred users with locations, and only thirteen have over one thousand such users. In contrast, our much larger Meetup dataset is more representative: it contains 2,635,724 events in 17,360 cities in 146 countries.

Why do we want to use complete cultural data (or as complete as possible)? If we are only interested in extracting general patterns, characteristics, and types—for example, the ten most common types of content on Instagram—we certainly do not need all data. But such summarization and aggregation of cultural data that disregards local patterns (in space, time, topics, etc.) is only one way to conduct quantitative cultural research. In my view, the *data aggregation approach that we inherited from the past does not take advantage of the scale and resolution of the data about cultural processes, dynamics, interactions, and artifacts we have today.*

As I explained earlier, in the case of a continuous distribution of characteristics of some cultural sample, a statistical average is only meaningful if the distribution has a bell-like or similar shaped curve. If a distribution is different, the average value may not correspond to any real group of items. What if we have discrete categories—say, different types of content in Instagram photos? Imagine that we identify the ten most frequently occurring types. Together they account for only 20 percent of all photos. This still leaves us with possibly hundreds of different types in the other 80 percent. Therefore, the meaningfulness of such results also depends on the shape of the distribution of discrete categories. Most popular, most frequent, or typical may correspond to 90 percent of all data, or only 10 percent.

In general, if the underlying phenomenon is global and diverse, even large samples can easily miss regional variations, patterns that may occur only for short times, and thousands of smaller clusters. Therefore, one of the main principles of cultural analytics is that *we ideally should try to obtain and analyze the complete data generated by any cultural process*, be it the career of a single professional photographer or all images shared on the web worldwide.

In our own work, we followed this principle to use all available data whenever it was possible. In our projects, we considered every painting of Vincent van Gogh available as a digital image, every photo in MoMA's photo collection, every frame in a number of films created by Dziga Vertov, every cover of *Time* magazine for 1923–2009, every page of the *Popular Science* and *Science* magazines during the first decades of their publication. We also followed this principle in working with social media. In 2014, Twitter awarded us a research grant in its Twitter Data competition and asked what part of Twitter data we wanted to get for our research. I asked for all geocoded tweets with images publicly shared worldwide on Twitter. We received this data, which contained 270 million image tweets. (Earlier in this chapter, I discussed patterns in image sharing during 2011–2014 revealed by the analysis of this dataset.)

I have already I pointed out a few reasons for having full data as opposed to small samples: taking into account small cultural clusters, studying cultural diversity, and detecting unique artifacts. For another example of what else complete data can show, I will use our analysis of approximately five thousand paintings by French impressionists. As I noted earlier, according to estimates, during their whole careers the original impressionists (a dozen artists who organized eight impressionism exhibitions in Paris between 1872 and 1886) created approximately thirteen thousand paintings and pastels, so the dataset we were able to assemble is not complete. However, it is more inclusive than usual representations of impressionism in art books, online galleries, and other places. James Cutting and his students looked at many books on impressionism and modern art and discovered that out of these thirteen thousand, only 140 paintings are reproduced repeatedly. (Cutting wrote a wonderful book that traces the history of the formation of this impressionism canon.[40])

If our idea of impressionism comes from these 140 works, representing 1 percent of the complete impressionist output, what can we learn by looking at 5,000 works (38 percent)? A visualization of these images is shown in plate 3. A close-up of this visualization is shown in plate 4. The images are organized automatically by visual similarities, including their color, lightness, texture, and composition characteristics. (For technically minded readers, the visualization uses first two components of principal component analysis, run on two hundred features extracted from all images.) The well-known characteristics of impressionist paintings—light tones, use of many colors, new modern subjects—turn out to be present in only about 25 percent of all the works in the dataset (lower left part of the visualization). The rest are more traditional in their appearance—either very dark or predominantly brown or dark red and dark yellow. Such more monochromatic pallets are typical in nineteenth-century paintings.

What version of impressionism is correct? The canonical one with only 140 works or the one with 5,000? We don't need to answer such a question: what is valuable is that we now have an alternative to the canonical version. The canon corresponds to the vision of culture articulated in 1875 by Matthew Arnold—culture as "the best." The alternative version shows us continuities between impressionists and other nineteenth-century artists and makes visible the larger context of the impressionist canon.

6 Metadata and Features

Statistics may be regarded as (i.) the study of populations, (ii.) as the study of variation, (iii.) as the study of methods of the reduction of data.
—Ronald Fisher, *Statistical Methods for Research Workers*, 1925[1]

As a mode of observation, statistics meant classifying, counting, and averaging. It seemed, as Balzac complained in Le curé au village, to depict society as a heap of atomic individuals.
—Theodore Porter, "Reforming Vision: The Engineer Le Play Learns to Observe Society," in *Histories of Scientific Observation*, 2011[2]

The constitution of tables was one of the great problems of scientific, political and economic technology in the eighteenth century. . . . The table of the eighteenth century was at once a technique of power and a procedure of knowledge.
—Michel Foucault, *Discipline and Punish: The Birth of the Prison*, 1977[3]

Our Working Hypothesis is that the status of knowledge is altered as societies enter what is known as the postindustrial age and cultures enter what is known as the postmodern age. . . . The nature of knowledge cannot survive unchanged within this content of general transformation. It can fit into the new channels, and become operational, only if learning is translated into quantities of information. We can predict that anything in the constituted body of knowledge that is not translatable in this way will be abandoned and that the direction of new research will be dictated by the possibility of its eventual results being translatable into computer language. . . . Along with the hegemony of computers comes a certain logic, and therefore a certain set of prescriptions determining which statements are accepted as "knowledge" statements.
—Jean-François Lyotard, "The Field: Knowledge in Computerized Societies," in *The Postmodern Condition: Report on Knowledge*, 1979[4]

From a World to a Dataset

In the previous two chapters, we looked at the types of cultural phenomena (media artifacts, behaviors, interactions, events) and sampling strategies. These strategies allow us to decide what to include when we are starting a new analytics project. They also help us think critically about existing collections or datasets we may be asked to work with. In this chapter, we explore a new step in the cultural analytics workflow: representing chosen cultural phenomena as data.

Data representations can include numbers and categories; texts, images, videos, audio, and 3-D shapes; recordings of human eye and body movements; spatial locations and network relations; and many other things. But all these types of media and records have to be organized in particular ways, as I will discuss ahead. Only then can we use computers to store, analyze, visualize, and share the results with others. And if you want to question existing conventions of data representation or try to invent new ones, you first need to learn what they are.

Let's begin by defining a data representation. A *data representation of a cultural phenomenon consists of a number of data objects and the characteristics of these objects encoded according to some system.* Creating such a representation involves answering three key questions.

First, what are the boundaries of this phenomenon? For example, if we are interested in studying contemporary societies, how can we make this manageable? Or, if we want to study the subject of modern art, how do we choose what to include—which time periods, countries, artists, artworks, publications, exhibitions, or other information? In another example, let's say that we are interested in contemporary photography. Shall we focus on looking at professional photo competitions, or photo enthusiast groups on Flickr, or is it better to collect larger samples of images from global social media networks since everybody today has a mobile phone with a built-in camera and thus is a photographer?

Second, what are the objects we will represent? This question was covered in chapter 4, but let's now look at some concrete examples. For example, if we want to represent the phenomenon of twentieth-century visual art, we may include the following data objects: artists, artworks, correspondence between artists, lists of their exhibitions, reviews in art journals, passages in art books, auction prices, and exhibitions where the works were shown. The entrance to the 2012 *Inventing Abstraction* exhibition at the MoMA in New York featured a large static network visualization showing connections among eighty-five artists in this exhibition based on the number of letters they exchanged.[5] In this representation, modern abstract art was represented as a network of artists linked by the letters—but alternatively the museum could have used computer algorithms to analyze all works these artists made and display the artist network based on similarities in visual language.

Data science uses a number of equivalent terms to refer to *data objects*. These terms come from other fields that were using data much earlier and which data science draws on. They are *data points, records, items, samples, measurements, independent variables*, and *target variables*. This is useful to know if you want to read data analysis publications, learn data skills using online tutorials, or do data analysis using programming languages such as Python and R.

Third, what characteristics of each object we will include? Characteristics of objects may be also referred as *properties, attributes, metadata*, or *features*. For example, to represent the phenomenon of "contemporary society," we can construct a sample of people chosen at random, and include their demographic and economic characteristics, their connections to each other, their daily physiological patterns recorded by sensors they wear, their social media posts (if they give us permission), and so on. If we want to understand patterns of work in a hospital, as our data objects we may use both people (doctors, nurses, patients) and medical procedures performed, tests, forms, doctors' notes, medical images produced, and so on.

Although it is logical to think of these three questions as three stages in the process of creating a structured representation that a computer can analyze—limiting the scope, choosing objects, and choosing their characteristics—it is not necessary to proceed in this linear order. At any point in the research, we can add new objects, new types of objects, and new characteristics. Or we can find that characteristics we wanted to use are not practical to obtain, so we have to abandon our original plan and limit analysis to characteristics we do have. In short, the processes of creating a data representation and analyzing this data often proceed in parallel.

Depending on our perspective, we could assume that a phenomenon such as "contemporary society" objectively exists regardless of how we study it. Alternatively, we can assume that a phenomenon is constructed by the researchers—that is, it is a set of objects and their properties used in all different qualitative and quantitative studies, publications, and communication about it to this point (books, articles, popular media, academic papers, etc.). In other words, a phenomenon is constituted by its representations and the conversations about it. This includes created datasets, research questions used in studies, and results of the analysis of these datasets.

Given that in the universities people often start with already existing research and either refine it or add new methods and questions, this perspective makes good sense. So the Facebook phenomenon as it is defined in computer science and computational social science is all published research on Facebook to date. However, my description of three questions that needed to be answered to create digital cultural data assumes the first perspective—that the world exists outside our research. The advantage of this perspective is that it can help us see the limitations of existing research, and help us notice other aspects of the phenomena. This first perspective maybe called empiricist, while the second is closer to Michel Foucault's concept of *discourse*, in which statements constitute the objects of knowledge.

The ideas in Foucault's *The Archeology of Knowledge* published in 1969[6] are very relevant for computational analysis of cultural phenomena. If statistics and quantitative social science call for us to seek unity and continuity in the data, Foucault's discourse concept allows for a different perspective in which our collected data—*statements* in Foucault's terms—may contain contradictions and multiple positions, and represent not a coherent system but a system in transition. So, for example, if we find correlations or patterns that describe only part of the data, this does not mean that our method is weak. Instead, we can expect that an institution or social or cultural process generates a large body of statements that may follow different logics and not correspond to each other.

Also relevant is another of Foucault's ideas: that we should analyze discourse on the level of "things said," as an *archive* of statements that are related to each other rather than to something outside. For me, large samples of user-generated content are such archives. Rather than always asking how user-generated content (e.g., Instagram images shared by a group of people in a given area and their tags and descriptions) does or does not reflect the urban, social, economic, and demographic reality outside, it is equally productive to instead consider this content as its own universe of visual subjects, styles, texts, and network relations. After all, it is a social network technically constructed in ways that encourage users to establish multiple links between its elements via assigning hashtags, following other users or tags, searching for tags, and so on.

To use Foucault's concepts, in this and the next chapter we will do a partial *archeology of data science*, exploring a few of data science's core concepts and learning about the conditions that allow it to generate its statements about the world.

In the opening pages of his visionary 1979 book *The Postmodern Condition: Report on Knowledge*, Lyotard wrote: "Along with the hegemony of computers comes a certain logic, and therefore a certain set of prescriptions determining which statements are accepted as 'knowledge' statements." But what does the "hegemony of computers" really mean? Computers act as vehicles and messengers of ideas, intellectual paradigms, and social practices that often were developed earlier. They later were coded into computer technologies and today appear as commonsense because they are used so widely. Among these paradigms, data science is one of the most important today. I promised in the book's introduction that critical examination of data science methods and their assumptions is one of the key goals of cultural analytics, and this chapter starts this examination.

Metadata and Features

I explained earlier that a cultural dataset contains a number of objects and their characteristics. Different fields adopted different terms to refer to such characteristics. In humanities fields, cultural heritage, and library science, people refer to both objects' characteristics that are already available in the data (because somebody already recorded them) and additional characteristics we have added via, for example, manual tagging as *metadata*. In social sciences, the process of manually creating structured descriptions of objects is called *coding*. In data science, researchers use algorithms to automatically *extract* various statistics (i.e., summarized compact descriptions of characteristics) from objects. These statistics are referred to as *features* and this process is called *feature extraction*.

In 2016, MoMA released on GitHub an artist dataset that "contains 15,644 records, representing all the artists who have work in MoMA's collection and have been cataloged in our database." The dataset "includes basic metadata for each artist, including name, nationality, gender, birth year, death year, Wiki QID, and Getty ULAN ID."[7] Names, nationalities, and birth years are examples of *metadata*. This is information about objects that already existed and was transferred into a computer, so now it is available as part of the data we can analyze.

Now imagine that we have used computer algorithms to automatically measure the composition, colors, and texture of these paintings and detect their genres. And if paintings show human figures and faces, we can also detect them and measure body positions and facial expressions. These are examples of features. In contrast to metadata that already exists as part of a dataset or a collection, *features* are new information created via algorithmic analysis of the objects. Often features are represented as numbers, but they can also use other data formats. For example, when we use computer vision algorithms to analyze images detecting the presence of object types, composition types, photo techniques, or abstract concepts, the outputs are presented as a list of words. Spam-detection algorithms may use binary categories to classify emails: each email message is considered to be either spam or not spam. Here is another example: a computer can analyze a set of emails, extract information on who emails who and how often, and represent this as a network of relations. In summary, both metadata and features can be encoded using many data types: integers, real numbers, discrete categories, free text, network relations, spatial coordinates, dates, or times.

Plate 5 shows a screenshot from Selfiexploratory, an interactive visualization interface for exploring an image collection using metadata and features that our design team created for the *Selfiecity* project. A user can filter the photos by city, gender, age, and a number of photo measurements extracted by software. City name is an example of metadata: since we collected photos in particular cities, we have this information for each photo. For all other characteristics, the interface shows their distributions (i.e., histograms), and a user can make multiple selections by selecting parts of these distributions. In this example, we see the application screen after I selected London, Age > 30, and Tilt Left between 10 and 70 degrees. Whenever a selection is made, the graphs are updated in real time, and the bottom area displays all photos that match. The result is a fluid method of browsing and spotting patterns in large media collections. Describing this interface and larger project, we wrote:

> In our project we wanted to show that no single interpretation of the selfie phenomenon is correct by itself. Instead, we wanted to reveal some of the inherent complexities of understanding the selfie—both as a product of the advancement of digital image making and online image sharing and a social phenomenon that can serve many functions (individual self-expression, communication, etc.). . . . While art historians and historians of photography traditionally engage in a close reading of a singular image, Selfiecity instead focuses on patterns in a larger set of images, employing computational analysis of many characteristics such as pose (for example, looking up/down, left/right), facial expression, and mood. It is a paradox of photography in social media: each individual image is and is not important.[8]

Which of the two terms—metadata and features—more appropriate for cultural analytics? Depending on the field people do not always use these two terms in the same way. In the humanities, often all characteristics of objects are referred to as metadata because this is a standard term in library science. Libraries were the first to organize information about their collections in systematic ways, and libraries ran many early humanities computing projects, so digital humanities inherited this term. In contrast, in data science, researchers and engineers often refer to any data characteristics as features. The reason is that data science is about algorithmic methods for data analysis and the algorithms don't care about the data origins. I will also follow this usage. Thus, I will use the term *features* to refer to both new information that can be extracted from data objects via computer analysis and the metadata that came with the data.

Now we need to add another concept to the discussion. In natural sciences and quantitative social sciences, characteristics of objects under study are commonly referred to as *variables*. These are the conditions being isolated and manipulated in experiments.

The term also implies particular ways of analyzing the data—creating statistical models that use *independent variables* to predict *dependent variables*. In this paradigm, one or a number of independent variables are used for prediction of one or a few dependent variables. (The common type of these models is linear regression.) For example, we may use some measures of a company's environmental policy as independent variables and a measure of employee satisfaction obtained via a survey as a dependent variable. We can then create a statistical model that partially predicts employee satisfaction based on a company's policy.

Medical research that is responsible for the largest part of science publications today uses the same paradigm. Often a group of patients chosen according to sampling methods so that it represents a larger population is given some treatment. Later the patients are evaluated to see if the treatment had an effect. The treatment group is compared to control group—patients who were not given any treatment. Sometimes a few patient groups are given different versions of the treatment and then they are compared. Either way, statistical methods are used to evaluate and report the results of all these studies. The effects of the treatment or a new drug are evaluated quantitatively by measuring various physiological indicators or other body conditions, and statistical tests are performed to make sure that the changes observed are not due to chance.

The paradigm in which the values of dependent variables are predicted from the values of independent variables has been dominating natural, social, and life sciences for many decades. It can be also used in the cultural sphere: for instance, to predict the attendance of a museum's exhibitions (dependent variable) given demographic information about city inhabitants, the type of exhibition, and the time of the year (independent variables). As we already saw, computer scientists use the same paradigm with large social media datasets: for example, predicting likes of Instagram photos based on their filters or content. In a 2014 study of one million Instagram photos, researchers found that "photos with faces are 38% more likely to receive likes and 32% more likely to receive comments."[9]

But do we want to use this paradigm to explain many contemporary cultural phenomena? And what exactly does it mean to "explain" culture? The idea of isolating some variables and proposing that they influence other variables reminds me of the Marxist sociology of culture that looked at art as an expression of class struggles and the economic organization of society. Today the highly reductive logic of this approach is obvious. However, a number of Marxist thinkers such as György Lukács, Theodor Adorno, and Fredrick Jameson managed to create very interesting cultural interpretations that went beyond such reductionism. I think that statistical models for interpreting culture also can be productive if we use them in original and self-reflective ways.

(I will come back to these questions at the end of the book in the "Do We Want to Explain Culture?" section of the conclusion.)

And this is another reason why I prefer using the term feature rather than variable—because the former does not imply the use of a particular paradigm for analysis and explanation, such as creating a statistical model. It only means that we are using objects' characteristics that were already available or were measured or predicted by a computer—but it does not say anything about what we do with these characteristics. (For example, instead of making a model, we can create a public interactive visualization so that other researchers, students, and the public can explore the data.)

Data = Objects + Features

A *number of objects and their features constitute a dataset* that can be analyzed, visualized, *sonified* (i.e., represented as images or as sounds), merged with other datasets, discussed, and more. This is how data science works in general, and the same is true for cultural analytics. If we want to use quantitative and visualization methods for the study of any cultural phenomenon, we need to represent that phenomenon as a dataset—that is, a number of objects described by some features.

Humanities and social science researchers have been pointing out that data is something that is *constructed*: it does not just exist out there but is a result of a series of choices. In the introduction to the edited collection *"Raw Data" Is an Oxymoron*, Lisa Gitelman and Virginia Jackson write:

> At first glance data are apparently before the fact: they are the starting point for what we know, who we are, and how we communicate. This shared sense of starting with data often leads to an unnoticed assumption that data are transparent, that information is self-evident, the fundamental stuff of truth itself. If we're not careful, in other words, our zeal for more and more data can become a faith in their neutrality and autonomy, their objectivity. . . . How are data variously "cooked" within the varied circumstances of their collection, storage, and transmission? What sorts of conflicts have occurred about the kinds of phenomena that can effectively—can ethically—be "reduced" to data?[10]

Certainly, this perspective is also important for thinking about and working practically with any cultural data. We should always consider how the existing metadata was arrived at, what characteristics the features describe, and what is left undescribed. A cultural analytics approach can be very helpful in this questioning because it aims to *destabilize existing categories*. These categories are often encoded in institutional metadata. For example, many art museum websites allow you to search a collection using a number of genre categories. But can all modern figurative paintings fit perfectly into categories such as portrait, landscape, city view, still life, and a few others? There are lots of paintings that are portraits but also include landscapes, an interior space, and some objects, and these elements may be as interesting for us as the person shown.

Rather than staring with existing and seemingly natural and logical categories, the cultural analytics approach is to extract low-level features and find clusters of objects that are based on these features. These clusters may correspond to existing categories, partly overlap with them, or be completely different.

Although feature extraction can help us to look at phenomena in a fresh way, suspending existing categories, this approach has its own limitations. No matter how many features we may have, with most cultural phenomena they still can't capture everything relevant for exploring all possible research questions. However, for particular questions, they can also represent everything we need; for example, the analysis of changes in composition of Mondrian's paintings over a number of years only needs a few features describing dimensions, proportions, and colors of the rectangles making up his paintings.

In general, it is good to assume that a data representation includes some aspects of the phenomena and omits others. This is not a new development. For example, any two-dimensional map used for navigation represents only some characteristics of a physical territory. But such a map does not need to show everything. It presents the information we need to accomplish certain tasks and omits the rest. This can be seen as a fundamental limitation of representations in general—but after people started making representations with interactive computer media, things work differently. While the information shown in physical maps was fixed, in interactive digital maps available on the web and in apps, we can select what layers and details to show, search for places, switch on a real-time traffic view, get navigation instructions, and more—so their utility as instruments is greatly expanded, though visually they may use the same conventions as older paper maps. (However, we can't change everything; for example, the projection type used is typically fixed.) We can also participate in creating digital maps, such as the very popular OpenStreetMap, which "is built by a community of mappers that contribute and maintain data about roads, trails, cafés, railway stations, and much more, all over the world."[11]

In thinking about data representations of contemporary phenomena and their limits, you also need to remember that these representations are not fixed. Their limitations often can be corrected—so long as we have the resources to do so. For example, let's say that we did a survey of social media usage in a particular area by asking a random sample of people a series of questions. (Pew Research center regularly conducts such surveys in the United States.[12]) We can enlarge the geographical coverage by carrying out more surveys in other areas. We can also do a new survey in the same area and ask additional questions, and so on. Earlier I mentioned a good example of such a practice: the Gallup US daily poll. Gallup conducted five hundred interviews across the United States every day with randomly selected people; this adds up to fifteen thousand interviews per month and 175,000 per year.[13]

How are *data representations* of some cultural phenomena different from other kinds of cultural representations humans have used until now, be they cave paintings, representational paintings, photographs, literary narratives, epic poems, or diagrams? First, a data representation is *modular*. It consists from separate distinct elements: objects and their features. Second, the *features are encoded in such a way that we calculate on them*. I already listed such formats earlier—integer numbers, floating point numbers, spatial coordinates, time units, and so on. Third, only one format should be used for each feature because this is what all analytical and visualization tools expect. For example, when representing dates, we can't mix exact numbers (1877), ranges (1875–1988), and words ("around 1875"). We need to choose a single format and translate all dates into this format. The same goes for geographic information. Software tools used today to analyze and visualize data assume that these conventions are followed. A big part of most data science projects is "data cleaning" that includes transforming data into such standard formats.

Of course, the danger of any conventions is that they may make it difficult to conceive of other possibilities. For example, imagine a dataset in which a single characteristic of objects is represented sometimes as numbers, sometimes as categories, and other times as free text. From the point of view of standard data science practices, this is not clean data and we need to fix it before working with it. But if we are investigating a cultural phenomenon, we may want to have exactly such a dataset, even when working with it will take more effort.

Data representation also needs to follow another fundamental constraint in order to exist inside a digital computer: it can only contain a *finite set of objects and a finite number of features*. For example, computational analysis of music typically starts by dividing a music track into very small intervals, such as 100 ms, and then measuring the sound characteristics of each interval. Names of artists, titles of their works, text biographies of artists in an encyclopedia, dates the works were created, digital images, and eye movements of an individual viewing a work are all examples of individual data objects. Note that such objects vary in size and complexity—from a few words making up a title to an fMRI recording of brain activity during a period of time. More complex or larger objects are often represented in a more compact way; for instance, a biography of an artist in an encyclopedia can be represented as a single number measuring its length in words or as all the unique words in the text. However, you can go back to the original full data and create new features from it, which will enable new explorations. (The length of entries in encyclopedias published over a long historical period has been examined in a number of studies. In one such study, the researchers looked at the different lengths of articles about the same Renaissance artists in several encyclopedias published over a significant period as a measure of their changing reputation.[14])

In summary, computer data is not just any arbitrary collection of items inscribed in any medium such as papyrus or index cards. In a computational environment, *data is a representation a computer can read, transform, and analyze*. This imposes certain constraints on what and how can be represented. What we choose as objects, what features are chosen, and how these features are encoded—these three decisions are responsible for creating data representations and, consequently, making them *computable, manageable, knowable*, and *shareable* though data science techniques.

If you've never worked with data before, the following overview of the basic practical conventions and formats for managing datasets will be useful. I keep it short on purpose because these topics are covered in detail in many data science and data analysis textbooks, online guides, and tutorials. Practically, objects and features can be organized in a number of ways. One of the most common ones is a *table*. An Excel or Google spreadsheet containing one worksheet is an example of a table. A table can be also stored as a standard text file if we separate the values by some characters, such as tabs or commas (these are stored as TXT or CSV files, respectively). Typically, each row represents one object, and each column represents one feature.

A collection of objects with their features stored in a table-like format is perhaps the most frequently used representation of data today, adopted in every professional and scientific field. It is the way our *data society understands phenomena and individuals and acts on them*. Here we can consider what Foucault wrote about the importance of tables in the eighteenth century: "The constitution of tables was one of the great problems of scientific, political and economic technology in the eighteenth century. . . . The table of the eighteenth century was at once a technique of power and a procedure of knowledge."[15] But now tables are even more important: they are used everywhere, and technologies such as spreadsheets have naturalized this way of thinking.

Other common data formats include XML and JSON. XML has important advantages over tables: data can be organized in a hierarchy and is accompanied by descriptions (tag and attribute names) and a schema describing file format. JSON does not have all these features, but it does provide a data hierarchy. If you are working with digital archives or social networks, you may often encounter data stored in these formats and made available via APIs. For analysis, the data can be converted from these formats into tables. Another fundamental computer technology used to store, access, and process data is *databases*. While single tables are common for smaller data (up to a few million rows), databases are required for big and more complex data. A common type is a *relational* database—a number of tables connected through shared elements (e.g., MySQL). Relational databases were invented in 1970. Large-scale web applications rely on newer database technologies to store and process billions of objects, such as MongoDB (2007), Cassandra (2008), and other NoSQL databases. Such databases store and serve data for Facebook Messenger, Spotify music recommendations, and numerous other applications. For example, Baidu, a search engine widely used in China and the fourth-largest site in the world in terms of web traffic (as of July 2016), stores two hundred billion objects in its MongoDB database.[16]

Data science also uses many other data formats and database types, and their development is a big research area. But regardless of the technology, the concept that data analysis techniques are designed to work with is the same: a collection of artifacts, a phenomenon, or a process represented as a set of objects and a set of features. Thus, while human societies have used data-like representations for thousands of years, the adoption of statistics, digital computers, and later machine-learning methods have led to this more limited concept of data. Datasets are not just any collection of information; they are objects structured in ways that allow them to exist within a computational medium and be analyzable by particular methods.

In this section, I discussed the most general principles that define computer data, regardless of what this data represents. Another commonly used paradigm for understanding data is to divide it into a number of types, such as geospatial data, networks, 3-D volume data, 3-D polygonal models, time-series data, digital images, digital videos, digital sound, and free text. Each of these types is important for certain industries, professions, and services: geospatial data for maps and geographic information system (GIS) analysis, network data for social networks, 3-D volume data for medical field and autonomous cars, and so on. There are separate techniques for computational analysis of each data type, while other techniques are shared. You will find many studies of cultural text data in the digital humanities, geospatial data in digital history, and music collections in the music information retrieval field. In this book, I am using many examples of our lab projects that use image data, and therefore I will discuss some of the ideas and techniques for analysis of this data type developed in the fields of image processing and computer vision. To learn the concepts and techniques for the analysis of other data types, you need to turn to the appropriate area: natural language processing for texts, network science for network data, GIS for geospatial data, time-series analysis for temporal data, and so on. But regardless of what types of cultural

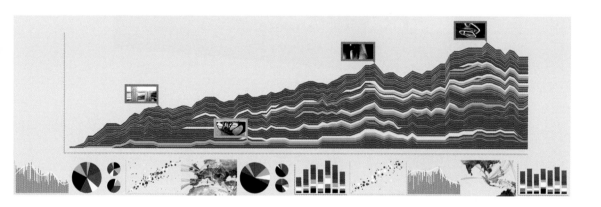

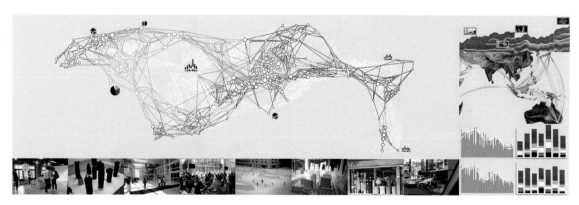

Plate 1
Designs for the Cultural Analytics Research Environment, 2008.

Plate 2
Lab member Jeremy Douglass shows the designs for the Cultural Analytics Research Environment on their intended system: the visualization supercomputer created at Calit2.

Plate 3
Visualization of five thousand impressionist paintings organized by visual similarity.

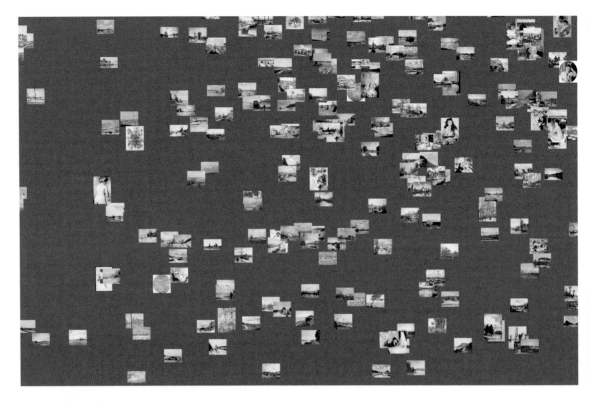

Plate 4
Close-up of the visualization of five thousand impressionist paintings, showing lighter and color-ful paintings that we associate with impressionism.

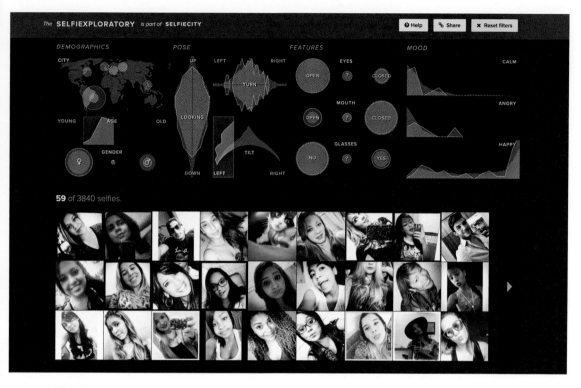

Plate 5

A screenshot of the Selfiexploratory application from the *Selfiecity* project. Authors: Lev Manovich, Moritz Stefaner, Daniel Goddemeyer, Dominikus Baur, Jay Chow, Alise Tifentale, Mehrdad Yazdani, and Nadav Hochman, 2014.

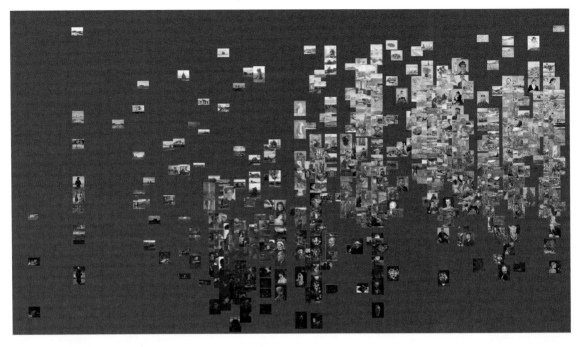

Plate 6
Image plot showing changes in average brightness in van Gogh's paintings over time. 776 images are organized according their dates (x-axis) and brightness measurement (y-axis).

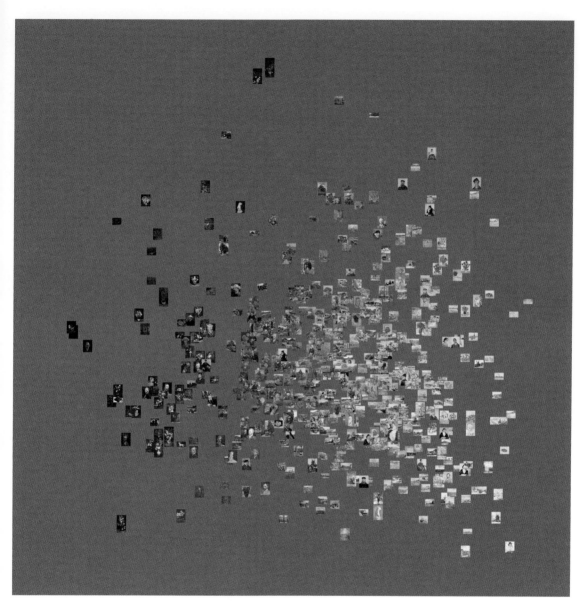

Plate 7
Image plot showing distribution of 776 van Gogh's paintings according to their median brightness (x-axis) and median saturation (y-axis).

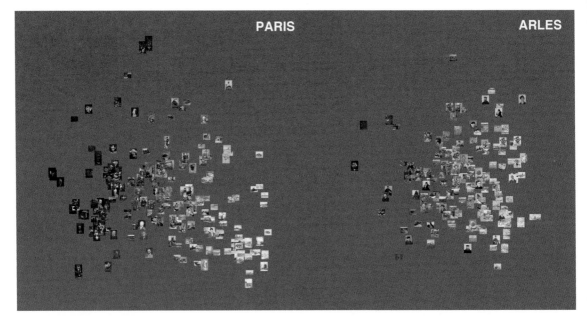

Plate 8

Comparing van Gogh's paintings created in Paris and in Arles according to their median brightness (x-axis) and median saturation (y-axis).

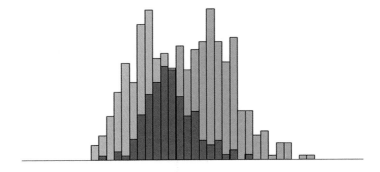

Plate 9
Plots comparing shoujo and shōnen manga pages. Blue: shōnen manga; pink: shoujo manga. *Top:* 1,074,790 manga pages shown as points and organized according to their brightness standard deviation (x-axis) and brightness entropy (y-axis). *Bottom:* Histograms of mean brightness values of the same 1,074,790 manga pages.

Plate 10
Lab members use Calit2's visual supercomputer to explore a visualization of one million manga pages, 2010.

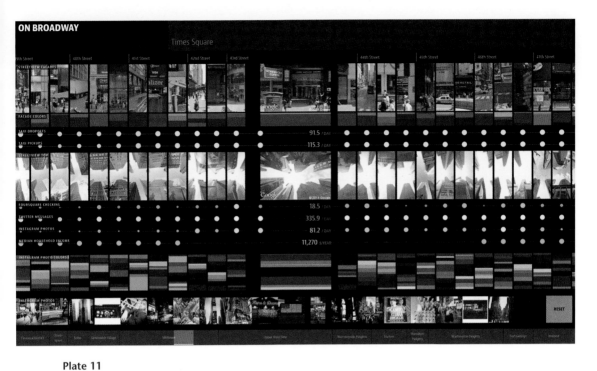

Plate 11

The *On Broadway* project's interface. Authors: Moritz Stefaner, Dominikus Baur, Daniel Godde-meyer, and members of Cultural Analytics Lab, 2014.

Plate 12
Image montage of 4,535 *Time* magazine covers of all issues published from 1923 to 2009, organized by publication date (left to right and top to bottom).

Plate 13

Slice visualization of 4,535 covers of *Time* magazine, using a single-pixel-width vertical line from each cover. The slices are positioned in order of publication, 1923–2009.

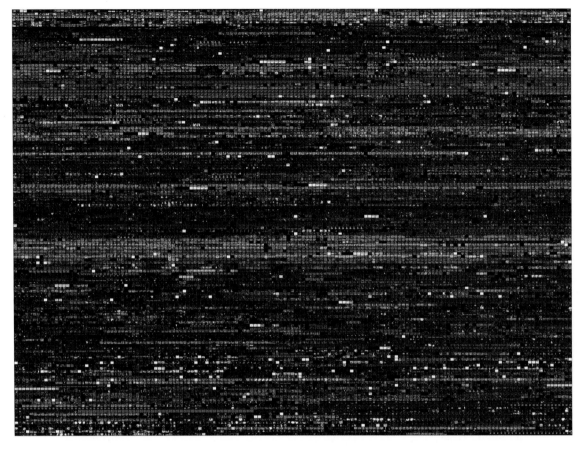

Plate 14
Image montage representing 62.5 hours of *Kingdom Hearts* gameplay via 22,500 video frames sampled from the complete screen video recording and organized according to gameplay progression (left to right and top to bottom).

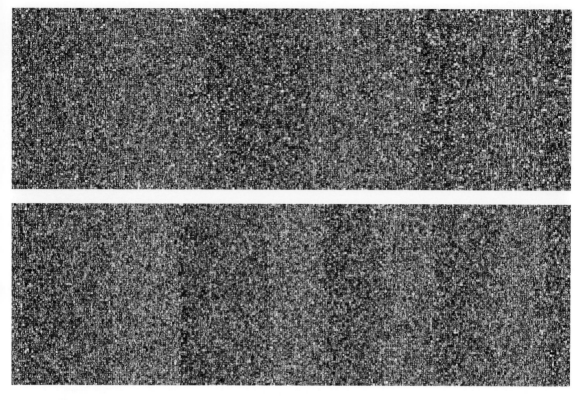

Plate 15

Image montages comparing fifty thousand images shared on Instagram during a few days in one city and the same number of images shared in Tokyo, also over a few days. *Top*: New York City. *Bottom*: Tokyo.

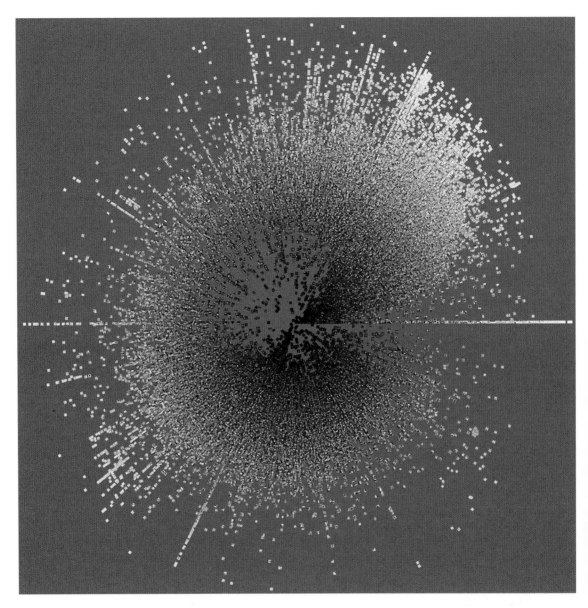

Plate 16
Radial image plot showing fifty thousand Instagram images shared in Bangkok, sorted by median hue (angle) and brightness mean (distance to the center) measurements.

data you're interested in, there is also one discipline that you will encounter in most quantitative studies of culture. It controls contemporary data imaginary by providing the language—that is, the concepts and techniques—for data analysis. This discipline is statistics.

Statistics in the Nineteenth and Twentieth Centuries: From a Single to Multiple Variables

Statistics comes from the word state, and its rise in the eighteenth and nineteenth centuries is inseparable from the formation of modern bureaucratic, Panopticon societies concerned with counting, knowing, and controlling their populations and their economic resources. Only in the middle of the nineteenth century does the meaning of statistics change: it becomes a name for an independent discipline concerned with producing summaries and reasoning about any collections of numbers, as opposed to only numbers important for the state.

The following very short and selective presentation of statistics history, which will help explain the specificity of contemporary data analysis methods, is divided into three stages. Other accounts of statistics may divide its history in different ways. The history of statistics in the context of modern society and academic fields has not yet been told in every detail, and different scholars give priority to different people and time periods.[17] (If you read only one work in that area, my recommendation is *The Politics of Large Numbers*.[18]) For our purposes, what is important is not who exactly invented what and when, but a few general ideas.

The first stage encompasses period from the seventeenth century to the middle of the nineteenth century. During this period, statistics means collecting and tabulating various social and economic data. At the end of the eighteenth century, William Playfair developed a number of graphing techniques to represent such collections visually. Playfair is credited with introducing four fundamental techniques: the bar chart and line graph (1786) and the pie chart and circle graph (1801). The titles of the books in which Playfair first used these techniques exemplify the kinds of number gathering that motivated their invention: *The Commercial and Political Atlas: Representing, by Means of Stained Copper-Plate Charts, the Progress of the Commerce, Revenues, Expenditure and Debts of England during the Whole of the Eighteenth Century* (1786); and *Statistical Breviary; Shewing, on a Principle Entirely New, the Resources of Every State and Kingdom in Europe* (1801).

These four techniques for visually representing quantitative data invented by Playfair are still the most popular today, despite later invention of other data visualization methods. These techniques visualize only *a single characteristic of objects (or a single variable)* under study. Built into all statistical and graphing software, they continue to shape how people use and think about data today—although computers can do so much more.

In the nineteenth century, topical maps were also popular. An example is a map of country wherein the tone of each area represents some statistic about it, such as literacy rate, crime rate, and so on.[19] Although such maps are two-dimensional graphical representations, they still only represent a single variable. A single characteristic of objects represented as numbers determines the brightness or graphic style for each part of the territory shown on a map.

In the second stage of statistics history (1830s–1880s), analytical and graphical techniques are being developed to study the relations *between two characteristics of objects* (i.e., two variables). In the 1880s, Francis Galton introduces the concepts of *correlation* and *regression*. Galton was also the first to use a graphic technique that we now know as a *scatter plot*.[20] Today, scatter plots remain the most popular technique for graphing two variables together.

In the early 1830s, Belgian statistician Adolphe Quetelet measured the height and weight of a large number of children and adults at different ages. He collected his study into a book that became famous after it was published in 1836: *A Treatise on Man and the Development of His Facilities or Social Physics*. Although in this book Quetelet was only looking at averages and frequency rates, later he realized that he can analyze the distributions of his measurements. He discovered that these characteristics measured in large numbers of people follow a bell-like curve that had been known since the beginning of the nineteenth century in other contexts. Along with analyzing height and weight as single separate variables, Quetelet also studied their relations in many people, creating in 1832 the modern body mass index. He found that, on the average, "the weight increases as the square of the height."[21] This is an example of statistics that quantifies the relation between two variables.

Paul Lazarsfeld, who founded the quantitative study of mass communication in the 1940s, explains how Quetelet went from his statistical results to the idea of social physics:

> In his earlier publications Quetelet had been primarily interested in the fact that the averages of physical characteristics and the rates of crime and marriage showed a surprisingly stable relation over time and between countries with age and other demographic variables. It was these relations which he had pointed to as the "laws" of the social world. By now, however, he was concerned with distributions about the averages. He was convinced that if he could make enough observations, his distributions would always have the normal or binomial form.

The notion of "law" was now extended: the distributions themselves and their mathematical derivations, as well as their constancy over time and place, became laws.[22]

While fundamental statistical concepts and methods were being established in particular research contexts, it took some time for them to become adapted in different disciplines. *Suicide* by Émile Durkheim (1897) is considered to the founding text of sociology.[23] The book has dozens of data tables. Durkheim used such summary statistics to compare suicide rates in different population groups (Protestants vs. Catholics, single vs. married, soldiers vs. civilians, etc.) and then to propose theoretical explanations for these differences. But this foundational work of social science still does not have a single statistical graph or any statistical tests of the significance of the differences between suicide rates in different countries because such tests were not yet invented.

In the third stage (1900–1930), the statistical concepts and methods for the analysis of one or two variables were further refined, extended, systematized, and given a rigorous mathematical foundation. These include summarizing a collection of numbers (measures of central tendency, such as mean and median, and measures of dispersion, such as variance and standard deviation), and analyzing relations between two variables (correlation and regression). During the same period, the methods for designing experiments and doing inferential statistics on the basis of such experiments—that is, predicting characteristics of the population using smaller samples—were also formalized. The key contributions in this period were made by Karl Pearson, Charles Spearman, and Ronald Fisher working in England and Charles Sanders Peirce in the United States. Andrey Markov in Russia developed new fundamental methods for the analysis of temporal random processes. Another famous Russian mathematician, Andrey Kolmogorov, published the foundations of modern probability theory in 1933.

In contrast to British and American mathematicians, some Russian and European scholars were very interested in applications of statistics to the analysis of culture. Markov presented his methods (Markov chains, now a standard part of data science) in 1913 using the analysis of Pushkin's *Eugene Onegin*;[24] Andrey Kolmogorov published a number of articles on the analysis of poetry using the probability theory in the 1960s. Italian sociologist Alfredo Niceforo applied statistics to the study of literature and art; in 1921, he published a book about the "measurement of civilization and progress." He referred to his project as "social symptomatology."[25]

Ronald Fisher's 1925 book *Statistical Methods for Research Workers* is a very influential presentation of statistics as it developed up until that time. The book chapters cover diagrams (Fisher's term for statistical graphs), distributions, regressions, correlations, variances, and statistical tests.

The content of contemporary introductory textbooks on statistics for undergraduate or graduate students in social sciences is very similar to the content of Fisher's book—and we may wonder why we keep using the concepts and tools developed long *before* computers to analyze big data today. People who were consolidating statistics in the beginning of the twentieth century were influenced by practical considerations about the time needed to perform computations manually. These considerations played a key role in shaping the discipline and consequently still form the data imaginary of our contemporary society.

Looking at Fisher's textbook, we do not see any methods for analysis of data with more than two variables. Today we refer to such data using the term *multivariate data*; statistical methods for its analysis are referred to as *multivariate statistics*. One such method was already developed in the first three decades of the twentieth century: factor analysis. English psychologist George Spearman discovered that the scores of school-children on a number of different tests were correlated. He proposed that a general mental ability that he named *g* is responsible for this performance on multiple tests. Spearman wrote: "All branches of intellectual activity have in common one fundamental function, whereas the remaining or specific elements of the activity seem in every case to be wholly different from that in all the others."[26] In 1904, he published a statistical method for the analysis of each person's multiple test scores. This method was later named *factor analysis*. It was gradually expanded further to become a general method that reduces multiple variables we measure such as test results to a smaller number of unobserved variables called *factors* (or *latent variables*). British psychologist Raymond Catell applied factor analysis to other areas in psychology such as the measurement of personality and attitudes;[27] American psychologist L. L. Thurstone used it to study mental abilities (1934);[28] and Lazarsfeld popularized its use in social psychology (1950).[29]

Interpretation, Explanation, Automation

In the 1930s–1960s, statisticians and social scientists gradually developed other methods for the analysis of multivariate data.[30] In addition to factor analysis, other methods introduced in this period and widely used today in data science include discriminant analysis, cluster analysis, multivariate regression, and multidimensional scaling.[31] The use of digital computers for data analysis after World War II facilitates these developments. In the 1950s, as computers got faster and started to become available in many universities, analyzing more and more variables together became more practical.

Introductory statistical classes being taught today still often only cover techniques for the analysis of one or two variables; in their studies, social scientists may sometimes use a few dozen variables, but usually far fewer—although computers can process practically unlimited numbers of them. In contrast, data science applications extract and process hundreds or thousands of features from every object in a dataset (or a data stream, if the data arrives continuously). The assumption that data objects should be described using a large number of features is standard in data science. (Neural networks that started to be widely used for certain tasks in 2010s have a different approach to features, and I will address this later in this chapter.) This is one of the differences between data science and quantitative social science, in which the numbers of variables considered in a typical study are very small—although both use many of the same multivariate analysis methods.

Why do data scientists and social scientists use such different representations? The answer has to do with the fundamental differences between the goals of quantitative social science and of data science. This difference is also crucial for cultural analytics, as we will discuss ahead. To understand it, we need to first cover a number of additional concepts.

The development of many statistical methods and their applications in the twentieth century often were motivated by research questions in social science. Quantitative social science sees *explanation* as one of its main goals, and its method is systematic experiments. The goal of experiments is to study and quantify how some varying conditions (i.e., independent variables) are affecting certain varying phenomena or processes (i.e., dependent variables, which can be also referred to as *effects*). Here, explanation has a different meaning than the common use of the word: to explain a phenomenon in quantitative social sciences means to able to quantify the effect of some things on other things.

In the field of experimental psychology, experiments are conducted in a lab to carefully control all conditions. This origin of this field is often traced to the work of German scientist Ernst Weber, who carried out a series of experiments starting in the 1820s to measure the relations between physical quantities such as weight and experienced sensation. If it is not possible to conduct such controlled experiments, as is often the case in sociology and economics, researchers instead isolate some variables and study their relationships. For example, how does a person's place of birth, ethnicity, or education affect her current professional position and salary? How does an athlete's preparation and diet affect her performance in multiple sports competitions?

If there are many conditions and effects, it is not easy to understand what is affecting what. Therefore, in an ideal twentieth-century experiment, a researcher measures only one condition and one effect. All other factors ideally would be fixed so they cannot vary. In an experiment, a condition is systematically changed, values of a single effect are recorded, and visualization and statistical techniques such as plots, correlation, and regression are used to study and quantify the possible relationships.

Social scientists often analyze a few conditions and a few effects together, but they keep the overall number of variables small. Otherwise, it becomes impossible to understand what affects what. The most popular method in social science for quantifying relations between a number of variables is *multiple regression analysis*. An effect is represented as a linear combination of values of a number of conditions. For example, a person's salary is predicted using a combination of values describing that person's education, age, gender, and years of employment.

Although humanities publications, museum websites, and exhibition catalogs frequently talk about the influence of some external conditions on the style and content of a body of works and the ideas of an artistic group or a cultural movement, I am not aware of humanities publications that have tried to quantify this effect using regression, correlation, or some other standard statistical method. And if humanities scholars would try to do this today, the reaction without a doubt will be negative. Yet given that millions of studies in sociology, political science, psychology, economics, and other social science fields have been using these methods for many decades, there is no theoretical reason that we cannot apply them to cultural data.

Why has this not happened? In the early nineteenth century, the Romantic movement in Europe developed the modern concepts of *artist* and *art*. If earlier artists were treated as skilled craftsmen who created objects according to rules and traditions, with details of what will be created often specified in contracts,[32] now art was redefined as something that exists outside society and the economy and therefore cannot be understood in rational terms. This paradigm apparently remained strong enough in the twentieth century to prevent people from analyzing quantitatively possible effects of various social, economic, political, and geographic conditions on art and culture or from developing statistical models to see how much of artistic and cultural variability can be explained using a combination of some external variables.

The goal of the humanities and qualitative social science has been *interpretation*. As we already saw, the goal of quantitative social science has been *explanation*, which in this context means quantitatively predicting values of some variables by using a combination of other variables. But data science has a different goal—*automation*. In this, data science often overlaps with artificial intelligence, which started to develop fifty years earlier. Like AI, data science is employed to automate certain kinds of human cognition: finding the right information, making the best decision given lots of relevant data, predicting future behaviors or states of a system, producing new knowledge from available information. Automation means not only efficiency and speed, but also consistency—producing the same decisions given the same input. (Although they don't look like traditional algorithms, neural networks also work in this way, producing the same output given the same input.)

We can think of this algorithmic decision-making as extension of modern bureaucracies that developed in many societies in the nineteenth century. Bureaucracy means making decisions on the basis of well-defined rules, without any exceptions. Instead of being based on social connections or a power of the ruler, in a bureaucracy decision-making is supposed to become rational and "algorithmic." Data science applications then can be seen as the next step in this algorithmizing of decision-making. They keep decision-making impersonal and formal—but substitute inflexible rules with more flexible real-time decisions that can vary depending on input data and automatically respond to various real-time conditions.

The popularity of the supervised machine learning approach and neural networks that started to replace more traditional algorithms after 2013 means that often we may not fully understand how a system arrives at decisions. But in industry applications, what matters is the speed and accuracy of automatic decisions and the ability to process larger and larger real-time data streams. Contemporary data science applications often sacrifice transparency for efficiency, accuracy, and performance. The models that can be understood by users are called *interpretable*; the models that cannot are called *uninterpretable*. In many application areas, such as law, hiring, medical decisions, and others, the ability to understand how a computer system arrived at a decision or recommendation is crucial, and the topic of *interpretability* has attracted lots of attention.[33]

And in general, do we want to live in a society in which numerous decisions are arrived at automatically without us being able to understand how it happens? Perhaps as a society we need to sacrifice speed and efficiency in favor of transparency, and only use fully interpretable models? (This problem may be solved in the future: many computer scientists are actively working on methods to reverse-engineer deep learning models to understand what and how they are learning.[34])

The Semantic Gap

The goal of cognitive automation is made difficult by a *semantic gap*. This term from computer science refers to a difference between the information that a human can extract from some data and how a computer sees the same data. For example, a human reader understands the ideas in the text, its style and genre, but a computer can only "see" a sequence of letters separated by spaces. Looking at a digital photograph of a person, we can immediately detect a face, separate a figure from the background, understand what a person is wearing, and interpret the facial expression. But a computer can only see the numbers that that make up the image.

What are these numbers? A digital image is a matrix of discrete pixels. The color of each pixel is defined by its RGB values—that is, the relative contributions of red, green, and blue. A digital photo with four thousand pixels horizontally and six thousand pixels vertically contains twenty-four million pixels together. Because each pixel is defined by red, green, and blue values, such a photo consists of seventy-two million numbers.

This is the *signal* (another data science term) a computer is given. It has to use these seventy-two million numbers to identify and locate separate objects, identify the type of the scene, find faces, detect and understand text, or perform other tasks. The research on algorithms to solve these questions takes place in the area of computer science called computer vision, which was born in the late 1950s.

We rely on computer vision algorithms every day—for example, when we take photos with our phones or standalone cameras. The algorithms automatically correct contrast, tone, and colors in images; locate faces and take a picture when the people are smiling; and adjust all exposure parameters after identifying the type of scene. They are also at work in apps such as Photos for iOS, Google Photos, and others that automatically classify images into subject categories such as city, beach, sky, selfie, screenshot, and more.

For example, in 2016, Apple's iPhone 7 was already using machine learning to identify objects, people, and bodies and then set "exposure, focus, white color, tone mapping, [and] noise reduction" accordingly.[35] It analyzes depth information from images in its two cameras and uses this to blur backgrounds for photos showing faces and people. And it automatically and seamlessly combines images from its wide angle and telephoto lenses to provide more details in parts of a photo.[36] Also in 2016, the slogan that appeared on the walls of the Berlin offices of EyeEm (one of the first companies to employ computer vision techniques to curate stock photo offerings) said, "You don't take a photograph, you make it."[37] This was the perfect summary of the shift from lens-based to *computational photography*. Certainly, the lens remained, but its centrality in photo making was now displaced by algorithms. To put this in the terms I used in 1997 in my analysis of the same shift taking place in cinema, *post-production* became more important than *production*.

ImageNet is an international competition in which the top research labs working on computer vision algorithms compete every year in different categories. In the competitions that ran in the 2010s, the performance of algorithms was compared in each of three tasks: image classification (algorithms identify object categories present in the image), object detection (algorithms identify all objects and their position in an image), and single object localization (algorithms identifies one example of each type of content present).[38] Between 2010 and 2015, a number of factors—use of convolutional deep networks, faster computers with more RAM, the same datasets that all teams compete on, and sharing of code online by most teams—led to fast progress in these computer vision tasks. For example, in a single object localization category, the overall error rates dropped from 28.2 percent in 2010 to 6.7 percent in 2014.[39] However, the performance varies significantly depending on image content. Using the state-of-the-art Google Vision API[40] with Instagram photos in the summer of 2016, we found that face detection was almost 100 percent correct. But for some categories, the proportion of errors was over 50 percent.

Now we can go back and answer the question I posed earlier: Why do data science algorithms use very large numbers of features? Trying to *close the semantic gap* (a standard phrase from computer science) is the main motivation behind this. We don't know exactly how a human instantly recognizes what a photo represents, understands the meaning of a spoken sentence, or performs other cognitive tasks. We compensate for our lack of knowledge by extracting lots of possible features in the hope that they will provide enough information for a computer to do what a human can do.

For example, features for email spam detection may include the frequency of certain terms, use of all capitals, grammatical correctness of the email, length of sentences, and presence of particular phrases in headers.[41] In many other data science applications, such as text analytics, detection of copyrighted videos, or prediction of loan default rates, large numbers of features are used for the same reason.

Let's look in more detail at the evolution of feature extraction in computer vision. (Chapter 9 will focus on the use of features for media visualization.) Today the general goals of computer vision relevant for cultural analytics include understanding image content, locating particular objects, detecting faces and predicting their demographic characteristics, identifying the photographic style, describing the content of the image using natural language, and predicting its emotional effect.[42] In the middle of the 1990s when computers were slower and had smaller memories (i.e., less RAM), researchers usually only extracted a few dozen visual features describing grayscale, color, and shapes in images. Using more features was not practical. In the 2000s, two algorithms that became very popular were SIFT (1999) and SURF (2006).[43] They were already using thousands of features per image. In our work with analyzing image collections, we used another popular algorithm, the histogram of oriented gradients (HOG; 2005). It also can generate thousands of features.

The first algorithm that was able to achieve good face detection performance in under thirty seconds was published in 2001.[44] It could process 120 images in two hours to detect only one type of content—a face. To see the progress in computer vision, consider this example: in 2015, it took us only two hours to classify one million photographs into one thousand content categories on a single PC with a GPU using the open-source code distributed by Google.

This is why I was only able to start thinking about cultural analytics in 2005, even though I took graduate classes in computer vision from 1986 to 1988 while I was in a PhD program in experimental psychology at New York University. I could not imagine at that time that one day a single computer would be analyzing millions of images per hour. Indeed, looking today at examples of computer vision papers published in the late 1980s, I discover that they often reported results of their algorithms applied to single images—something that looks very uncanny today when teams participating in ImageNet competitions have to process millions of images.[45]

In the 2010s, many computer science researchers and industry applications started to use a different approach to automatically understand the content of images, voice, text, and other media and to automate other tasks. This approach is called *deep learning* (or *deep neural networks*). I mentioned this shift before, but now let's look at neural networks more closely. Rather than manually designing and fine-tuning many different features in the hope that together they will allow algorithms to close a semantic gap, a scientist uses a *training set* of examples that are labeled (e.g., a set of emails labeled as spam) to train a system to learn how to automatically classify new data. A system extracts a large set of generic low-level features from the input and processes them in a number of steps to arrive at a smaller set of high-level features that describe it in a more compact way.[46] In the case of object recognition in photos, the system starts with raw pixel values and progressively learns how to find edges, corners, color gradients, parts of objects, and eventually whole objects. Thus, at each step it learns a more high-level representation of input data. The numbers of these extracted low-level features often are even larger than in the older approach that uses individually crafted features.[47] Deep learning currently is a very active area of research. For example, an important 2012 paper on deep learning applied to image recognition was cited 6,100 times by the middle of 2016 and 27,080 times by the middle of 2018.[48]

The proponents of the deep learning paradigm criticize the earlier approach for having to manually craft many different features. In deep learning, the network learns itself what higher-level features to construct from the standard low-level features. But in the new paradigm, scientists still have to test and fine-tune the architecture of neural networks and its many details, and this still involves lots of experiments. Either way, a computer has to perform lots of steps—either extracting different kinds of features or extracting only one kind but then creating new features from it via deep learning—to try to close the semantic gap.

Feature extraction using algorithms is a fundamental component of modern data science, enabled by digital computers. In the next chapter, we will continue exploring the topic of features. I will discuss two of our projects to demonstrate how metadata and features—that is, existing high-level information about images, such as time periods and genres, and measurements of characteristics of individual images—can be combined in analysis.

Let's conclude this chapter with a summary of its main points. Before we can use a computer to analyze cultural phenomena, behaviors, or collections of artifacts or samples, they have to be represented as data. We learned that such representation has to follow a number of conventions and requirements that have developed over long histories of statistics and computational data processing:

1. A phenomenon is represented as a *set of objects* (also called *data points, measurements, samples, records*) and their *features* (also called *attributes, characteristics, metadata, variables*). The features may include already available metadata, as well as measurements of objects' characteristics we generate using algorithms. (The latter process is called *feature extraction*.)

2. Together, the objects and their features form a *dataset*.

3. The number of objects in a dataset has to be *finite*.

4. Features are encoded using *data types*: whole and fractional numbers, categories, spatial coordinates, spatial shapes and trajectories, dates, times, text tags, or free text.[49]

5. Each feature can use only one data type.

6. The number of features in the dataset has to be finite.

How many and what features do we need to include in a data representation? This depends on the goals this representation will serve. Because the goal of quantitative social science is explanation, social scientists typically use a small number of features. The researchers want to explain and quantify the effects of some features (independent variables) on other features (dependent variables). If too many variables are included, it becomes hard to interpret a model. In data science, the goal is *automation* of knowledge creation and decision-making. Because it is often not clear how a human makes decisions—for example, how you judge that a particular email is spam—the data science methodology is to extracts lots of different features in the hope that together they contain the right information to make the correct decision. And what about cultural analytics? What kinds of features should we extract from cultural artifacts and user activities, and what can we learn with these features? These questions will be discussed in chapters 7 and 9.

7 Language, Categories, and Senses

Our goal is not to treat existing classifications as "ground truth" labels and build machine learning tools to mimic them, but rather to use computation to better quantify the variability and uncertainty of those classifications.

—Peter M. Broadwell, David Mimno, and Timothy R. Tangherlini, "The Tell-Tale Hat: Surfacing the Uncertainty in Folklore Classification," 2017[1]

In reality, the whole point of numbers is to handle questions of degree that don't admit simple yes or no answers. Statistical models are especially well adapted to represent fuzzy boundaries—for instance, by characterizing an instance's mixed membership in multiple classes, or by predicting its likelihood of membership in a single class as a continuous variable. One important reason to map genre algorithmically is that it allows us to handle these fuzzy boundaries at scale.

—Ted Underwood, *Understanding Genre in a Collection of a Million Volumes*, 2014[2]

Data Types

The conventions for data representation covered in the previous chapter are constraints of computational thinking. If we want to use digital computers to represent and then analyze any cultural phenomenon as data—be it a collection of video recordings of all performances at the Eurovision Song Contest (1956–), a list of all exhibitions in the MoMA during its history (1929–)[3], or the experiences of all visitors to a particular exhibition—we need first to translate this phenomenon into a *medium of data* that algorithms can work on. This translation is not a mirror of the phenomenon. Only some characteristics of the artifacts, users' behaviors, and their sensorial, emotional, and cognitive experiences can be captured and encoded as data.

Data is a medium. Like photography, cinema or music, it has both affordances and restrictions. It allows us to represent many kinds of things in many ways, but it also imposes limits on what we can represent and express and how we think about it. In particular, it dictates that we chose one of the available data types to represent any characteristic of the phenomenon. There are a number of ways to categorize available data types. There are three commonly used schemes—we already talked about the first in previous chapter, but not the other two.

In the first scheme, *data types* refer to the types of phenomena and media being represented. In this scheme, we have geospatial data (which can be further broken into spatial coordinates, trajectories, shapes, etc.), 3-D data (polygonal, voxels, point clouds), 2-D image data (raster and vector), temporal data, network data, sound data, text data, and so on.

The second scheme distinguishes between *categorical* and *quantitative* data. Quantitative data can be further divided into *discrete and continuous*.[4] The same phenomenon often can be represented using any of these data types, and the choice of representation strongly influences how we can think about it, imagine it, and analyze it.

For example, we can represent cultural time using discrete temporal categories, such as centuries or periods, like Renaissance and Baroque. Such representation may encourage us to think about each period as one entity, and to start comparing such entities. (The foundational book of modern art history—1915's *The Principles of Art History* by Heinrich Wölfflin—is a perfect example of such an approach.) But if we represent time in culture as continuous or discrete data—for example, as years—this more neutral and detailed scale makes it easier to conceive of culture in terms of gradually changing values. Suddenly, labels such as Renaissance and Baroque, modernism and postmodernism, or Russian avant-garde and socialist realism fade away, allowing us to see continuities and gradual evolution.

Let's look at another example that does not involve time. We can represent colors in an image using the terms provided by natural languages or as sets of numbers using RGB, HSL, HSV, or other color models. For example, the X11 color system supported by browsers has names for nine red colors—LightCoral, IndianRed, FireBrick, and so on. These same colors can be specified as RGB values: (240, 128, 128), (205, 92, 92), and (178, 34, 34). But numerical representation has a key advantage over natural language. Using three numbers between 0 and 255, we can represent 16,777,216 different color values; no human language can come close to this. This example illustrates how a choice of one data type over another allow us to represent some phenomena with more fidelity—which will then shape how a phenomenon can be analyzed. If we compare mature paintings by Piet Mondrian, a few color categories will be sufficient, but for paintings of Giorgio Morandi, which use very desaturated colors that are close to each other in brightness, numerical representation is much better.

The third scheme distinguishes among *structured*, *unstructured*, and *semi-structured data*. Structured data is organized according to a predefined model. For example, to analyze and visualize patterns in a large collection of art images, we create a table containing information about each image. Each column contains only the type of information stored in a particular format: for example, image filename, creation date, title given by the author, and some extracted visual features. Such a table is ready for statistical analysis and visualization. Other examples of structured data include web logs, point-of-sale data, stock trading data, and sensor data.

Examples of unstructured data include text, music, digital images, and videos. Historically computational data processing dealt only with structured data, so everything else that does not fit into a table or a database format was called unstructured data.

Semi-structured data falls in between the structured and unstructured types. An example of such data is an email. The email has a body of text (an unstructured part) and a number of elements stored by a computer in fixed formats, such as sender and recipient email addresses and the date and time the email was sent.

The choice of a particular data representation type may strongly influence our understanding of the phenomenon we want to study. Once we encode it in a particular way, it becomes more difficult to imagine alternatives. For example, if we represent time using regular intervals, this mechanical view of time prevents other views of time, such as cyclical.[5] If we represent a space as a set of discrete points defined by numerical coordinates (i.e., the Cartesian coordinate system introduced by Descartes in 1637), it is more difficult to envision it different ways. The discrete geometric representation will be suitable for the geometric abstractions of Kazimir Malevich or Bridget Riley, but not for those of Francis Bacon or Park Seo-Bo, which "modulate" a surface. (The two types of representation correspond to the difference in computer graphics between vector and raster images or between polygons and voxels.)

The choice of data type imposes additional constraints on the representations, but it can also open up unique possibilities. Some methods become hard to think about it, but others become easy to work with. In fact, in statistics some methods only make sense for continuous variables, while others only work for categorical data. For example, calculating mean or standard deviation is only appropriate for quantitative data.

The adoption of the data science paradigm by many new professional and research fields and industries seen in the first two decades of the twenty-first century is likely to continue to grow. This affects how contemporary society represents knowledge and information. Until the twenty-first century, only selected knowledge areas (i.e., natural sciences, biological sciences, and quantitative social sciences) and business have relied on quantitative data. But the "datafication" of many other fields and areas of human life means that they also now use quantitative representations. And this makes them subjectable to the same techniques of data mining, statistical modeling, and predictive analytics. These techniques now form the "senses" and the "mind" of contemporary society: how it perceives itself and makes endless decisions.

This adoption of data science may lead to a more nuanced view of phenomena as we shift from categorical to continuous data. However, systems of categories defined using words from natural languages (e.g., as color terms) that traditionally have been humans' preferred way of representation did not go away. They remain central to political, social, and cultural life. In the second part of this chapter, I will look at the contemporary *society of categories* and at some ways to analyze systems of cultural categories.

Measurement Scales

How do we create data? One common method used especially in the sciences is measuring a phenomenon. Regardless of what we measure, we need to use some system to encode these measurements. In 1946, psychologist Stanley Stevens defined *scales of measurements*. Although alternative scales have been proposed by others, Stevens's system is the one used the most widely. The system contains four scales. The *nominal* scale describes qualitative measurements (i.e., categories); the other three scales—*ordinal*, *interval*, and *ratio*—describe quantitative measurements.[6]

Steven's theory of scales is very important. It specifies how phenomena can be represented as different data types and what kinds of descriptive statistics can be used with each type. This applies equally to *physical, psychological, social, and cultural phenomena*. For instance, in the psychology of art and sociology of culture fields, researchers study audience perceptions of artifacts by representing these perceptions using one of these scales. Perceptions can be measured by asking people to fill out questioners; by analyzing videos of their faces during the events to automatically measure the types, levels of expressiveness, and valence of their emotions; or by other methods.[7]

Depending on the measurement scale, different statistical techniques can be used to summarize numerical data. For example, *mode* is used to represent the central tendency of nominal data: it is the most commonly occurring number. Another summary representation is the *median*—a number that separates the data evenly into two parts. Both mode and median can be used for ordinal data. With interval and ratio data, we are allowed to use mode, median, mean, and also measures of dispersion: *standard deviation* and *range*.

Let's continue learning about measurement scales and how they apply to cultural analytics research. We will start with nominal data. One example of such data is parts of speech types: verbs, nouns, adjectives, and so on. Nominal values have *no order and no hierarchy*. Many categorical systems are like this: all categories are equally important and there is no inherent order among them. However, things are different in social and cultural realms. Some of the most important systems of categories used by many societies—such as sex, race, gender, and ethnicity—are *hierarchical*. The struggles against these hierarchies have been central to political, social, and intellectual agendas of many countries for a number of decades, while in other countries this started only more recently.

Standard accounts of culture today are also deeply hierarchical. When we start analyzing some cultural data, its metadata often has categories that encode such historical or contemporary hierarchies. This means that category members are implicitly or explicitly ranked according to perceived importance, prestige, and value. European academic art of the seventeenth and eighteenth centuries had a strict hierarchy of genres of paintings, with historical paintings considered to be the most important and still lifes the least important. The culture of the twentieth century was based on a number of binary categories, with one category considered more valuable than another: fine arts versus decorative arts (or design), high culture versus popular culture (or mass culture), avant-garde versus kitsch.[8] Our social, lifestyle, and technological systems have changed significantly even just in the last two decades, but such cultural dichotomies established in the nineteenth and twentieth centuries continue to structure how we think about culture. In fact, the dominant view of culture today as used by museums, foundations, and government agencies has not changed from the one expressed by British critic Matthew Arnold in his 1875 book—"culture being a pursuit of our total perfection by means of getting to know, on all the matters which most concern us, the best which has been thought and said in the world . . ." This formulation establishes hierarchical categories. Culture refers to "the best"; everything else is not "culture." The endless world outside this "best" now has some labels for its different vast continents—culture industries, creative industries, user-generated content, mass media, and so on—but it can't enter the art museums that carefully guard Arnold's hierarchy. So you are unlikely to see any respectable art museum presenting an exhibition of great advertising designs, interface designs, Instagram photography, fashion, or any other vibrant area of contemporary culture. This is only possible in design or applied arts museums, such as the London Design Museum, the Victoria and Albert Museum, the Museum of Applied Arts in Vienna, and the Cooper Hewitt Smithsonian Design Museum, or an art museum that has a design or fashion department (the MoMA and the Metropolitan Museum in New York).

It is relevant to recall here that the modern Western opposition between high and low cultures was not universally accepted in the twentieth century. In communist countries—Russia after 1917, and Eastern Europe, China, Cuba, and a number of other countries later—this opposition was not part of the intellectual discourse. Instead, a different opposition was at work—between professional creators and everybody else. The professionals were educated in state schools and belonged to creative unions run by the state. They also had access to resources and were given state commissions. The Western opposition between art and mass media was also not meaningful because the system of professional education, membership in creative unions, and access to resources was the same for painters, composers, film directors, actors, and architects.

We already saw how oppositions between high culture and mass culture and professional versus amateur creators structure the work with big cultural data today. Researchers in computer science and social sciences study social networks, media sharing networks, online forums, blogs, discussion sites (e.g., Reddit and Quora), recommendation sites (e.g., Yelp), and professional networks (e.g., Behance). For me, this is the *contemporary culture*, and its scale, diversity and global reach is what makes it so interesting to study. But for many academic humanists and people who professionally work in high culture, such as art curators, critics, or festival organizers, social media is mass culture (or pop culture) and should not enter museums and galleries, or be the subject of academic studies. In such a perspective, an artist is only somebody who has a degree from an accredited art program and an exhibition career that includes commercial galleries, art centers, and art museums.

As an example, in 2017, after I delivered a lecture about our lab projects in a seminar organized by PhD students in art history at one of the most prestigious private US universities, one student asked me: "Why study Instagram at all?" I answered that for me it is a unique window into contemporary photography and global visual imagination. The student responded: "Instagram is a company, and like every company, its goal is to make money. Therefore, it is irrelevant for us art historians." Unfortunately, I have encountered many people in the academy and the arts with this attitude. Of course, professional artists, collectors, galleries, and art fairs are also concerned with making money, so what is the real difference? I think that academics and high culture professionals do not consider people sharing their creations on social networks or sites such as DeviantArt to be professional artists because they don't have art degrees or exhibition histories. And therefore they all are automatically dismissed as not worth paying attention to.

The examples I just discussed show how deeply hierarchical categories are ingrained even in the communities (such as particular academic fields) engaged in thinking critically about culture or society. More generally, many social and cultural categories may appear to not have any order, but in reality they do. When you are using such already

existing categories as part of your dataset metadata, you may unintentionally reproduce their hierarchy in your analysis.

You probably noticed that many of my examples of such hierarchical categories
are binary: male/female, high culture/mass culture, art/design, and so on. Although
Stevens's scheme does not separate them into a special type, such binary categories are
extremely important in human history and culture. Structuralism in particular empha-
sized the role of binary oppositions in language, literature, and myths. According to the
anthropologist Claude Lévi-Strauss, who was the most influential structuralist, binary
oppositions are essential to human thinking.

Another analysis of binary oppositions was developed by linguists Roman Jakobson
and Nikolai Trubetzkoy in the 1930s. It is called the theory of *markedness*. In many
linguistic phenomena, one term dominates another term. This first, unmarked term
is seen as more common or as requiring less mental effort; the second, marked term
is defined in opposition to it. For example, in the opposition *honest/dishonest*, the first
term is unmarked and the second one is marked. Another example is *old/young*: in
English, a question about somebody's age usually uses the unmarked term (How old
are you?). In his 1972 article, Jakobson suggested that "every single constituent of
a linguistic system is built on an opposition of two logical contradictories: the presence of an attribute ('markedness') in contraposition to its absence ('unmarkedness')."[9]
The theory of markedness was adopted by social sciences and humanities to critique
how oppositions such as gender function in society and language. For example, as one
researcher pointed out, "In English order matters. Therefore, what comes first is seen as
first in the metaphorical sense—higher ranked. Thus, in the phrase 'men and women'
women do indeed come second."[10]

Let's now look at the other measurement scales in Stevens's scheme. Data that uses
an *ordinal* scale has an explicit order. For example, questionnaires often ask people to
choose one option using a scale that has the following five choices: strongly agree,
agree, disagree, neutral, and strongly disagree. This type of ordinal scale was introduced
by American social psychologist Rensis Likert in his 1932 PhD thesis.[11] Social sciences,
marketing research, and opinion and attitude measurements are among the fields
that use questionnaires organized according to Likert's scale. The other two important
characteristics of ordinal data are that it has no absolute zero and that the distances
between the points cannot be quantitatively defined.

For data that has an *interval scale*, we can quantify a *degree of difference*, but there is
no absolute zero. An example of interval data is spatial coordinates. Every point on
Earth's surface can be defined via its longitude and latitude. The choice of zero for longitude and latitude is an accepted convention that allows us to quantify distances and

positions of points and regions on the Earth's surface. Spatial coordinates are often used in cultural analytics when we compare cultural characteristics of different geographic areas, study geographic diffusion of new inventions or cultural phenomena, analyze spatial distributions of social media posts, or visualize movements of cultural creators (for an excellent use of this idea, see "A Network Framework of Cultural History"[12]).

Finally, we come to the ratio scale. Data that uses a *ratio scale* can both be qualitatively compared and be measured in relation to zero. Examples of ratio data include weight, length, and angle. Zero weight, zero length, and zero angle are all meaningful concepts corresponding to phenomena in physical reality. As I will discuss in the next section, *using ratio data whenever possible as opposed to only nominal and ordinal data (i.e., categories) is a key part of the cultural analytics methodology.* Rather than only relying on discrete categories that natural languages provide for describing analog dimensions of culture, we can use numerical measurements that better represent values on these dimensions (such as brightness or saturation of a color in an image, or speed and trajectory of movement in a dance).

Language and Senses

Most representations of physical, biological, and cultural phenomena constructed by artists, scholars, and engineers so far only capture some characteristics of these phenomena. A linear perspective represents the world as seen from a human-like viewpoint, but it distorts the real proportions and positions of objects in space. A contemporary one-hundred-megapixel photograph made with a professional camera captures details of human skin and separate hairs—but not what is inside the body under the skin.

If the artifacts are synthetic, sometimes it is easy to represent them more precisely. Engineering drawings, algorithms, and manufacturing details used to construct such artifacts are already their representations. However, nature's engineering can be so complex that even all representational technologies at our disposal can barely capture a miniscule proportion of information. For example, currently the best fMRI machines can capture a brain scan at a resolution of 1 mm. This may seem like a small enough area—yet it contains millions of neurons and tens of billions of synapses. The most detailed map of the universe produced in 2018 by Gaia (the European Space Agency craft) shows 1.7 billion stars—but according to estimates, our own galaxy alone contains hundreds of billions of stars.

And even when we consider a single cultural artifact created by humans and existing on a human scale—a photograph you took, a mobile phone you used to take it with, or your outfit made of items you purchased at Zara or COS—data representations of these artifacts often can only capture some of their characteristics. In the case of a digital photograph, we have access to all the pixels it contains. This artifact consists of 100 percent machine data. However, these pixels to us will look a bit different from one display to the next, depending on its brightness, contrast, and color temperature settings and its technology. Moreover, what we can do with this image is only partially determined by its data. In my 2011 article "There Is Only Software," I argued that "depending on the software I am using, the 'properties' of a media object can change dramatically. Exactly the same file with the same contents can take on a variety of identities depending on the software being used."[13]

A digital pixel image is a synthetic artifact fully defined by only one type of data in a format ready for machine processing (e.g., an array of numbers defining pixel values). But what about physical artifacts, such as fashion designs that may use fabrics with all kinds of nonstandard finishes; combine multiple materials, textures, and fabrics; or create unusual volumes? This applies to many collections created by fashion designers by Rei Kawakubo, Dries Van Noten, Maison Margiela, Raf Simons, and Issey Miyake, among others. How do we translate such clothes into data? The geometries of pattern pieces will not tell us about visual impressions of their clothes or the experience wearing them. Such garments may have unique two-dimensional and three-dimensional textures, use ornaments, play with degrees of transparency, and so on. And many fashion designs are only fully "realized" when you wear them, with the garment taking on a particular shape and volume as you walk.

The challenge of representing the experience of material artifacts as data is not unlike calculating an average for a set of numbers. While we can always mechanically calculate an average, this average does not capture the shape of the distribution, and sometimes it is simply meaningless.[14] In a normal distribution, most data lie close to the average, but in a bimodal distribution, most data are away from it, so the average does not tell us much.

Similarly, when we try to capture our sensorial, cognitive, and emotional experience of looking at or wearing a fashion garment, all methods we have available—recording a heartbeat, eye movements, brain activity, and other physiological, cognitive, and affective processes, or asking a person to describe their subjective experience and fill out a questionnaire—can only represent some aspects of this experience.

But this does not mean that any data encoding automatically loses information or that our intellectual machines (i.e., digital computers) are by default inferior to human machines (i.e. our senses and cognition). For example, let's say I am writing about artworks exhibited in a large art fair that features hundreds of works shown by hundreds of galleries. What I can say depends on what I was able to see during my visit and what

I remembered—and therefore is constrained by the limitations of my senses, cognition, memory, and body, as well as by the language (English, Russian, etc.) in which I write.

In humanities, the common method of describing artifacts and experiences was to observe one's own reaction as filtered by one's academic training and use natural language for describing and theorizing these experiences. In social sciences and practical fields concerned with measuring people's attitudes, tastes, and opinions, researchers used questionnaires, group observations, and ethnographies, and these methods remain very valuable today. Meanwhile, since the 1940s engineers and scientists working with digital computers have been gradually developing a very different paradigm—describing media artifacts such as text, shapes, audio, and images via numerical features. (These descriptions use the ratio scale in Steven's scheme; alternatively, they fall into the continuous data category if we use a continuous vs. discrete data scheme.) Cultural analytics adopts the same paradigm, and it is crucial to understand why it is such a good idea. My explanation is summarized in the next paragraph, and the rest of the chapter expands it.

Numerical measurements of cultural artifacts, experiences and processes, give us a new language to describe and discuss culture. This language is closer to how the senses represent analog information. The senses translate their inputs into values on quantitative scales, and this is what allows us to differentiate among many more sounds, colors, movements, shapes, and textures than natural languages can describe. So when we represent analog characteristics of artifacts, interactions, and behaviors as data using numbers, we get the same advantages. This is why a language of numbers is a better fit than human languages for describing analog aspects of culture. (For the examples of our visualizations that use computational measurements of images, see plates 3–8, 10 and 16, and figures I.2 and 10.1.)

Natural languages was the only mechanism in humanities for describing all aspects of culture until the recent emergence of digital humanities. *Natural* or *ordinary language* refers to a language that evolved in human evolution without planning. Although the origins of natural languages are debated by sciences, many suggest that they developed somewhere between two hundred thousand and fifty thousand years ago. Natural languages cannot represent small differences on analog dimensions that define aesthetic artifacts and experiences such as color, texture, transparency, types of surfaces and finishes, visual and temporal rhythms, movement, speed, touch, sound, taste, and so on. In contrast, our senses capture such differences quite well.

The aesthetic artifacts and experiences the human species created over many thousands of years of its cultural history exploit these abilities. In the modern period, the arts started to systematically develop a new aesthetics that strives to fill every possible "cell" of a large multidimensional space of all possible values on all sense dimensions, taking advantage of the very high fidelity and resolution of our senses. Dance innovators from Loie Fuller and Martha Graham to Pina Bausch, William Forsythe, and Cloud Gate group defined new body movements, body positions, compositions, and dynamics created by groups of dancers or by parts of a body, such as fingers, or by speeds and types of transitions. Such dance systems are only possible because of our eyes' and brains' abilities to register tiny differences in shapes, silhouettes, and movements.

In the visual arts, many modern painters developed lots of variations of a *white on white* monochrome painting—works that feature only one field of a single color or a few shapes in the same color that differ only slightly in brightness, saturation, or texture. These include Kazimir Malevich (*Suprematist Composition: White on White*, 1918), Ad Reinhardt (his "black paintings"), Agnes Martin, Brice Marden, Lucio Fontana, Ives Klein, members of the Dansaekhwa movement in South Korea, and many others.

In the twenty-first century, works by contemporary product designers often continue the explorations that preoccupied so many twentieth-century artists. For example, in the second part of the 2010s, top companies making phones—Huawei, Xiaomi, Samsung, Apple—became obsessed with the sensory effects of their designs. Designers of phones started to develop unique surface materials, colors, levels of glossiness of a finish, and surface roughness and waviness. As the phone moves closer and closer to becoming a pure screen or transparent surface, this obsession with sensualizing the remaining material part may be the last stage of phone design before the phone completely turns into screen—although we may also get different form factors in the future, in which the small material parts become even more aestheticized.[15]

For instance, for its P20 phone (2017), Huawei created unique finishes, each combining a range of colors. Huawei named them Morpho Aurora, Pearl White, Twilight, and Pink Gold. When looking at the back of a phone at different angles, different colors would appear.[16] The company proudly described the technologies used to create these finishes on its website: "The Twilight and Midnight Blue HUAWEI P20 has a high-gloss finish made via a 'high-hardness' vacuum protective coating and nano-vacuum optical gradient coating."[17] (Huawei Mate 20 Pro I have been using during 2019 had such a screen.)

What about the minimalism that has become the most frequently used aesthetics in the design of spaces in the early twenty-first century, exemplified by all-white or raw concrete spaces, with black elements or other contrasting details? From the moment such spaces started to appear in the West in the second part of the 1990s, I have been seeking them out so I can work in them—hotel areas, cafes, lounges. Today you can find such places everywhere, but in the late 1990s there were quite rare. In my book *The Language of New Media*, completed at the end of 1999, I thanked two such hotels because large parts of that book were written in their public spaces—the Standard and Mondrian, both in Los Angeles. While not strictly minimalist in a classical way (they were not all white), the careful choice of textures and materials and elimination of unnecessary details was certainly minimalist in its thinking. Later in 2006–2007, I spent summers in Shanghai working on a new book and moving between a few large minimalist cafes there; at that point, Shanghai had more of them than Los Angeles.

On first thought, such spatial minimalism seems to be about overwhelming our perception—asking us to stretch its limits, so to speak, in order to take in simultaneously black and white, big and tiny, irregular and smooth. I am thinking of the famous Japanese rock gardens in Kyoto (created between 1450 and 1500), an example of *karesansui* ("dry landscape"): large black rocks placed in a space of tiny grey pebbles. In 1996, a store for Calvin Klein designed by London architect John Pawson opened in New York on Madison Avenue around Sixtieth Street, and it became very influential in the minimalist movement. Pawson was influenced by Japanese Zen Buddhism, and an article in the *New York Times* about his store used the phrase "less is less."[18] The photographs of the store show a large open white space with contrasting dark wood benches.[19] So what is going on with these examples?

I think that minimalist design uses both sensory extremes for aesthetic and spatial effect, and small subtle differences that our senses are so good at registering. The strong contrast between black and white (or smooth and textured, wood and concrete, etc.) helps us to better notice the variations in the latter—the differences in shapes of tiny pebbles in Kyoto Garden or the all-white parts of the 1996 Calvin Klein store space, which all have different orientations to the light coming in from very large windows.

The most famous early twenty-first-century examples of minimalist design are the all-white and or silver-grey Apple products designed by Jonathan Ive in the 2000s. The first in this series was the iPod in 2001, followed by the PowerBook G4 in 2003, iMac G5 in 2004, and iPhone in 2007. In his article "How Steve Jobs' Love of Simplicity Fueled a Design Revolution," Walter Isaacson quotes Jobs talking about his Zen influence: "'I have always found Buddhism—Japanese Zen Buddhism in particular—to be aesthetically sublime,' he told me. 'The most sublime thing I've ever seen are the gardens around Kyoto.'"[20] In the most famous Kyoto garden, which I was lucky to visit, the monochrome surface made from small pebbles contrasts with a few large black rocks. In Apple products of the 2000s, the contrast between the all-white object and the dark, almost black screen when the device is turned off, made from different materials, works similarly. It makes us more attentive to the roundness of the corners, the shadows from the keys, and other graduations and variations in the graytones and shape of the device.

In general, minimalism is everything but minimal. It would be more precise to call it *maximalism*. It takes small areas on sensory scales and expands them. It makes you see that between two grey values there are in fact many more variations than you knew (I call this aesthetics common in South Korea today "50 shades of grey"): that the light can fall on a raw concrete surface in endless ways; that the edge in the textured paper cut into two parts by hand contains fascinating lines, volumes, and densities. Our senses delight in these discoveries. And this is likely one of the key functions of aesthetics in human cultures from prehistory to today—giving our senses endless exercises to register small differences, as well as bold contrasts. Minimalism cleans our visual, spatial, and sound environment from everything else, so we can attend to these differences between a few remaining elements. To enjoy that less is less.

Senses and Numbers

For thousands of years, art and design have thrived on human abilities to discriminate between very small differences on analog dimensions of artifacts and performances and to derive both pleasure and meaning from this. But natural languages do not contain mechanisms to represent such nuances and differences. Why? Here is my hypothesis. Natural languages emerged much later in evolution than the senses, to compensate for what the latter cannot do—represent the experience of the world as categories. In other words, *human senses and natural languages are complementary systems*. Senses allow us to register tiny differences in the environment, as well as nuances of human facial expressions and body movements, whereas languages allow us to place what we perceive into categories, to reason about these categories and communicate using them.

Evolution had no reason to duplicate already available functions, and that is why each system is great at one thing and very poor at another. Our senses developed and continued to evolve for billions of years—for instance, the first eyes developed around five hundred million years ago during the Cambrian explosion. In comparison, the rise of human languages and their categorization capacities is a very recent development.

When we use a natural language as a *metalanguage* to describe and reason about an analog cultural experience, we are doing something strange: forcing it into small number of categories that were not designed to describe it. In fact, if we can accurately and exhaustively put into words an aesthetic experience, it is likely that this experience is an inferior one. In contrast, using numerical features instead of linguistic categories allows us to much better represent nuances of an analog experience. (In Stevens's scheme, *numerical* means data that uses ordinal, interval, and ratio scales. Or, if we use a simpler scheme of continuous versus discrete data, *numerical* means continuous.)

Our sensors and digital computers can measure analog values with even greater precision than our sense organs. You may not be able to perceive a 1 percent difference in brightness between two image areas or 1 percent difference in the degree of smile between two people in a photo, but computers are able to measure these differences. For example, for *Selfiecity* we used computer vision software that measured the degree of smile in each photo on a 0–100 scale. I doubt that you will be able to differentiate between smiles on such a fine scale.

Consider another example—representation of colors. In the 1990s and 2000s, digital images often used twenty-four bits for each pixel. In such a format, each pixel can encode grayscale using a 0–255 scale. This representation supports sixteen million different colors—while human eyes can only discriminate among approximately ten million colors. Today many imaging systems and image editing software programs use thirty, thirty-six, or forty-eight bits per pixel. With thirty bits per pixel, more than one billion different colors can be encoded. Such precision means that if we want to compare color palettes of different painters, cinematographers, or fashion designers using digital images of their works, we can calculate it with more than sufficient accuracy. Certainly, this precision goes well beyond what we can do with the small number of terms for colors available in natural languages.[21] Some natural languages have more terms for different colors then other languages, but no language can represent as many colors as digital image formats.

In summary, a data representation of a cultural artifact or experience that uses numerical values or features computed from these values can capture analog dimensions of artifacts and experiences with more precision than a linguistic description. However, remember that a natural language also has many additional representation devices besides single words and their combinations. They include the use of metaphors, rhythm, meter, intonation, plot, and other devices that allow us to represent experiences, perceptions, and psychological states in ways that single words and phrases can't. So though natural languages are categorical systems, they also offer rich tools to go beyond the categories. Throughout human history, poets, writers, and performers have used these tools, and the best hip- rap artists today such as Oxxymiron and Tatarka create exceptional works by employing them as well.

Not everybody can invent great metaphors. Numerical features allow us to measure analog properties on a scale of arbitrary precision and they can be extracted automatically from any number of aesthetic artifacts using computers. But this does not mean that data representations of artifacts, processes, and performances that use numbers can easily capture everything that matters.

In the beginning of the twentieth century, modern art rejected figuration and narration and decided instead to focus on sensorial communication—what Marcel Duchamp referred to as "retinal art." But over the course of the twentieth century, as more possibilities were fully explored and later became new conventions, artists started to create works that are harder and harder to describe using any external code, be it language or data. For example, today we can easily represent the flat geometric abstractions of Sonia Delaunay, František Kupka, and Kasimir Malevich as data about shapes and colors and sizes of paintings and drawings—and we can even encode details of every visible brushstroke in these paintings. (Computer scientists have published many papers that describe algorithmic methods to authenticate the authorship of paintings by analyzing their brushstrokes.) But this becomes more difficult with new types of art made in the 1960s and 1970s: light installations by James Turrell, acrylic 3-D shapes by Robert Irvin, earth body performances by Ana Mendieta, and happenings by Allan Kaprow (to mention only the most canonical examples), as well as the works of thousands of other artists in other countries, such as the Движение art movement in the USSR. The works of the latter included *Cybertheatre*, staged in 1967 and published in the *Leonardo* journal in 1969.[22] The only actors in this theatre performance were fifteen to eighteen working models of cybernetic devices (referred to as *cybers*) capable of making complex movements, changing their interior lighting, making sounds, and omitting colored smoke. For something less technological, consider *Imponderabilia* by Marina Abramović and Ulay (1977): for one hour, the members of public were invited to pass through the narrow "door" made by the naked bodies of the two performers.

The experience of watching the documentation left after an art performance is different from being present at this performance. What can we measure if an artwork is designed to deteriorate over time or quickly self-destructs, like Jean Tinguely's *Homage to New York* (1960)? Similarly, while the first abstract films by Viking Eggeling, Hans Richter, and May Ray made in the early 1920s can be captured as numerical data as easily as geometric abstract paintings by adding time information, how do we represent Andy Warhol's *Empire* (1964), which contains a single view of the Empire State Building projected for eight hours? We certainly can encode information about every frame of a film, but what is crucial is the physical duration of the film, its difference from the actual time during shooting, and very gradual changes in the building's appearance during this time. The film was recorded at twenty-four frames per second and projected at sixteen frames per second, thus turning a physical six and a half hours into eight hours and five minutes of screen time. (Very few viewers were able to watch it from beginning to end, and Andy Warhol refused to show it in any other way.)

Measuring Perceptions

Modern art of the last sixty years is one of the cultural areas that presents a challenge for cultural analytics methods. What about other cultural expressions that exploit three-dimensional textures, transparency, volumes, and our senses of touch, taste and smell—for example, fashion, perfume, food, architecture, and space and object design? I have already discussed the challenges of capturing in numbers the experiences of seeing or wearing many fashion items that work with dimensions that can't be easily read from fashion photographs—volumes, structures, differences in material surfaces. This is how Hadley Feingold describes a famous dress from Hussein Chalayan's 2000 spring/summer collection in her post "Sculptural Fashion": "'Remote Control' (often referred to as the Airplane dress) . . . is made of fiberglass and resin composite and has flaps that open via remote control. What is revealed beneath is a soft mass of tulle. What is truly striking here is the modular fabrication, at once sleek and impersonal, that opens up to a soft, more human-like interior that is at the same time no less structured."[23]

How can we capture as data at least some of the unique characteristics and subtle differences in numerous designed products and experiences? Think of descriptions of new perfumes, cars, or drinks offered to consumers: here writers employ adjectives, historical references, and metaphors. Now think of the product development, marketing, advertising, and other departments of companies that make and offer these products in many markets. They perform user studies by employing questionnaires, focus groups, in-depth interviews, ethnographic methods, self-reports; they analyze people's behaviors and interactions with brands and ads on social networks using interaction data; they capture biometric and brain activities using a variety of techniques ranging from hear rate measures to fMRI.

Many techniques used in consumer marketing research, advertising research, and brand management are the same as in sociology, anthropology, human-computer interaction, political science, and especially psychology. In all areas, methods such as surveys, questionnaires, and physiological recordings are used to quantify aspects of human experiences and human understanding of themselves, other people, products, and situations. These methods compensate for our inability to directly measure human cognitive and emotional processes and states. For example, rather than using some objective measurements of pain, a doctor asks you to characterize your experience of pain on a 1–10 scale. (In 2013, researchers were able to successfully measure levels of pain using fMRI, but given its cost and equipment required, you will not see this method in a regular doctor's office today.[24]) Over time, new technologies and improvements in existing ones gradually improve our ability to directly measure such states, but this is a slow process.

What does this mean for cultural analytics methods? *Instead of measuring cultural artifacts, we can instead measure human perceptions and experiences of these artifacts and our interactions with them.* In this paradigm, human experience becomes the common denominator that allows us to bypass the challenge of measuring multisensory or ephemeral offerings. To do this, we can rely on methods used in HCI,[25] marketing research, attitude and opinion measurements, and experimental psychology, as well as draw on theories of cultural reception in humanities. So if we feel that important dimensions of certain types of cultural objects such as fashion, food, designed spaces, and music can't be captured directly, we can instead measure people's perceptions of these objects and experiences with them.

But will such a paradigm shift—from measuring artifacts and communication (i.e., extracting features from texts, music, images, video, 3-D designs, etc.) to measuring sensations, perceptions, emotions, feelings, meanings, and attitudes—fully solve the problem? Focusing on a human receiver rather than on artifacts and messages (e.g., blog posts) brings its own challenges.

If we measure body or brain activities using various technologies such as eye tracking, EEG, fMRI, and so on, the output are numerical metrics. This data can be then analyzed algorithmically to create more compact numerical representations or mapped into categories. For example, Emotiv makes consumer and professional headsets that records EEG readings and translate them into measurements of levels of interest, excitement, relaxation, focus, and stress. The measurements are presented as values on a 0–100 scale.[26] Another company, Affectiva, infers emotional and cognitive states using video and audio of a person. One of its products is the Automotive AI, which measures degrees of alertness, excitement, and engagement, levels of drowsiness, joy, anger, surprise, and laughter, and overall positivity or negativity of mood. Such monitoring can be used for alerts and recommendations when the driver is engaged, and also can automatically hand control from a driver to a car in semiautonomous vehicles.[27]

At present the theories behind such measurements do not differentiate among many kinds of stimuli that cause the same kinds and levels of emotions, focus, or relaxation. They can't help us understand how interactions between a person and an interactive art installation are different from interactions between a driver and a car—or distinguish among the interactive computer installations of Myron Krueger, David Rockeby,

Jeffrey Shaw, Masaki Fujihata, or Char Davies (to use examples of important artists who pioneered this genre);[28] our responses to fashion collections by Rei Kawakubo and Rick Owens; or buildings by Zaha Hadid and MAD. The same goes for popular sentiment measurements of texts: they can't distinguish between you reading a political speech and reading Tolstoy's *Anna Karenina*.

In general, our technological measurements and data representations of human emotional and cognitive states, memories, imagination, or creativity are less precise and detailed than our measurements of artifacts. While computer vision algorithms can extract hundreds of different features from a single image, EEG or FMRI at present measure fewer dimensions of human cognitive processes. The gradual progress of technology will allow for more precision and specificity—but it can take decades. In contrast, measures of artifacts' properties are very easy to obtain on a large scale, which is important for cultural analytics. Think of histograms of three color channels (R, G, and B) that your camera or editing software constructs for any photo. Now imagine similar histograms for line orientations, texture, shapes, faces and objects, and dozens of other dimensions computed over millions of photographs. And now compare this to the measurements of seven "universal human emotions" or levels of excitement and engagement popular today. The difference in fidelity is obvious. Perhaps most importantly, I can carry out image measurements of these millions of photographs on my computer—as opposed to recruiting humans to participate in research that uses EEG, FMRI, and other such technologies[29] or getting their permission to use data captured by personal devices such as fitness trackers.

The challenge of precisely characterizing human responses to cultural objects and situations and doing it at scale can't be solved in a simple way. This is why in our own lab we have been privileging analysis of objects rather than reactions—which I also could have been doing due to my background in experimental psychology. However, I think that quantitative analysis of responses, participation, and interaction will eventually become a popular or even the most important method for studying culture. In academic disciplines concerned with culture—from literary studies, architecture theory, and visual culture to media studies, urban anthropology, and internet studies—researchers so far have not adopted the techniques for cognitive and emotional measurements widely used in interaction design or marketing research (this field is called *neuromarketing*). So if you want to get two degrees—one in humanities, social sciences, or design, and the second in neuroscience—you will be equipped to participate in the future theoretical and practical shift from studying objects to studying perceptions and experiences. For example, imagine a film review that does not talk about the film's story and characters; instead, it will analyze human perception, cognition, and emotional data.

Top-Down and Bottom-Up Analysis

I have argued that extracting numerical features is often a better way to represent cultural phenomenon than using linguistic categories. However, would you want to visit a museum of contemporary art that does not use any categories at all and instead organizes all its objects regardless of their origins only by numerical measurements, such as image size, proportions, colors, grayscale histogram, or line curvatures? Actually, I would. To suspend all categories in this way would be a refreshing experience. However, given the role played by languages in how we understand the world and communicate with others and the fact that natural languages developed evolutionarily to categorize, cultural categories are not going to disappear tomorrow.

Cultural categories are instruments of powers, used to include, exclude, dominate, and liberate. Evolution of human culture includes changes in categorical systems and "wars of categories." For example, during the Cold War (1947–1991), countries were categorized as belonging to the first world (capitalist countries), the second world (developed communist countries), or the third world (developing nonaligned countries). After the collapse of communist governments in 1989–1991, the third world eventually came to be called the Global North—as opposed to the Global South. This new term "emerged in part to aid countries in the southern hemisphere to work in collaboration on political, economic, social, environmental, cultural, and technical issues."[30]

As a part of this reconfiguration of conceptual geography, the distinction between the first and second world faded away. Was it appropriate to dissolve their differences? How do we account for the hysteresis effect of the communist past of the former second world today? Recently, the term Global East has been used to refer to these countries.[31] Like Global South, the new term aims to increase visibility and to compensate for "a double exclusion in analysis, whereby post-socialist cities are neither at the centre nor the periphery, neither mainstream nor part of the critique."[32]

Categories structure our views of social, economic, and cultural phenomena. They can reshape both how we view the past and the futures we construct—by channeling our energy and resources in particular directions. The goal of cultural analytics is not to abandon all historical, genre, media, and other cultural categories. Instead, we want to examine systems of cultural categories that are taken for granted. This means asking a number of questions:

1. Is a particular system of discrete categories sufficient to capture the diversity of a phenomenon?

2. Do the categories that likely were established some time ago still represent the phenomenon adequately, or do they need to be updated? (For example, in *Software Takes Command*, I examine the modern category of *medium* and argue that another category, *metamedium*, is more appropriate for the computer era).[33]

3. Can we use continuous features instead of discrete categories to represent variation in the phenomenon?

Given that all cultural institutions still use categorical systems to structure their own and our understandings of cultural artifacts, as well as their production, exhibition, and archiving, examination of these categories is an important part of the cultural analytics program. For example, Wikipedia's "List of Subcultures" article has 130 entries,[34] while Japan's manga industry classifies manga using four categories of readers defined by age and gender, and further by a few dozen genres. Whenever you are working with existing or creating new cultural datasets, remember that you can modify existing categories for research purposes or define new ones. You should also consider how the existing categories are organized (e.g., as a hierarchy or as a flat system), how they developed and changed over time, the differences in categories used in different geographic regions and different institutions, and the relations between categories used by professionals, academics, and general audiences.

Similar questions are often asked in humanities and social sciences, so is there something unique that cultural analytics brings here? I think so. In their influential 1999 book *Sorting Things Out: Classification and Its Consequences*, Geoffrey Bowker and Susan Leigh Star write: "*A classification is a spatial, temporal or spatio-temporal segmentation of the world. A classification system is a set of boxes (metaphorical or literal) into which things can be put in order to then do some kind of work—bureaucratic or knowledge production.*"[35] The idea of segmentation is very relevant. Cultural phenomena and their particular dimensions are often continuous, but the representations of these phenomena by cultural and academic institutions and discourses segment them into discrete categories. However, because we can now measure continuous dimensions with algorithms and represent them as numbers with arbitrary precision, discrete categories are no longer the only choice. Instead, we can represent cultural phenomena as distributions of continuous features. These distributions then can be compared with existing discrete categories for the same phenomena.

One of the key ideas of cultural analytics is to combine two directions of analysis: top-down analysis using existing categories and bottom-up analysis using extracted continuous features. *Bottom-up* here means extracting features and then visualizing the phenomenon using these features. We can visualize distributions of single features (histograms), two features together (scatter plots or heatmaps), or multiple features (pair-wise scatter plots; parallel coordinates; scatter plots that use MDS, PCS, t-SNE, UMAP, or other dimension-reduction techniques). *Top-down* here means superimposing existing cultural categories for our data onto these visualizations (using color or another technique). In addition to visualization, we have a number of unsupervised machine learning methods for examining the structure of feature space, such as cluster analysis and dimension reduction. These methods are part of the cultural analytics toolkit. We used them in many of our lab projects (e.g., see the visualization in plate 3). They are covered in numerous data science classes, textbooks, and tutorials, so you can learn them on your own. The section called "Analysis Examples" later in this chapter illustrates using top-down and bottom-up analysis together.

I believe that the majority of cultural artifacts and phenomena in human history have continuous dimensions best represented by numerical features. In contrast, the majority of our conceptual landscapes of cultural fields today and in the past consist of discrete categories. By superimposing these discrete categories on continuous distributions of features, we can better see how the categories divide the phenomena and if they are adequate. For example, the categories may correspond to breaks in features' distributions, which means that they do capture real divisions. Or they may arbitrarily divide a continuous distribution, leading us to think that there are distinct classes when in reality they don't exist. Or the distributions may have distinct breaks, but they are not reflected in the categories (see plate 9).

We can now add two more questions to the three listed earlier:

4. How do existing categories divide continuous distributions of a phenomenon's features?

5. Does examination of features' distributions and relationships suggest the need for new categories?

Only *after* we ask these questions can we with some confidence decide what is more appropriate for describing a given phenomenon: categories or numerical features.

Prescriptive Aesthetics and Modernisms

Let's say you receive a cultural dataset from a museum, a public depository on the web, or any other source. The dataset lists some artifacts and includes some categories. Will you focus on analysis of data using categories, without having to extract features? Or is it better to extract various features right away? I believe that you can begin with one of the following two hypotheses as a starting point.

Hypothesis 1: If the cultural artifacts were created using *prescriptive aesthetics*, the existing categories are likely to be meaningful. This is often the case with historical cultural phenomena before the twentieth century. However, you may still want to extract numerical features from your dataset to examine the variations within each category and to check how good the fit is between categories and features. Following this analysis, the categories may need to be revised.

Hypothesis 2: If the cultural artifacts were created by authors that did not follow any prescriptive aesthetics (i.e., there were no explicit rules) and we can easily observe significant variability in the dataset, representing these artifacts using continuous features is appropriate. This is often the case for the modernist period after 1870 when the goal of many artists was to keep inventing the new. (However, many others continued to practice prescriptive aesthetics.)

As an example of prescriptive aesthetics, consider architectural orders in Ancient Greek and Roman civilizations. Originally the Greeks used three orders—the Doric, Ionic, and Corinthian. Romans added two more: the Tuscan and the Composite. The orders define details of building columns, including their proportions, type of decoration and profiles, and other building elements. Like Instagram filters today, choosing a particular order does not dictate the complete design of the building—but it does give it a particular "look." In European art, prescriptive aesthetic systems were particularly important during the seventeenth and eighteenth centuries. For example, in theatre, French playwrights followed a system of rules that called for unity of time, unity of place, and unity of action. The action has to unfold within a single twenty-four-hour period, in a single location, and follow a single plot line.

Modernist artists revolted against prescriptive aesthetics and conventions. But this revolt took a strange direction: groups of artists aided by art theorists or journalists started to create their own new prescriptive aesthetics, and each group claimed that their aesthetics was the only true modern art. These movements included futurism, fauvism, cubism, orphism, rayonism, expressionism, vorticism, constructivism, surrealism, and others.

A few of these styles, such as cubism, constructivism, and surrealism, became popular and were adopted by other artists. Still, all twentieth-century artworks that follow various isms account for only a tiny part of professional art produced during the century. This larger part is omitted from the standard art historical narrative of modern art presented as progression through isms. All these other artists did not write manifestoes and did not create brands. We only have a single category for these millions of artworks: figurative art (or realist art). Obviously, this one category can't capture all the different visual languages, types of content, feelings, and sentiments seen in figurative artworks created in different countries during the century. Creating large datasets of these artworks, extracting numerical features, and then visualizing and clustering them using these features may allow us to develop more inclusive maps of modern art.

Modernism also gives rise to many prescriptive aesthetic systems. The twelfth tone technique in music (1921–), neoplasticism, writing by members of the Oulipo group (1960–), Dogma 95 cinema movement (1995–), Apple's Human Interface Guidelines (1987–), and the flat design movement in UI (2006–) are some of the relevant examples. It is important to remember that a prescriptive aesthetic, design, or communication system does not lock down all elements of the work; it only limits parameter variations on some dimensions or only a single dimension, such as the original 140 characters restriction in Twitter or the original square image format in Instagram. Extracting features and using numerical data representation allows us to capture variations across many works that follow some prescriptive aesthetics.

However, introducing subcategories inside existing categories or adding new categories to an existing system can be also a radical move. If we have a system of five categories describing some cultural field, and we enrich it by adding fifteen more, this increases the resolution of the map these categories provide. Sometimes we may need five hundred categories, and other times five hundred thousand. Today the processes of creating such large categorical systems are algorithmic (e.g., cluster analysis), so we don't need to decide a priori how many we will have or fix the criteria.

Thus, categorical systems function in new ways in the data science era—they can be *generated on the fly, changed at any time,* and *have as many members as necessary.* As opposed to always being rigid and constraining, categories acquire dynamism, flexibility, and plasticity. Therefore, it is wrong to assume that cultural analytics aims to always in all situations replace existing cultural categories by continuous numerical features. Quantifying a phenomenon and using data science methods to establish a more detailed categorical system can be as productive. In this respect, cultural analytics is the opposite of the movement in structuralism to reduce the variety of cultural phenomena to a small number of fundamental structures and binary oppositions (de Saussure, Lévi-Strauss, Greimas). Instead of such reduction, cultural analytics wants to multiply and diversify categories, replace rigid categories by fuzzy ones, and recategorize the phenomena using computational methods.

For a good example of such algorithmic recategorization, consider *maps of science*— network graphs showing connections among many publications in academic fields.[36] One such well-known map created in 2007 used 7.2 million papers published in sixteen thousand academic journals and indexed in Elsevier's Scopus (2001–2005) and

Thomson Reuters's Web of Science indexes for science, social science, and arts and humanities (2001–2004).[37] The map shows connections among research paradigms with colors indicating larger divisions, such as social sciences, humanities, brain research, and so on. Rather than using standard lists of academic disciplines, the authors proposed a new method for algorithmically discovering science paradigms. In the words of the researchers: "The problem is simple: disciplines don't capture the unique multi-disciplinary activities of sets of researchers. Researchers at a university or located in a region (state or nation) tend to self-organize around sets of multi-disciplinary research problems."[38] Therefore, rather than taking a system of academic disciplines for granted, the authors clustered individual articles using joint citations. The clustering produced 554 research paradigms. The comparison of the maps of science generated by new and old methods showed that the former better captures the research strengths of a single university or a country. One of our 2008 designs for a hypothetical cultural analytics interface uses a map of science layout, with clusters of works or types of aesthetics acting as the equivalent of academic research paradigms (see plate 1).

Today we encounter computationally generated categories in our everyday digital lives. The following example illustrates this using the targeting option in Twitter Ads—a Twitter service available to all its users. Targeting means selecting a particular audience for advertising messages. In Twitter's case, this may mean showing my particular tweets to additional Twitter users in addition to my followers, who may see these tweets anyway. The standard targeting method is to select the audience by using explicit categories: for example, I want my tweets to be shown to people of both genders, age 25 to 34, in particular countries. But Twitter also offers a newer algorithmic method (2014–) to select "follower look-alikes." Facebook also has "lookalike audiences" option. To use this method, I first need to specify some users—for example, by uploading a list of particular accounts. The algorithm then automatically finds a new audience with characteristics similar to these users on the list. Alternately, I can ask Twitter to build a new audience of users with characteristics similar to my existing followers.

Importantly, the category of follower look-alikes is not defined explicitly; that is, I don't need to select any values on any parameters. Twitter's algorithms compute features of my followers automatically and find users with similar characteristics. And if this system uses supervised machine learning, it's likely that nobody can tell what these features are and how they are combined because this information is distributed over the millions of connections of a neural network. Here we have a new type of category: it is not defined by a human and can change at any moment. According to many reports, this method works better than traditional audience selection, so it's used by millions of people and businesses advertising on social networks every day.

Imagine that one million people are using the look-alike method today, so Twitter's algorithms build one million categories. We don't know how they are defined exactly, but they perform. This is quite a radical departure from traditional category systems.

Humanists like to refer to a quote from a 1942 essay by Jorge Luis Borges entitled "The Analytical Language of John Wilkins" that became famous after Foucault used it in his book *The Order of Things: An Archeology of Human Sciences* (1966).[39] The story says that "according to some Chinese encyclopedia . . . animals are divided into: (a) belonging to the Emperor, (b) embalmed, (c) tame, (d) suckling pigs, (e) sirens, (f) fabulous, (g) stray dogs, (h) included in the present classification, (i) frenzied, (j) innumerable, (k) drawn with a very fine camelhair brush, (l) *et cetera,* (m) having just broken the water pitcher, (n) that from a long way off look like flies." This quote is often invoked to support the idea that categories can be arbitrary, be nonsystematic, and differ from culture to culture. This is all true—but to me it is more interesting to ask about how categories function differently in our data society and how this is different from earlier periods. Using algorithms that can process very large datasets almost instantly allows generation of dynamic categories, categories that are not defined explicitly but use patterns that computers detect in the data, and systems that can have lots of categories as opposed to only a few.

Analysis Examples: 776 van Gogh Paintings and One Million Manga Pages

Having introduced the idea that top-down and bottom-up analysis can be combined, I will now illustrate this with two examples from our lab projects. The first example uses a dataset of 776 digital images of paintings Vincent van Gogh created between 1881 and 1890. The images were collected by students in my classes in 2010 from public websites. We included this dataset in the free distribution of our ImagePlot visualization software (2011–).[40] Along with metadata for each painting, such as the title, I added a number of visual features extracted from each image: mean, median, and standard deviations of brightness, saturation, and hue; numbers of distinct shapes; and average shape size. (A *shape* here is any area in the image that is perceived as distinct because it has a different color or brightness from other shapes.) We developed software that uses MATLAB and OpenCV to extract hundreds of other visual features, but since the van Gogh dataset was meant for learning ImagePlot, I wanted to keep the list of included features short.

I decided to use digital images of van Gogh's paintings for a few reasons. With many artists, we don't know exactly when their works were created. But for van Gogh, we know the year, the month, and often even the week for most paintings because he described his new paintings in over seven hundred letters to his brother, who supported the artist financially. (All letters with links to the images of the paintings they describe are available from the excellent vangoghletters.org website.) Because we know the month when each painting was created, these 776 paintings covering only ten years (1881–1890) are perfect for studying gradual changes in the artist's visual and semantic language.

The second reason is the existence of well-established categories for understanding and presenting van Gogh's art. These categories are places where he lived: Belgium and Netherlands (1880–1886), Paris (March 1886–January 1888), Arles (February 1888–April 1889), Saint-Rémy (May 1889–May 1890), and Auvers-sur-Oise (May–July 1890). Many art historical and popular accounts divide van Gogh's artistic biography into style periods corresponding to these places. Thus, geographic categories are used to rationalize stylistic categories.

For instance, this is how the Vincent van Gogh Museum in Amsterdam describes the changes in van Gogh's style after he moves to Paris in 1886: "Soon after arriving in Paris, Van Gogh senses how outmoded his dark-hued palette has become. . . . His palette gradually lightens, and his sensitivity to color in the landscape intensifies . . . his brushwork [becomes] more broken."[41] And this is a description of the artist's works that he created after he moved to Arles in the South of France in 1888: "Inspired by the bright colors and strong light of Provence, Van Gogh executes painting after painting in his own powerful language. Whereas in Paris his works covered a broad range of subjects and techniques, the Arles paintings are consistent in approach, fusing painterly drawing with intensely saturated color."[42]

Are the descriptions of the differences between these periods accurate? Do changes in the artist's style indeed perfectly correspond to his moves from one place to another? And is it appropriate to think of his (or any other artist's) development as a succession of distinct periods? If art historians acknowledge that some changes are gradual ("his palette gradually lightens"), can we make these statements more precise and quantify such changes? These are all good questions for the combined top-down and bottom-up analysis, which I will illustrate with three visualizations.

In the first visualization, in plate 6, we see images of 776 van Gogh paintings positioned according to their average brightness (y-axis) and their dates, represented by year and month (x-axis). Here I use the median as the measure of the average brightness. Although we are only considering a single visual dimension, it already becomes clear that the well-established view—that the artist's style systematically changes as he moves from place to place—does not hold. During van Gogh's time in Paris, Arles, and Saint-Rémy, he continues to create some very dark paintings typical of his earlier years.

Moreover, even within short periods of time, the range in brightness in the paintings the artist makes is significant. This to me suggests two ideas. One is that *we should not think of a style as a narrow line that moves through time*. Instead, it is more like a wide river that does change directions, but only gradually. The second idea is that the new visual inventions by van Gogh made in each place where he comes to live do not apply to all his works created there. Instead, the new coexists with the old (e.g., very dark paintings that we still find after van Gogh moves to France).

The second visualization, shown in plate 7, allows us to compare all 776 images using two visual features together: median brightness (x-axis) and median saturation (y-axis). On the brightness axis, the earlier paintings created from 1881 to 1885 are mostly on the left; the paintings created from 1885 to 1890 occupy the center and the right part. On the saturation dimension, his mature paintings occupy the lower part; that is, their average saturation is not high. Even his famous Arles paintings still rarely fall into the upper part. This is a surprising finding given the museum characterization of these paintings as having "intensely saturated color." The statement is not wrong, but it is imprecise. Some of the Arles paintings are more saturated than the Paris ones, but not all of them.

To investigate further the differences between the Paris and Arles periods, I created a third visualization, which compares all Paris and all Arles paintings in our dataset side by side (see plate 8). We use the same features as in the previous visualization: median brightness (x-axis) and median saturation (y-axis). Notice how the brightness and saturation values of the Paris and Arles paintings significantly overlap. This strengthens what the first visualization already suggested: the commonly accepted division of van Gogh's works into stylistic periods based on places where he was living may need to be reconsidered.

One of the reasons for the conventional opinion that van Gogh's style was radically changing is that we are used to looking at a small number of works. In general, often when we think about a particular artist, we consider only their most famous works. Such works may exaggerate the differences among periods. The history of the historical formation of van Gogh's canon—his most often reproduced works—is complex and long, but it is possible that one of the reasons that certain works were selected over others is that they emphasize these differences. When we systematically compare most of the paintings created in Paris and Arles by visualizing them using extracted features, we can see that the differences between the two sets are smaller than we could have expected by only looking at the famous works.

We can also now better understand the nature of these differences. First, van Gogh's paintings created in Paris have significantly more variability in both brightness and saturation values than the paintings created in Arles. Second, the center of the "cloud" formed by all of Arles paintings in plate 8 is shifted to the left and to the top. In other words, the Arles paintings are overall both lighter and more saturated than the Paris paintings. However, this difference is smaller than the usual narrative about van Gogh's art may suggest. Calculating averages of the mean and standard deviations of brightness and saturation for the paintings from the two periods quantifies these observations. The brightness averages of all paintings created in the two cities are 129.83 (Paris) and 158.51 (Arles); the averages of saturation are 95.70 and 109.28, respectively (on a 0–255 scale). The standard deviations of brightness values are 51.65 (Paris) and 34.71 (Arles); the standard deviations of saturation values are 40.59 and 36.30, respectively.

The measurements of the spread of brightness and saturation values support one of the statements on the museum site: "Whereas in Paris his works covered a broad range of subjects and techniques, the Arles paintings are consistent in approach, fusing painterly drawing with intensely saturated color."[43] Indeed, standard deviations of both brightness and saturation averages across all Paris paintings are smaller than those of all Arles paintings. We also now understand that the intensity of many Arles paintings is achieved by changes in two visual characteristics working together, as opposed to only changes in saturation. In other words, van Gogh simultaneously increases both saturation and brightness of his colors. In fact, the average change in brightness is larger than the change in saturation: 18 percent versus 12.4 percent.

Of course, these two features do not cover all aspects of van Gogh paintings; if we want to characterize his visual languages more fully, we will need to create a number of such representations using different combinations of features.[44] (Three different visualization programs we wrote in the lab support the rapid creation of such multiple visualizations.) Alternatively, we can use unsupervised machine learning methods that project many features onto a lower-dimension 2-D or 3-D space that we can see directly. Together these methods are referred to as *dimension reduction*. For example, the visualization in plate 3 uses a method called principle component analysis (PCA), applied to two hundred features we extracted from images of impressionist paintings. In contrast to plots that sort images according to two features (e.g., average brightness and saturation), PCA and other dimension-reduction methods can group images according to many features at the same time.

Let's now look at the second example of using existing cultural categories and feature extraction together. One prominent example of cultural categories is genres. In digital humanities, the quantitative analysis of literary genres in history led to some of the most interesting work in the field. They include the investigation of patterns in the rise and fall of forty-four genres of British novels from 1740 to 1990 by Franco

Moretti;[45] tracing the gradual separation of the literary languages of novels, poetry, and drama from the ordinary everyday language in 1700 to 1900 by Ted Underwood and Jordan Sellers; and other projects.[46]

But genres are also important for contemporary culture. We can look at genre categories established in the culture industry, using as a starting point many theories of genres proposed by theorists of popular music, cinema, and other fields. We can also apply computational text analysis to discussions in online fan communities and media sharing sites to study how audiences understand and use genre categories. In all these cases, applying top-down and bottom-up analysis allows us to compare two maps of a cultural field: one with discrete categories and another showing continuities using extracted features. I will describe our lab project *One Million Manga Pages* (2010–2011) to illustrate how these ideas work in practice.[47]

The project analyzes 883 manga publications, using data and over one million images downloaded from the fan site OneManga (onemanga.com) in 2009.[48] At the time, this was the most popular site for *scanlation*—manga publications scanned by fans, with the text translated into different languages. The manga publications are structured as series of chapters that may appear over periods ranging from a few months to many years. The metadata for each series we downloaded included names of authors and artists, publication periods, the intended audience, and tags describing their genres.

The Japanese manga publishing industry divides the market for manga into four categories based on age and gender: teenage girls, teenage boys, young women, and young men (*shoujo*, *shōnen*, *seinen*, and *josei*). Each manga publication series was assigned one of these categories. The fans used thirty-five genre categories to tag manga series on the site. Many series had multiple tags. For example, the very popular series *Naruto* was tagged as action, adventure, anime, comedy, drama, and fantasy; *Bleach* had all these tags, plus supernatural; *Nana* was tagged as anime, drama, live action, and romance. I found that the average number of genre tags was 3.17 for shoujo manga and 3.47 for shōnen manga, indicating more genre diversity in tags used for titles intended for male teenagers.

Figure 7.1 shows a network graph representing connections among all genre categories. Line thicknesses indicate the strength of a connection—that is, how often the two tags are used together. The size and brightness of the genre name indicates the frequency of each tag: more frequent ones are bigger and darker. We can see that some genres are connected to many others; others are connected to only a few. Thus, this graph maps what we can think of as *genre affordances*: which combinations are very popular, which combinations are still possible although they not popular, and which combinations are impossible.

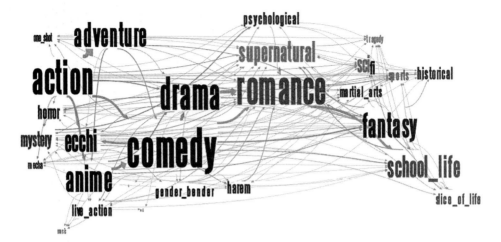

Figure 7.1
Visualization of the connections among thirty-five genre categories used by fans on onemanga
.com, 2009.

Figure 7.2 is a graph showing connections between genre categories and audience
categories. To make the graph easier to see, I included only the twelve most frequent
tags. Some connections are predictable (male teenagers and young men prefer action),
but others are less so. For example, both male and female teenagers turn out to prefer
comedy, but not young men. The connection between the romance and drama genres
is stronger than for romance and comedy; most romances are set in schools (tagged as
school life). Interestingly, none of the top genres is exclusive; all of them are connected
to other genres. Serious manga fans and industry professionals are maybe aware of such
patterns—but likely not all of them since some patterns only appear when we map
hundreds of titles together.

In addition to the metadata for 883 manga publications, we also used for analysis
the images of all pages of these publications available on the site—1,074,790 unique
pages in total. Each manga page contains a few frames featuring grayscale drawings.
In figure I.1, you see an image plot all of all pages organized by two visual features.
Together, a number of pages make one chapter, and a number of these chapters
together make up one publication. Each publication is drawn by a single author (sometimes with the help of assistants) and has a consistent visual style. We wanted to see
if there are connections among these styles, the four audience segments of the manga
industry, and the forty-one genres tagged by fans. In other words, are there systematic
differences in some aspects of the style of manga publications authored for different

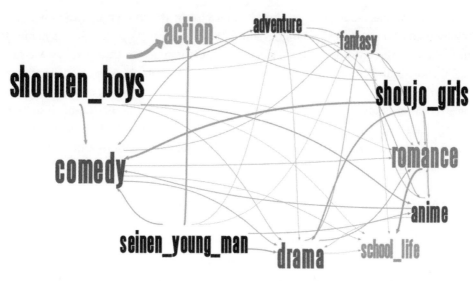

Figure 7.2
Visualization of the connections among the three most frequent audience tags and the eight most frequent genre tags from onemanga.com, 2009.

audiences? And are there also some systematic differences among manga in different genres?

Defining and measuring aspects of visual style is a challenging problem, and we were able to only start exploring this for manga in the *One Million Manga Pages* project. However, these initial explorations led to interesting results. We extracted eight grayscale features from each page in our dataset and compared their summary statistics for publications designed for female and male audiences. The average brightness of all manga drawings in our dataset from shoujo publications (for teenage girls) was 203.17 (measured on a 0–255 scale). For manga drawings from shōnen publications (for teenage boys), it was significantly darker: 184.19. The difference was even stronger between manga aimed at young females and young males (josei and seinen manga): 205.45 versus 184.44. Comparing the average values for all other visual features confirmed the presence of statistically significant differences.

This analysis shows that visual style in manga is used to construct gender differences. However, the gender spaces defined by style do not form absolute sets. Instead, they have a strong overlap. This for me was the most interesting result because it reveals a more complex picture of gender/style spaces. This picture is revealed when we plot distributions of features. Plate 9 shows histograms of the average grayscale for shoujo and shōnen manga pages and a scatter plot in which each manga drawing is represented by a point. A standard deviation of a drawing's grayscale values is mapped to the x-axis; the entropy of the grayscale values is mapped to the y-axis. As we can see, the distributions for shoujo and shōnen features overlap. (The two types of manga are marked using blue and pink colors in the visualizations.) Not all shoujo manga is lighter than shōnen manga; some are also rather dark in tone. Similarly, not all shōnen manga is always darker; some titles are relatively light. Each distribution has a bell-like shape. Use of numerical features allows us to plot these distributions and see how discrete categories (manga audiences) and continuous features are related to each other.

More Examples: One Million Artworks and 42,571 Movies

I have shown how the use of categories in the data and extracted numerical features allows us to make interesting discoveries using examples of one artist's career (e.g., van Gogh) and a popular cultural field (e.g., manga). Let's now look at two other strategies for investigating cultural categorical systems.

One strategy is to examine how such systems change over time. Does the number of artifacts that belong to each category become smaller or grow bigger? Are there new categories that were added in particular moments? As an example, we can look at the growth in the types and numbers of programs in creative fields in universities and specialized art schools and academies around the world. Consider Nanjing University of the Arts, the first modern art academy in China, established in 1918. In 2018, it was offering twenty-five undergraduate disciplines and seventy postgraduate disciplines ranging from critical history of design and new media to three specializations in traditional Chinese painting (mountains and rivers, human figures, and flowers and birds).[49] In the same year, the New School in New York City, which includes the famous Parsons School of Design (established in 1896), was offering forty-five undergraduate majors and many minors ranging from food studies and creative coding to sustainable cities—in addition to older disciplines such as fashion design and photography.[50] When were each of these creative disciplines and specializations first offered, and what are their growth patterns over time and in space (i.e., when do they appear in different cities and countries)? Collecting, analyzing, and visualizing such data will be a very interesting project.

While analyzing one million artworks shared on deviantart.com from 2001 to 2010, we looked at categories that were gradually introduced by contributors and administrators to organize the artworks.[51] Since the launch of DeviantArt in 2000, the number of top-level categories and subcategories systematically grew to accommodate the variety of techniques and subjects in artworks submitted by contributors. The category system is organized as a tree, with a number of top-level categories containing further subcategories. By 2011, many branches of this tree had up to six levels of subcategories under them, and the total number of all subcategories was over 1,700.

For the temporal analysis, we zoomed into the two top categories: "traditional art" and "digital art." We then compared patterns of growth of their subcategories and numbers of artworks shared by artists over the ten-year period studied. Because subcategories can describe content, medium, or techniques, analysis of the development of subcategories and numbers of shared artworks in each subcategory allows us to better understand the effects of digital tools on art. Many media theorists, critics, and artists have written about this topic, but our study was the first to examine such effects quantitatively using large samples of digital artworks created over time.

Although both categories had a similar growth rate, the number of digital art subcategories was always approximately two times larger than the number of traditional art subcategories. By the end of 2001, traditional art had ten subcategories, while digital art had twenty-two; in 2005, these numbers were eighty-one and 162; and in 2010, they were 113 and 216. One possible explanation for this difference is that digital art has more categories that describe specific digital techniques (vector graphics, pixel art, 3-D art, fractals, etc.) and artistic scenes corresponding to these authoring techniques and specific software tools or applications. By *scenes* I mean groups of nonprofessional and semiprofessional artists who are passionate about particular digital techniques and authoring applications and who exchange information and learn from each other using publications, local interest groups, and online networks such as DeviantArt. While the tools of traditional art did not change for decades, the digital tools kept changing during our analysis period, leading to the formation of such scenes around new tools and new techniques.

My inspiration for quantitative analysis of systems of cultural categories comes from the fields of *bibliometrics* and *scientometrics* that developed in the 1960s.[52] They offer many methods, tools, and research examples that can be carried over from their original context—analysis and measurement of academic publications, patterns and relationships among scientific fields, and growth of innovation—to many areas of culture. For example, many scientometrics researchers quantitatively analyzed the growth of science as a whole and its particular disciplines. In one study, the authors used 38,508,986 publications from 1980 to 2012, looking at the numbers published each year, and also at 256,164,353 cited references covering the years 1650–2012. The analysis identified three stages in science growth: less than 1 percent until the middle of the eighteenth century, 2–3 percent until World War II, and 8–9 percent after that to 2012. They also found that the growth in numbers of publications was very similar among different disciplines.

The key challenge for using this paradigm in cultural analytics is the lack of formal methods for citation in culture that would be equivalent to those for science. In design, architecture, fashion, cinema, literature, or visual arts, authors borrow visual ideas and elements from other works, but this is not documented. However, in some fields, such as pop music, numerous "citations" are explicit because the authors and publishers have to get the rights to any samples or whole works they want to use. In pop music, the use of electronic and later digital recording media for all published works made sampling central to its functioning since the early 1980s, when hip hop producers such as Grandmaster Flash started using sampled breaks. The organizations that do music rights management include ASCAP (ten million works by 680,000 songwriters, composers, and publishers), BMI (twelve million works by 750,000 members), Sony/ATV (four million works), and Universal Music Publishing Group (UMPG; 3.2 million).[53] Such a structured practice of rights for samples does not exist in other cultural areas, but we can invent ways to get around this limitation. In the landmark project *Culturegraphy* (2014), visualization designer Kim Albrecht used references between films recorded in the Internet Movie Database (IMDB). As the project's designer explains, IMDB contains "nine different reference types (alternate language version of, edited from, features, follows, references, remake of, spin off from, spoofs & version of)," with "119,135 such connections from 42,571 movies."[54] One of the project's fascinating results was the first quantitative and graphic view of the "rise of the post-modern cinema"—specifically, the relative quantities of references in later films to earlier films.[55] This view revealed that the quantities of such references quickly grew after 1980. This trend was noticed earlier by film scholars, but Albrecht's project for the first time demonstrated that it was not limited to particular movies. You should look at this and other detailed visualizations in the project yourself; they "connect the macro view with the micro view and show the references of each movie that give rise to the larger pattern of the graphic."[56]

By considering categories used in institutional collections and the number of items in each category, we can make visible the "shapes" of these collections. In 2013, the Museum of Modern Art in New York gave my lab access to approximately twenty thousand digitized photos from its photography collection, covering the history of photography from the 1840s to the present. One of many visualizations we created shows all photos sorted by the year of creation as recorded by MoMA (see figure 7.3). Although we may expect that a major institutional art or design collection, including that of MoMA, is more representative of some periods and some types of images

Figure 7.3
Visualization of twenty thousand photographs from the photography collection of the Museum of Modern Art (New York). Images are sorted by year (from 1844 to 1989, top to bottom).

than others, the extreme unevenness in this coverage, revealed by our visualization, is rather striking. The period between the First and Second World Wars dominates over all other periods—and in this period, modernist artistic photography dominates, with other types such as photojournalism, industrial, and amateur photography practically absent.[57]

What will be a more representative representation of photography history, if we are to start a new photography museum? We may want each temporal unit of equal size—for example, five- or ten-year intervals—to have approximately an equal number of artifacts. An alternative strategy is to progressively increase the numbers of artifacts in a collection as the field of professional photography was growing. Or we can employ another sampling strategy. The key thing is to have some strategy in order to construct a more representative history of a cultural field (photography in this case).

The Society of Categories

Categorical data is central to modern society's representation and "processing" of its people, cultures, and social interactions. It became even more important in the 2010s when the success of adopting supervised machine learning and neural networks for automatic classification led to use of such classification in new areas and on a new scale. Companies, nonprofits, and academic researchers use categorical data and analytical statistical techniques developed for this data to capture and analyze what people think and believe, how they understand social and economic phenomena, their perceptions of products and brands, and their interactions with each other. For example, ordinal scales such as Likert's five-point scale for questionnaires have been widely employed to analyze attitudes and opinions for many decades. Today, companies and nonprofits such as Nielsen, Gallup, Pew Research Center Project, and numerous others continue to use such questionnaires in their surveys.

The use of polls to determine public opinions was popularized by Gallup. The company was established in New Jersey in 1935; in 1939 it started to conduct market research for advertising and film industries. Nielsen was founded in Chicago in 1923; it started to measure the radio industry in the 1930s. The Gallup Global Well-Being survey asks one thousand randomly selected individuals from every country included in the survey to rate aspects of their lives on a ten-point scale. The description of the method Gallup publishes demonstrates the kinds of decisions and choices being made in such measurements—which, of course, affects the published results: "Gallup measures life satisfaction by asking respondents to rate their present and future lives on a 'ladder' scale with steps numbered from 0 to 10, where '0' indicates the worst possible life and '10' the best possible life. Individuals who rate their current lives a '7' or higher *and* their future an '8' or higher are considered thriving. Individuals are suffering if they report their current and future lives as a '4' or lower. All other individuals are considered struggling."[58] The people being polled are asked to use an interval scale: numbers from zero to ten. Their responses are then mapped into an ordinal scale that has only three categories: thriving, struggling, and suffering. This is a good example of how measurement scales are used to collect and represent information and how the final reported information is a result of a number of mappings from scale to scale. If the thresholds used for mapping from interval to ordinal scales were set differently, the proportions of people in each country reported in three categories would be different. Here are the examples of the results from the 2010 survey for three countries, with the proportions of people in the thriving, struggling, and suffering categories: Costa Rica (63, 35, and 2), United States (57, 40 and 3), and Cuba (24, 66, and 11).

In the twentieth century, many statistical methods were invented to analyze categorical data obtained with questionnaires and surveys. For example, all later works by famous French sociologist Pierre Bourdieu used the technique of correspondence analysis developed by statistician Jean-Paul Benzécri.[59] These techniques are also central to the most influential book in the sociology of culture—Bourdieu's *Distinction: A Social Critique of the Judgement of Taste* (1979). The book's empirical analysis uses the results of two surveys of the tastes of the French public carried out in the 1960s.

Cotemporary digital social networks are engineered to have their hundreds of millions of users create *discrete signs* of attention and interest. Favorites, likes, and shares are the signs that are already *a priori quantified* by the networks' interfaces. In other words, they are asking people to translate their feelings into categorical data. On Facebook, we can see counts of likes and shares for every post. Weibo shows the numbers of fans, discussions, and reads for every topic. (For example, in the second week of August 2016, the most popular post of the week on Weibo was shared 1,155,243 times and liked 575,389 times.[60]) These counts, along with the usernames of people who added their likes or shared posts, are available to network and third-party algorithms that drive social media monitoring and publishing dashboards, contextual advertising, and other media analytics applications. (They are also often available to researchers via social networks' APIs.) To use the data science terms, the networks convert users' attention, interests, social connections, and tastes into structured data, which is easier to analyze than unstructured data, such as texts of social media and blog posts, images and videos they share, or even video interviews conducted in a research study. Certainly, these unstructured forms of human media encode our feelings, thoughts, attitudes, desires, and imaginations, but both human receivers and algorithms often struggle to decode them. This ambiguity of human expression and communication is delightful, desirable, and satisfying for us in many situations—but not for the industry and its algorithmic decision-making systems controlling marketing, advertising, logistics, prices, and other elements of business.

In fact, the world of social media networks can be compared to a massive global marketing study in which people are presented with numerous cultural objects—products, songs, movies, images, influencers, normal users, and everything everybody posts—and they have to choose the ones they prefer, expressing their preferences in a binary way: I like this, I share that. But social networks and normal marketing research also differ in important ways. Historically they developed only to host user-generated content, and commercial content came later. In their present state, user-generated content and commercial content appear next to each other on users' walls and in their streams.

As it became clear that a few people click on ads presented next to personal content in social networks and apps (this measure is called *click rate*), advertisers started to further blur the boundary between these categories. One method to do so is *native advertising*, in which ads match the normal formats and styles of the platforms on which they appear.[61] Types of native advertising include ads shown in search results, recommendation widgets ("you may also like"), and stories written as though they come from the platform editors. Another method is paying social media "stars" and "influencers" (people who have many followers) to feature particular products in their regular posts, an update on the older product placement method. (In 2016, a person who had over ten thousand followers on Instagram could already be compensated to promote products.[62])

Shall we conclude that by forcing people to use the same mechanisms of appreciation, such as ratings, likes, and shares, on all posted content, the networks are "commodifying" human relations? Or maybe it is the opposite: products are humanized and "emotionalized" because they are appreciated and liked in exactly the same way as photos of your friends or posts about their important life events? Or does this humanize business objects and simultaneously dehumanize expressions of individuals? Regardless, there is an uncanny symmetry today between the networks collecting and making available perfectly organized structured data of users' likes and shares and the computational analysis of this data by companies, advertisers, marketers, nonprofits, and political parties. The formats in which opinions and interests are collected match statistical methods and algorithms developed much earlier.

It is tempting to conclude that all these formats were coldly engineered so that companies can extract our preferences and interests—but this is not correct. For example, the original motivation for a web hyperlink comes from early hypertext and UI research in the 1960s, decades before the web emerged and started to be used commercially. But even something that may look like it was designed only to collect data—the Like button—was not. Facebook engineers started to prototype the button in the summer of 2007. The idea was to create a design element that would allow users to express that they liked a post. After seeing a protype, people from platform marketing, the feed team, and the ads team got interested and began imagining how they could use such feature for their own purposes. But it took two years before it was launched in early 2009.[63] Some of the initial ideas for the use of the button did not work. Only after the design team was able to show that the presence of the button did not take away from a number of post's comments was the decision made to implement the button for all the users.

The preceding reflections add a new angle to the popular discussions of artificial intelligence and its future. AI can anticipate our behaviors only when we are acting in predictable ways. Predictable here refers to having consistent routines and opinions and behavioral and shopping patterns. All users of AI and predictive analytics may prefer us to have complete consistency, but we also are expected to be spontaneous and periodically change so that we can discover and adopt new brands and offerings.

But we do not always behave or think in predictable ways. For instance, the 2015 study "Navigating by the Stars: Investigating the Actual and Perceived Validity of Online User Ratings" analyzed user ratings for 1,272 products across 120 product categories. The authors found that "average user ratings lack convergence with *Consumer Reports* scores, the most commonly used measure of objective quality in the consumer behavior literature."[64]

In the nineteenth and twentieth centuries, there was no social media with photos and posts about products and companies people could rate, like, or share. Organizations and companies had to administer questionnaires or have people do product comparisons in formal settings. (Today such methods are still widely used because they have a number of advantages over social media data, as I already mentioned.) This is one of the reasons that statisticians developed methods and concepts for using and analyzing different kinds of categorical data. So though basic statistics textbooks and most introductory classes today focus on analysis of quantitative (numerical) data, this is only one part of modern statistics. This primacy of quantitative data analysis reflects the developments of statistical methods in the second part of the nineteenth century and first third of the twentieth century in the context of numerical measurements— human physical characteristics (Quetelet), educational tests (Spearman), or agricultural experiments (Fisher).

Cultural analytics certainly can use both quantitative and categorical statistics. However, representing large-scale cultural phenomena or processes as either categorical or quantitative data is not always necessary for their computational analysis. As I will show in part III, visualization methods allow us to explore large collections of visual cultural artifacts or samples from a cultural process without measuring them.

In other words, we do not have to use either numbers or categories. The ability to explore collections of cultural data and information, see patterns at different scales, confront our stereotypes, and make discoveries—but without having to necessarily quantify them—is the reason that visualization is as important for cultural analytics as statistics and data science. Far from being only one of the tools in quantitative cultural analysis, *visualization is an alternative analytical paradigm*. It allows us to see patterns that we cannot observe by reading, viewing, or interacting with individual cultural artifacts directly one at a time or by quantifying collections of artifacts and using statistical and computational methods for analysis.

III Exploring Cultural Data

8 Information Visualization

I first drew the Chart in order to clear up my own ideas on the subject, finding it very troublesome to retain a distinct notion of the changes that had taken place. I found it answer the purpose beyond my expectation, by bringing into one view the result of details that are dispersed over a very wide and intricate field of universal history; facts sometimes connected with each other, sometimes not, and always requiring reflection each time they were referred to.

—William Playfair, *An Inquiry into the Permanent Causes of the Decline and Fall of Powerful and Wealthy Nations*, 1805, in reference to "The Chart, No. 1, representing the rise and fall of all nations or countries, that have been particularly distinguished for wealth or power, is the first of the sort that ever was engraved, and has, therefore, not yet met with public approbation."[1]

The pretty photographs we and other tourists made in Las Vegas are not enough. How do you distort these to draw a meaning for a designer? How do you differentiate on a plan between form that is to be specifically built as shown and that which is, within constraints, allowed to happen? How do you represent the Strip as perceived by Mr. A. rather than as a piece of geometry? How do you show quality of light—or qualities of form—in a plan at 1 inch to 100 feet? How do you show fluxes and flows, or seasonal variation, or change with time?

—Robert Venturi, Stefan Izenour, and Denise Scott Brown, *Learning from Las Vegas: The Forgotten Symbolism of Architectural Form*, 1972[2]

"Whole" is now nothing more than a provisional visualization which can be modified and reversed at will, by moving back to the individual components, and then looking for yet other tools to regroup the same elements into alternative assemblages.

—Bruno Latour, "Tarde's Idea of Quantification," in *The Social after Gabriel Tarde: Debates and Assessments*, 2010[3]

Information visualization is becoming more than a set of tools, technologies and techniques for large data sets. It is emerging as a medium in its own right, with a wide range of expressive potential.

—Eric Rodenbeck, keynote lecture at O'Reilly Emerging Technology conference, March 4, 2008[4]

Visualization is ready to be a mass medium.
—Fernanda B. Viégas and Martin Wattenberg, "Interview: Fernanda Viégas and Martin Wattenberg from Flowing Media," 2010[5]

In 2000, only specialists in a few professional fields knew about information visualization. Ten years later, this changed completely: In 2010, the Museum of Modern Art in New York presented a dynamic visualization of its collection on five screens created by Imaginary Forces. The *New York Times* regularly featured custom visualizations both in its print and web editions, created by its in-house interactive team. Numerous sophisticated visualization projects created by scientists, designers, artists, and students appeared online. If you searched for certain types of public data, the first result returned by Google linked to an automatically created interactive graph of this data.[6] If you wanted to visualize your own dataset, there were dozens of free online visualization tools and platforms such as Google Docs, Tableau Public, Plotly, and others. Three hundred years after William Playfair's amazement at the cognitive power of information visualization, it looks like many others finally are getting it.

(A note on my use of terms: Today the terms *information visualization* and *data visualization* are often used interchangeably. Historically the first term preceded the second. To emphasize that visualization has a long history and was not magically born only recently, I decided to use "information visualization" in this chapter.)

I can't address all aspects of information visualization as a new medium of visual communication and exploration in a single chapter. Nor can I teach you how to visualize your cultural datasets. There are numerous online tutorials, courses, and books that cover the craft of visualization, and you can learn from them and keep practicing until you achieve the desired results. Instead, this chapter focuses on a few ideas fundamental to visualization's identity as a medium and its history: visualization as a mapping from one domain to another; visualization as a reduction of information; and visualization as a predominantly spatial representation. I then identify a new paradigm that I call *media visualization*. Whereas traditional information visualization demands reduction—using points, lines, and other geometric elements to stand in for real-world objects and their relations—media visualization operates without such reduction. I discuss a few well-known experimental projects to illustrate media visualization possibilities and explain the relevance of this paradigm for explorations of large cultural visual datasets.

What Is Visualization?

What is information visualization? Despite the popularity of *infovis* (a common short-ening of *information visualization*), it is not so easy to come up with a definition that will work for all kinds of visualization projects being created today and at the same will clearly separate them from those of other related fields, such as scientific visualization and information design. Let's start with a provisional definition that we can modify later. We can define *information visualization* as a *mapping between data and a visual representation*. We can also use different concepts besides representation, each bring-ing an additional meaning. For example, if we believe that a brain uses a number of distinct representational and cognitive modalities, we can define infovis as a mapping from other cognitive modalities (such as mathematical and propositional) to an image modality.

This definition does not cover all aspects of information visualization—such as the distinctions among static, dynamic (i.e., animated), and interactive visualizations—the latter, of course, being the most important today. In fact, most definitions of info-vis by computer science researchers equate it with the use of interactive, computer-driven visual representations and interfaces. Here are two examples of such definitions: "Information visualization (InfoVis) is the communication of abstract data through the use of interactive visual interfaces,"[7] and "information visualization utilizes computer graphics and interaction to assist humans in solving problems."[8]

Interactive graphic interfaces in general, and interactive visualization applications in particular offer all kinds of new techniques for manipulating data elements—from the ability to change how files are shown on the desktop in a modern OS to the mul-tiple coordinated views made available in some visualization software such as Mon-drian.[9] However, regardless of whether you are looking at a visualization printed on paper or a dynamic interactive arrangement of graphic elements on your computer screen that you can change at any moment, in both cases this image is a result of map-ping. So what is special about the images that such mapping produces?

For some researchers, information visualization is distinct from scientific visualiza-tion in that the latter uses numerical data, while the former uses non-numerical data such as text and networks of relations.[10] Personally, I am not sure that this distinction holds in practice. Certainly, plenty of infovis projects use numbers as their primary data, but even when they focus on other data types, they still often use some numerical data as well. For instance, a typical network visualization may use both data about the structure of the network (which nodes are connected to each other) and quantitative data about the strength of these connections (e.g., how many messages are exchanged between members of a social network). As a concrete example of infovis that combines non-numerical and numerical data, consider *History Flow* ((Fernanda B. Viégas and Martin Wattenberg, 2003), one of the first projects to visualize large cultural data.[11] This project shows how a given Wikipedia page grows over time as different authors contribute to it. The contribution of each author is represented by a line. The width of the line changes over time, reflecting the amount of text contributed by an author to the Wikipedia page. To take another infovis classic, *Flight Patterns* (Aaron Koblin, 2005) uses numerical data about flight schedules and trajectories for all planes that fly over the United States to create an animated map displaying the patterns formed by their movement over a twenty-four-hour period.[12]

Rather than trying to separate information visualization and scientific visualization using some a priori idea, let's instead enter each phrase in a Google image search and compare the results. The majority of images returned by searching for information visualization are two-dimensional and use vector graphics—points, lines, curves, and other simple geometric shapes. The majority of images returned when searching for scientific visualization are three-dimensional; they use solid 3-D shapes or volumes made from 3-D points. The results returned by these searches demonstrate that the two fields indeed differ—not because they necessarily use different types of data but because they privilege different visual techniques and technologies.

Scientific visualization and information visualization come from different cultures (science and design); their development corresponds to different areas and eras of computer graphics technology. Scientific visualization developed in the 1980s along with the field of 3-D computer graphics, which at that time required specialized graphics workstations. Information visualization developed in the 1990s along with the rise of desktop 2-D graphics software and the adoption of PCs by designers; its popularity accelerated in the 2000s. The two key forces behind this acceleration were the easy availability of big datasets via APIs provided by major social network services from 2005 on, and new high-level programming languages specifically designed for graphics (i.e., Processing[13]) and software libraries for visualization (for instance, d3[14] and ggplot2[15]).

Can we differentiate information visualization from information design? This is trickier, but here is my way of doing it: *information design starts with data that already has a clear structure, and its goal is to express this structure visually*. For example, the famous London tube map designed in 1931 by Harry Beck uses structured data: tube lines, stations, and their locations over London geography.[16] In contrast, *the goal of information visualization is to discover the structure of a (typically large) dataset*. There is no a priori knowledge of this structure; a visualization is successful if it reveals this structure. A different way to express this is by saying that information design works with information, whereas information visualization works with data. As is always the case with actual cultural practice, it is easy to find examples that do not fit such a distinction—but a majority do. Therefore, I think that this distinction can be useful in allowing us to understand the practices of information visualization and information design as partially overlapping but ultimately different in terms of their functions.

Finally, what about the earlier practices of visual display of quantitative information in the nineteenth and twentieth centuries that are known to many via the examples collected in the pioneering books by Edward Tufte?[17] Do they constitute infovis as we understand it today? As I already noted, most definitions provided by researchers working within computer science equate information visualization with the use of interactive computer graphics.[18] Using software, we can visualize much larger datasets than was previously possible; create animated visualizations; show how processes unfold in time; share visualizations with others; and, most importantly, manipulate visualizations interactively. These differences are very important—but for the purposes of this chapter, which is concerned with the visual language of information visualization, they are less important. When we switched from pencils to computers, this did not affect the core idea of visualization: mapping some properties of the data into a visual representation. Similarly, while the availability of computers led to the development of new visualization techniques (scatterplot matrix, tree maps, various new types of network diagrams, etc.), the basic visual language of infovis remained the same as it was in the nineteenth century—points, lines, rectangles, and other graphic primitives. Given this continuity, I am using the term infovis to refer to both earlier visual representations of data created manually and contemporary, software-driven visualizations.

Reduction and Space

In my view, the practice of information visualization from its beginnings in the second part of the eighteenth century until today relied on two key principles. The first principle is *reduction*. Infovis uses graphical primitives such as points, straight lines, curves, and simple geometric shapes to stand in for objects and relations between them—regardless of whether these are people, their social relations, stock prices, income of nations, unemployment statistics, or anything else. By employing graphical primitives (or, to use the language of contemporary digital media, vector graphics), infovis is able to reveal patterns and structures in the data objects. However, the price being paid for this power is extreme reduction. We throw away 99 percent of what is specific about each object to represent only 1 percent in the hope of revealing patterns across this 1 percent of objects' characteristics.

Information visualization is not unique in relying on such extreme reduction of the world to gain new power over what is extracted from it. It comes into its own in the first part of the nineteenth century when in the course of just a few decades almost all graph types commonly found today in statistical and charting programs were invented.[19] This development of new techniques for visual reduction parallels the reductionist trajectory of modern science in the nineteenth century. Physics, chemistry, biology, linguistics, psychology, and sociology propose that both the natural and the social world should be understood in terms of simple elements—molecules, atoms, phonemes, just noticeable sensory differences, and the like—and the rules of their interaction. This reductionism becomes the default metaparadigm of modern science and it continues to rule scientific research today. For instance, currently popular paradigms of complexity and artificial life focus our attention on how complex structures and behavior emerge out of the interaction of simple elements.

Even more direct is the link between the nineteenth-century infovis and the rise of social statistics. Philip Ball summarizes the beginnings of statistics in this way: "In 1749 the German scholar Gottfried Achenwall suggested that since this 'science' [the study of society by counting] dealt with the natural 'states' of society, it should be called Statistik. John Sinclair, a Scottish Presbyterian minister, liked the term well enough to introduce it into the English language in his epic *Statistical Account of Scotland*, the first of the twenty-one volumes of which appeared in 1791. The purveyors of this discipline were not mathematicians, however, nor barely 'scientists' either; they were tabulators of numbers, and they called themselves 'statists.'"[20]

In the first part of the nineteenth century, many scholars, including Adolphe Quetelet, Florence Nightingale, Thomas Buckle, and Francis Galton, used statistics to look for the "laws of society." This inevitably involved summarization and reduction—calculating the totals and averages of the collected numbers about citizens' demographic characteristics, comparing the averages for different geographical regions, asking if they followed a bell-shaped distribution, and so forth. It is therefore not surprising that many—if not most—graphical methods that are standard today were developed during this time for the purposes of representation of such *summarized data*. According to Michael Friendly and Daniel J. Denis, between 1800 and 1850, "in statistical graphics, all of the modern forms of data display were invented: bar and pie charts, histograms, line graphs and time-series plots, contour plots, and so forth."[21]

Do all these different visualization techniques have something in common besides reduction? They all use *spatial variables*—position, size, shape, and, more recently, curvature of lines and movement—to represent key differences in data and reveal the most important patterns and relations. This is the second (after reduction) core principle of infovis practice as it was practiced for three hundred years—from the very first line graphs (1711), bar charts (1786), and pie charts (1801) to their ubiquity today in all spreadsheet software such as Excel, Numbers, Google Docs, OpenOffice, and the like.[22]

Infovis privileges spatial dimensions over other visual dimensions. In other words, we map the properties of our data in which we are most interested into topology and geometry. Other less important properties of the objects are represented through different visual dimensions—the tones, fill-in patterns, colors, transparency, size, or shape of the graphical elements.

As examples, consider two common graph types: bar chart and line graph. Both first appeared in William Playfair's *Commercial and Political Atlas*, published in 1786, and became commonplace in the early nineteenth century. A bar chart represents the differences between data objects via rectangles that have the same width but different heights. A line graph represents changes in the data values over time via the changing height of the line.

Another common graph type—a scatter plot—similarly uses spatial variables (positions and distances between points) to make sense of the data. If some points form a cluster, this implies that the corresponding data objects have something in common; if you observe two distinct clusters, this implies that the objects fall into two different classes; and so on.

Consider another example—network visualizations that function today as distinct symbols of "network society" (see Manuel Lima's authoritative gallery at visualcomplexity .com, which presents one thousand network visualization projects). Like bar charts and line graphs, network visualizations also privilege spatial dimensions: position, size, and shape. Their key addition is the use of straight or curved lines to show connections between data objects. For example, in *Distellamap* (2005), Ben Fry connects pieces of code and data by lines to show the dynamics of the software execution in Atari 2600 games.[23] In Marcos Weskamp's *Flickr Graph* (2005), the lines visualize the connections among users of Flickr.[24] (Of course, many other visual techniques can also be used in addition to lines to show relations; see, for instance, a number of maps of science created by Katy Borner and her colleagues at the Information Visualization Lab at Indiana University.[25])

I believe that the majority of information visualization practices from the second part of the eighteenth century until today follow the same principle—reserving the spatial variables for the most important dimensions of the data and using other visual variables for the remaining dimensions. This principle can be found in visualizations ranging from the famous dense graphic showing Napoleon's march on Moscow by Charles Joseph Minard (1869)[26] to the more recent *The Evolution of the Origin of Species* by Stefanie Posavec and Greg McInerny (2009).[27] Distances between elements and their positions, shape, size, line curvature, and other spatial variables code quantitative differences between objects and/or their relations (e.g., who is connected to whom in a social network).

When visualizations use colors, fill-in patterns, or different saturation levels, typically this is done to partition graphic elements into groups. In other words, these non-spatial variables function as group labels. For example, Google Trends uses line graphs to compare search volumes for different words or phrases; each line is rendered in a different color.[28] However, the same visualization could have simply used labels attached to the lines—without different colors. In this case, color adds readability, but it does not add new information to the visualization.

The privileging of spatial over other visual dimensions was also true of plastic arts in Europe between the sixteenth and nineteenth centuries. A painter first worked out the composition for a new work in many sketches; next, the composition was transferred to a canvas; and then shading was fully developed in monochrome. Only after that was color added. This practice assumed that the meaning and emotional impact of an image depends most of all on the spatial arrangements of its parts, as opposed to colors, textures, and other visual parameters. In classical Asian ink and wash painting, which first appeared in the seventh century in China and was later introduced to Korea and then Japan (in the fourteenth century), color did not even appear. Painters used exclusively black ink to explore the contrasts between objects' contours, their spatial arrangements, and different types of brushstrokes.

It is possible to find information visualizations in which the main dimension is color—for instance, a common traffic light that "visualizes" the three possible behaviors of a car driver: stop, get ready, go. This example shows that if we fix spatial parameters of visualization, color can become the salient dimension. In other words, it is crucial that the three lights have exactly the same shape and size. Apparently, if all elements of the visualization have the same values on spatial dimensions, our visual system can focus on the differences represented by colors or other nonspatial variables.

Why do visualization designers—be they the inventors of graphing techniques at the end of the eighteenth and early nineteenth centuries or the millions of people who now use these graph types in their reports and presentations or the contemporary authors of more experimental visualizations featured in museum exhibitions—privilege spatial variables over other kinds of visual mappings? Why are color, tone, transparency, and shape used to represent secondary aspects of data while the spatial variables are reserved for the most important dimensions?

The answer comes from studies of vision in experimental psychology. Visualization designers exploit the strengths of the human visual system. Human vision can perceive very well small differences in spatial arrangements of elements and very quickly compare the sizes, directions, orientations, and shapes of these elements. Consequently, most popular visualization techniques rely on our ability to see these differences in positions of points, directions and curvature of lines, and relative sizes of bars. This ability is used to interpret scatter plots, line plots, and bar plots.

In comparison, human vision's abilities to make quick comparisons among color hues, brightness levels, or levels of transparency are more limited. This is why visualization designers typically use these variables for secondary aspects of data. For example, you can assign around eight category values to different hues or tones. But if you try to do so for a larger number of values, it becomes more difficult to see patterns in a visualization. Similarly, if you want to represent values of a quantitative variable by using differences in color, tone, or transparency, you can do it successfully for a few dozen of values and sometimes maybe even a hundred, but not for a larger number. If you try to do this, you push beyond what human vision can easily process.

Why has the human visual system evolved to have superior spatial abilities? Why is the geometric arrangement of elements in a scene more important to human perception than other visual dimensions? Possibly this has to do with the fact that each object in the real world occupies a unique part of the 3-D space. Therefore, it is important for a human brain to be able to segment a visual field into spatially distinct objects that are likely to have different behaviors and uses for a human being—for example, animals, trees, fruits, or people; one animal versus a few; and so on. Object recognition also can benefit from an ability to register differences in structures of objects. Different types of objects have parts with different shapes. A tree has a trunk and branches; a human being has a head, a torso, arms, and legs. Identifying 2-D forms and their arrangements and registering small differences in size, shape, and orientation is thus likely to play an important role in object recognition. Yet another possible reason is the need to read facial expressions and recognize faces, which also requires high-resolution spatial perception. A face has eyes, nose, and mouth, plus other parts, and we need to be able to perceive tiny differences in their shapes, positions, and details.

A craftsperson, designer, or artist can create objects and compositions that focus our attention on nonspatial visual dimensions such as textures, colors or shades of one color, or reflective qualities of materials: think of ornaments in traditional human cultures, Matisse's paintings, fashion designs by Missoni, the minimalist spaces that became popular in the 1990s, or phone designs in the 2010s with surfaces that use subtle colors and levels of reflectivity. But in everyday perception, spatial dimensions are what matter most. How close two people are to each other and their body positions; the expressions on their faces; their relative size, which allows us to estimate their distance from us; the characteristic shapes of different objects, which allows us to recognize them—all these and many other spatial characteristics that our brains instantly compute from retinal input are crucial for our daily existence.

This privileging of spatial variables in human perception may be the reason that all standard techniques for making graphs and charts developed in the eighteenth to twentieth centuries use spatial dimensions to represent key aspects of the data and reserve other visual dimensions for less important aspects. However, we should also keep in mind the evolution of visual display technologies, which constrain what is possible at any given time. Only in the 1990s, when people started using computers to design and present visualizations on computer monitors, did color become the norm. Color printing is still significantly more expensive than using a single color—so even today many academic journals are printed in black and white. Thus the extra cost associated with creating and printing color graphics during the last two centuries was likely also a reason for privileging spatial variables in visualization design.

When hue, shading, and other nonspatial visual variables were used in visualizations created in the nineteenth century and most of the twentieth century, they usually represented only a small number of discrete values (typically nominal and ordinal scales). However, computer-based scientific visualization, geo-visualization, and medical imaging today often use such variables to represent continuous values (ordinal and ratio scales). Hue, shading, and transparency are now commonly employed in these fields to show continuously varying qualities such as temperature, gas density, elevation, gravity waves, and so on.

How is this possible? Consider hue. As I already noted earlier, today computers allocate anywhere from eight to forty-eight bytes to represent pixel values in a digital image, so computer displays can show more unique colors than human eyes can see if the monitor can render all these colors. Similarly, displays can show hundreds of levels of shading and transparency, which can also code continuous variables.

Does this contradict my statement that spatial arrangement is key to information visualization? We can solve this puzzle if we consider a fundamental difference between information visualization and scientific visualization/geovisualization, which I did not yet mention. Information visualization uses arbitrary spatial arrangements of elements to represent the relationships between data objects. Scientific, medical, and geovisualization typically show existing (or simulated) physical objects or processes such as a brain, a coastline, a galaxy, an earthquake, and so on. Because the spatial layout in such visualizations is already fixed and cannot be arbitrarily manipulated, color, shading, and other nonspatial variables are used instead to show new information. A typical example of this strategy is a *heat map*, which uses transparency, hue, and saturation to overlay information over a spatial map.[29]

The two key principles that I suggested—*data reduction* and *privileging of spatial variables*—do not account for all possible visualizations produced during last three hundred years. However, they are sufficient to separate information visualization (at least as it was commonly practiced until now) from other techniques and technologies for visual representation: maps, engraving, drawing, oil painting, photography, film, video, radar, MRI, infrared spectroscopy, and the like. They give information visualization its unique identity—the identity that remained remarkably consistent for almost three hundred years, until the second part of the 1990s.

Visualization without Reduction

The meanings of the word *visualize* include *make visible* and *make a mental image*. This implies that until we visualize something, this something does not have a visual form. It becomes an image through a process of visualization.

If we survey the practice of infovis from the eighteenth century until the end of the twentieth century, we indeed see that visualization takes data that is not visual and maps it into a visual domain. However, it seems to no longer adequately describe certain new visualization techniques and projects developed since the middle of the 1990s. Although these techniques and projects are commonly discussed as information visualization, is it possible that they represent something else—a fundamentally new development in the history of representational and epistemological technologies, or at least a new broad visualization method for which we do not yet have an adequate name.

Consider a visualization technique called a *tag cloud*.[30] The technique was popularized by Flickr in 2005 and today it can be found on numerous websites and blogs. A tag cloud shows the most common words in a text, and the size of each word corresponds to its frequency in the text. We can use a bar chart with text labels to represent the same information—which in fact would work better if the word frequencies are very similar. But if the frequencies fall within a larger range, we do not have to map the data into a new visual representation in this way. Instead, we can vary the size of the words themselves to represent their frequencies in the text. This is the idea of the tag cloud technique.

Tag clouds exemplify a broad method that I will call *media visualization*: creating new visual representations from the actual visual media objects or their parts. Rather than representing text, images, videos, or other media though new visual signs such as points, rectangles, and lines, media visualizations build new representations out of the original media. Images remain images; text remains text. (For examples of media visualizations, see plates 12–16.) In view of our discussion of the data reduction principle, we can also call this method *direct visualization* or *visualization without reduction*. In this method, the data is reorganized into a new visual representation that preserves its original form.

Usually, media visualization does involve some data transformation, such as changing data size. For instance, a text cloud visualization would not show every word that occurs in a long text; instead it only shows a smaller number of the most frequently used words. However, this is a reduction that is quantitative rather than qualitative. We do not substitute media objects for new objects (i.e., graphical primitives typically used in infovis), which only communicate selected properties of these objects (e.g., bars of different lengths representing word frequencies). My phrase "visualization without reduction" refers to this preservation of a much richer set of properties of data objects when we create visualizations directly from them.

Not all media visualization techniques, such as a tag cloud, originated in the twenty-first century. If we project this concept retroactively into history, we can find earlier techniques that operate within the media visualization paradigm. For instance, a familiar book index can be understood as a media visualization technique. Looking at a book's index, you can quickly see if particular concepts or names are important in the book because they will have more occurrences listed; less important concepts will take up less space.

Although both the book index and the tag cloud exemplify the media visualization method, it is important to consider the differences between them. The older book index technique relied on the typesetting technology used for printing books. Because each typeface was only available in a limited number of sizes, the idea that you can precisely map the frequency of a particular word to its font size was counterintuitive—so it was not invented. In contrast, the tag cloud technique is an example of what I call *software thinking*—the ideas that explore the fundamental capacities of modern software. Tag clouds explore the capacities of software to vary every parameter of a representation and to control it using external data. The data can come from a scientific experiment, from a mathematical simulation, from the body of the viewer in an interactive installation, from sensors, and so on. If we take these software capacities for granted, the idea to arbitrarily change the size of words based on some information—such as their frequency in a text—is something we may expect to be actualized in the process of cultural evolution. In fact, all contemporary interactive visualization techniques rely on the same two fundamental capacities: all parameters of a representation can vary, and their values can be controlled by external data.

The rapid growth in the number and variety of visualization projects, software applications, and web services since the late 1990s was enabled by advances in computer graphics capacities in both hardware (processors, RAM, displays) and software (C, Java, and Python graphics libraries, Flash, Processing, Flex, Prefuse, d3, etc.). These developments popularized information visualization and also fundamentally changed its identity by foregrounding animation, interactivity, and more complex visualizations that represent connections among many more objects than was possible previously.[31] But along with these three highly visible trends, the same advances also made possible the media visualization approach.

Artistic Media Visualization

In this section, I will discuss three well-known digital projects that for me exemplify the media visualization paradigm. These projects are *Cinema Redux*, *Preservation of Favored Traces*, and *Listening Post*.[32]

Cinema Redux was created by interactive designer Brendan Dawes in 2004.[33] Dawes wrote a program in Processing that sampled a feature film at the rate of one frame per second and scaled each frame to 8 × 6 pixels. The program then arranged these sampled frames in a rectangular grid, with every row representing a single minute of the film. Although Dawes could have easily continued this process of sampling and remapping—for instance, representing each frame though its dominant color—he chose instead to use the actual, scaled-down frames from the film. The resulting visualization represents a trade-off between the two possible extremes: preserving all the details of the original artifact and abstracting its structure completely. A higher degree of abstraction may make the patterns in cinematography and narrative more visible, but it would also remove the viewer further from the experience of the film. Staying closer to the original artifact preserves the original detail and aesthetic experience but may not be able to reveal some of the patterns.

Ultimately, what is important in the context of our discussion is not the particular sampling values Dawes used for *Cinema Redux* but that he *reinterpreted the previous constant of visualization practice as a variable*. Throughout visualization history, infovis creators mapped data into new diagrammatic representations consisting of graphical primitives. This was the default practice. With computers, a designer can now select any value on the original data/abstract representation dimension. In other words, a designer can now choose to use graphical primitives *or* the original images exactly as they are—or any format in between. Thus, though the project's title, *Cinema Redux*, refers to the idea of reduction, in the historical content of earlier infovis practice it can be actually understood as expansion: expanding typical graphical primitives (points, rectangles, etc.) into actual data objects (film frames).

Before software, creating a visualization typically involved a two-stage process: first counting or quantifying data and then representing the results graphically. Software allows for direct manipulation of the media objects without quantifying them. As demonstrated by *Cinema Redux*, these manipulations can successfully make visible the relations among a large number of these artifacts (thousands of film frames). Of course, such visualization without quantification is made possible by the a priori quantification required to turn any analog data into a digital representation. In other words, it is the reduction first performed by the digitization process that now allows us to visualize the patterns across sets of analog artifacts without reducing them to graphical signs.

For another example of media visualization, let's look at Ben Fry's *Preservation of Favored Traces* (2009).[34] This project presents an interactive animation of the complete text of Darwin's *On the Origin of Species*. Fry used different colors to show the changes made by Darwin in each of six editions (1859–1872) of his famous book. As the animation plays, we see the evolution of the book text from edition to edition, with sentences and passages deleted, inserted, and rewritten. In contrast to many animated visualizations that show some spatial structure constantly changing its shape and size in time, reflecting changes in the data (e.g., the changing structure of a social network over time), in Fry's project the rectangular frame containing the complete text of Darwin's book always stays the same; what changes is its content. This allows us to see how over time the pattern of the book's additions and revisions becomes more and more intricate as the changes from all the editions accumulate.

At any moment in the animation we have access to the complete text of Darwin's book—as opposed to only a diagrammatic representation of the changes. At the same time, it can be argued that that *Preservation of Favored Traces* does involve some data reduction. Given the typical resolution of computer monitors and web bandwidth, Fry was not able to show all the actual book text at the same time.[35] Instead sentences are rendered as tiny rectangles in different colors. But when you mouse over any part of the image, a pop-up window shows the actual text. Because all the text of Darwin's book is easily accessible to the user in this way, I think that this project can be considered an example of media visualization.

Let's add one more example—*Listening Post* by Ben Rubin and Mark Hansen (2001).[36] Usually this work is considered to be the finest example of the genre of computer-driven installations rather than an information visualization, but I think it is appropriate to also consider it as the latter, expanding classical infovis in a new direction (media visualization). *Listening Post* pulls text fragments from online chat rooms in real time, based on various parameters set by the authors, and shows them across a display wall made from a few hundred small screens in a six-act looping sequence. The work consists of six "acts" that follow each other. Each act uses its own distinct spatial layout to arrange dynamically changing text fragments. For instance, in one act the phrases move across the wall in a wave-like pattern; in another act words appear and disappear in a checkerboard pattern. Each act also has a distinct sound environment driven by the parameters extracted from the same text that is animated across the display wall.

We can argue that *Listening Post* is not a visualization because the spatial layouts in all acts are prearranged by the authors and not driven by the data. We can contrast this with classical infovis methods such as a scatter plot, in which the layout of points is derived from the data. This argument does make sense—but it is important to keep in mind that though layouts are prearranged, the data in these layouts is not; it is a result of the real-time data mining of the web. So although the text fragments are displayed in predefined layouts (wave, checkerboard, etc.), because the content of these fragments is always different, the overall result is also always unique. In contrast, in a scatter plot all points are often exactly the same, so information is only carried by their layout.

Note also that if the authors were to represent the text via abstract graphical elements, we would simply end up with the same abstract pattern in every repetition of an act. But because they show the actual text that changes all the time, the patterns that emerge inside the same layout are always different. This is why I consider *Listening Post* to be a perfect representative of media visualization thinking: the patterns it presents depend as much on what all the text fragments that appear on the screen wall actually say as on their predefined composition.

Whereas common visualization techniques such as scatter plots and bar charts only define a basic mapping method and the rest is driven by the data (positions of points, length of bars), visualizations of networks use a different principle. Like *Listening Post*, they use certain predefined layouts. Manuel Lima identified what he calls a *syntax* of network visualizations—commonly used layouts such as radial convergence, arc diagrams, radial centralized networks, and others.[37] The key difference between many of these network visualizations and *Listening Post* lies in the fact that the former often rely on the existing visualization layout algorithms. Thus, they implicitly accept the ideologies behind these layouts—in particular the tendency to represent a network as a highly symmetrical and/or circular structure. The authors of *Listening Post* wrote their own layout algorithms that allowed them to control the layouts' intended meanings. It is also important that they used six very different layouts that cycle over time. The meaning and aesthetic experience of this work—showing both the infinite diversity of web conversations and the existence of many repeating patterns—to a significant extent derive from the temporal contrasts between these layouts. Eight years before Bruno Latour's article (quoted at the beginning of the chapter) in which he argues that our ability to create "a provisional visualization which can be modified and reversed"[38] allows us to think differently because any "whole" we can construct now is just one among numerous others, *Listening Post* beautifully staged this new epistemological paradigm, enabled by interactive visualization.

Cultural Time Series

The three visualizatio projects I considered demonstrate that in order to highlight patterns in the data we do not have to dramatically reduce it by representing data objects as abstract graphical elements. We also do not have to summarize the data as is common in statistics and statistical graphics; think, for instance, of a histogram that divides data into a number of bins or a bar chart showing the numbers of items in multiple categories. This does not mean that in order to qualify as a media visualization an image has to show 100 percent of the original data—every word in a text, every frame in a movie, or so on. Out of the three examples I just discussed, only *Preservation of Favored Traces* does this. Both *Cinema Redux* and *Listening Post* do not use all the available data; instead they sample it. The first project samples a feature film at the fixed rate of one frame per second; the second project filters the online conversations using set criteria specific to each act. However, what is crucial is that the elements of these visualizations are not the result of remapping of the data into some new representation format; they are the original data objects selected from the complete dataset. Images remain images, text remains text. This strategy can be related to the traditional rhetorical figure of synecdoche—and specifically the particular case in which a specific class of thing refers to a larger, more general class.[39] (For example, in *Cinema Redux*, one frame stands for a second of a film.)

Although sampling is a powerful technique for revealing patterns in the data, *Preservation of Favored Traces* demonstrates that it is possible to reveal patterns while keeping 100 percent of the data. But you have likely employed this strategy—for instance, if you have ever used a magic marker to highlight important passages of a printed text (or the equivalent of this technique in a word processor). Although text highlighting normally is not thought of as visualization, we can see it as an example of a media visualization that does not rely on sampling. You sample selected sentences from the complete texts and highlight them so that later you can only look at these sentences.

Preservation of Favored Traces and *Cinema Redux* also both break away from the second key principle of traditional visualization: communication of meaning via spatial arrangement of elements. In both projects, the layout of elements is dictated by the original order of the data—shots in a film, sentences in a book. This is possible and also appropriate because the data they visualize is not the same as the typical data used in infovis. A film or a book is not just a collection of data objects: it is a narrative made from these objects. Of course, infovis designers also often work with sequential data (e.g., time measurements in an experiment, quarterly sales for some products, volumes of social media posts over time). But these are not a priori narratives. And usually we visualize only a single dimension of such data: quantities over time. But the book or a movie is a truly "thick" narrative in which changes take place over multiple dimensions, and events and scenes are connected to others appearing much earlier and later.

It is certainly possible to create effective visualizations that remap a narrative sequence into a completely new spatial structure, as in *Listening Post* (see also *Writing without Words* by Stefanie Posavec and *The Shape of Song* by Martin Wattenberg[40]). But *Cinema Redux* and *Preservation of Favored Traces* demonstrate that preserving the original sequences is also effective.

Preserving the original order of data is particularly appropriate in the case of cultural datasets that have a time dimension. I call such datasets *cultural time series*. Whether feature films (*Cinema Redux*), books (*Preservation of Favored Traces*), or long Wikipedia articles (*History Flow*), the relationships between the individual elements (a film's shots, a book's sentences) and between larger parts of a work (a film's scenes, a book's paragraphs and chapters) separated in time are of primary importance to the work's evolution, meaning, and user experience. We consciously or unconsciously notice many of these patterns while watching, reading, or interacting with the work, but projecting time into space—laying out movie frames, book sentences, magazine pages in a single image—gives us new possibilities to study them. Thus, *space* turns out to play a crucial role in media visualization after all: it *allows us to see patterns between media elements that are normally separated by time*.

Beyond Information Visualization

In an article on the then-emerging practice of artistic visualization written in 2002, I defined *visualization* as "a transformation of quantified data which is not visual into a visual representation."[41] At that time, I wanted to stress that visualization participates in the reduction projects of modern science and modern art, which led to the choice of the article's title: "Data Visualization as New Abstraction and Anti-Sublime." I think that this emphasis was appropriate given the types of infovis projects typically created at that time. (Although I used a somewhat different formulation for the definition that appears at the beginning of this chapter—a remapping from other codes to a visual code—the two definitions focus on the same concept: mapping.)

Most information visualization today continues to employ graphical primitives. However, as the examples in this chapter demonstrate, alongside this "mainstream" infovis, we can find another trend. These are the projects in which the data being visualized is already visual—text, film frames, magazine covers. In other words, these projects create new visual representations from the original visual data without translating it into graphic signs. They also show that the second key principle of normal infovis—mapping of the most important data dimensions into spatial variables—does not always have to be followed.

Does media visualization actually constitute a form of infovis, or is it a different paradigm altogether? We have two choices. Either we accept that this is something fundamentally different, or, alternatively, we can revise our understanding of what infovis is. Given that all media visualizations we looked at aim to make visible patterns and relations in the data, this certainly aligns media visualization with infovis as it developed during the last three hundred years. It is also relevant that some of the most well-known infovis projects of the last twenty years follow a media visualization approach. This is true of *Cinema Redux* and *Preservation of Favored Traces* and other seminal projects that I did not discuss, such as *Talmud Project* (David Small, 1999),[42] *Valence* (Ben Fry, 2001),[43] and *TextArc* (W. Bradford Paley, 2002).[44] This means that people intuitively identify them as infovis projects even though they consist not of vector elements but of media (text or images). In another example, a *phrase net* technique, which was developed by Frank van Ham, Martin Wattenberg, and Fernanda Viégas and awarded Best Paper at the IEEE InfoVis 2009 conference, also uses a media visualization paradigm.[45]

Does this mean that what we took to be the core principle of information visualization during its first three centuries—reduction to graphic primitives—was only a particular historical phenomenon, an artifact of the available graphics technologies? I think so. Similarly, the privileging of spatial variables over other visual parameters may also turn out to be a historically specific strategy rather than the essential principle of infovis. The new abilities brought about by computer graphics to precisely control—that is, assign values within a large range—color, transparency, texture, and many other visual parameters in any part of an image allow us to start using these nonspatial parameters to represent the key dimensions of data. This is already common in scientific, medical, and geovisualization—but not yet in information visualization.

Why did infovis designers continue to use computer-generated vector graphics during the 1990s and 2000s (i.e., using the visual language developed 170 to 200 years ago, but only now with computers) while the speed with which computers could render images was progressively increasing? Perhaps the main factor has been the focus on the World Wide Web as the preferred platform for delivering interactive visualizations. Web technologies made it relatively easy to create vector graphics and stream videos—but not to render large numbers of continuous tone images in real time. This required the use of a graphics workstation, a high-end PC with a special graphics card or a game console with optimized graphics processors, as well as time-consuming software development. Although video games and 3-D animation programs could render impressive numbers of pixels in real time, this was achieved by writing code that directly accesses hardware—something that very high-level media programming environments such as Processing and Flash/Flex could not do.

However, as the processing power and RAM size of personal computers and computer devices (desktops, laptops, tablets, phones, etc.) keeps increasing, these differences between the performance of programs written in high-level languages and the programs that work on lower machine levels become less important.

For example, in 2009 I developed ImagePlot visualization software for our work in the lab.[46] For a programming language, I used the high-level scripting language of ImageJ, a popular open-source application for image processing used in the sciences.[47] Running ImagePlot on my 2010 Apple PowerBook laptop (processor: 2.8 GHz Intel Core 2 Duo; memory: 4 GB), I rendered a media visualization showing the evolution of design and content in 4,535 *Time* magazine issues (1923–2009). The visualization resolution was 30,000 × 4,000 pixels, and it took only a few minutes to render it. Most of that time was spent scaling down the images from their original size to the small size used in the visualization (see plate 12).

Also, in 2009 we developed the HiperView[48] software together with Calit2's Center of Graphics, Visualization and Virtual Reality (GRAVITY). The software was created to run on visual supercomputers constructed by this lab. Its largest system at that time was a tiled display with a 286-megapixel resolution made from seventy 30-inch Apple monitors all running at 2,560 × 1,600 resolution and a number of PCs with high-end graphics cards. The software enabled a researcher to manipulate media visualizations interactively in real time showing up to ten thousand images of any size. For example, you could position all the *Time* covers by time (x-axis) and then instantly see temporal patterns on many dimensions by choosing this or that visual feature or metadata for the y-axis (gender and ethnicity of a person on a cover, average saturation and hue, etc.). You could also load a very high-resolution visualization of one million manga pages and instantly zoom in, pan to explore its details, and zoom out to see their context (see plate 10).

I believe that the media visualization approach is particularly important for humanities, media studies, and cultural institutions. Many of these only recently have started to discover the use of visualization but eventually may adopt it as a basic tool for research, teaching, and exhibition of cultural artifacts. (The first conference on visualization in the humanities took place at MIT in 2010.[49])

If all media and humanities scholars start systematically using visualization for research, teaching, and public presentation of cultural artifacts and processes, the ability to visualize media artifacts in full detail is crucial. Displaying the actual visual media in the dataset as opposed to representing it by graphical primitives helps the researcher to understand the meaning and/or cause behind the pattern she may observe, as well as to discover additional patterns.

Graphical reduction will continue to be used, but this is no longer the only possible method. The development of computers and the progress in their media capacities now makes possible a new visualization paradigm that I have called *media visualization*—visualization that does not reduce original media artifacts to points, bars, or lines. Instead, it displays all the artifacts in the dataset in their original form, and sorts, samples, and remaps them in many ways to make possible new discoveries.[50]

9 Exploratory Media Analysis

Looking at the table of contents of many data science textbooks, you can notice the similar pattern. Typically, the first chapter is devoted to the topic called *exploratory analysis* (or "exploratory data analysis"). This is the stage where you are supposed to get a feeling for your dataset. You check how many objects are in it, what data types are used, and what the available features are. You generate various plots to see how the features are distributed, how much variability they have, and if there are any correlations. You also look for any interesting patterns. The plots can be created quickly using interactive graphing functions available in popular languages used for data analysis such as Python and R, spreadsheet software such as Excel, and visualization software such as Tableau and Power BI. This exploratory analysis may lead to hypothesis that may require getting more data, extracting new features, and performing statistical tests and creating models to fit the data.

The concept of exploratory data analysis was developed by John W. Tukey in the 1960s and popularized in his book on the subject published in 1977.[1] Tukey was chairman of the Statistics Department at Princeton University and also a research scientist at Bell Laboratories, where his colleagues created the first statistical programming languages that supported interactive graphics devices in the middle of the 1970s. One of these languages was called S. In the 1990s, S was extended to become R language. In 2000, R was adopted by millions and became the standard tool for exploratory data analysis (most code written for S is still present in R).

Exploratory data analysis ideas and techniques were originally developed when scientists and statisticians were working with structured data, and contemporary presentation of these ideas in data science textbooks still assume the same. But how can we perform exploratory analysis of large collections of cultural artifacts such as texts, maps, audio, video, and images? These are all examples of unstructured data. We can extract many features and then explore them using the standard techniques of exploratory data analysis—but we will lose so much by doing this. Novels can't be reduced to lists of frequent topics; films can't be reduced to lists of characters, plots, and editing decisions; photographs can't be reduced to the types of objects in them or distributions of colors and grayscale values. Computational analysis of extracted features can only supplement careful reading, looking, hearing, and interacting with the original artifacts, but it can't replace it. And this brings us back to the opening question of the book: How can we see a billion images?

Luckily, in the case of visual media, it is possible to combine examining individual artifacts and seeing patterns across millions of them. This is the approach we have been successfully exploring in my lab for many years. Using a variation of the term *exploratory data analysis*, I came up with the term *exploratory media analysis* to describe this approach that relies on media visualization.

I have already introduced media visualization in chapter 8. In this and the following chapters I will present further arguments for why it is a good approach, discuss how we use digital image processing and computer vison for media visualization, and illustrate a number of its methods with examples. Media visualization can be used either with existing datasets or after extracting features—but in both cases, we retain original media and utilize abilities of human perception to process images in parallel and quickly notice many patterns.

Against Search

Early twenty-first-century media researchers have access to unprecedented amounts of media—more than they can possibly study, let alone simply watch or even search. Millions of hours of television programs are already digitized by national libraries and media museums, we have millions of digitized newspaper pages from the nineteenth and twentieth centuries,[2] there are over four hundred billion copies of web pages covering the period from 1996 until today,[3] and numerous other massive media collections are waiting to be dug into.

How do we take advantage of this new scale of media in practice? For instance, let's say that we are interested in studying how presentations and interviews by political leaders are reused and contextualized by TV programs in different countries. The following example comes from our application for the Digging into Data competition in 2011 run by U.S. National Endowment for the Arts. The relevant large media collections that were available at the time we were working on our application (June 2011) include 1,800 official White House videos of Barack Obama, five hundred of George W. Bush's presidential speeches, 21,532 programs from Al Jazeera English (2007–2011), and 5,167 *Democracy Now!* TV programs (2001–2011). Together, these collections contain tens of thousands of hours of video. We want to describe the rhetorical, editing, and cinematographic strategies specific to each video set, understand how different news producers may be using videos of political leaders in different ways, identify outliers, and find clusters of programs that share similar patterns. But how can we watch all this material to begin pursuing these and other questions?

Even when we are dealing with large collections of still images—for instance, three hundred thousand images in the Art Now Flickr group,[4] 150,000 professional and student design projects published on coroflot.com every month,[5] or over 170,000 Farm Security Administration/Office of War Information photographs taken between 1935 and 1944 and digitized by the Library of Congress[6]—such tasks are no easier to accomplish. The basic method that always worked when the numbers of media objects were small—see all images or videos, listen to all audio, notice patterns, and interpret them—no longer works.

Given the size of many digital media collections, even simply seeing what's inside them is impossible (before we even begin formulating questions and hypotheses and selecting samples for closer analysis). Although it may appear that the reasons for this are the limitations of human vision and human information processing, I think that it is actually the fault of current interface designs. Popular interfaces for large digital media collections such as lists of images, an image grid, and a detailed view presenting one image at a time (these examples are from the Library of Congress Prints and Photographs site) do not allow us to see the contents of a whole collection. These interfaces usually display only a small number of images at a time in a rigid order. This method does not allow us to understand the "shape" of the overall collection and notice interesting patterns.

Most media collections contain some kind of metadata such as author names, production dates, program titles, image formats, or, in the case of social media services such as Instagram and Flickr, upload dates and times, user assigned tags, locations, numbers of likes, and other information.[7] If we are given access to such metadata for a whole collection in an easy-to-use form such as a spreadsheet or a database, this allows us to at least understand distributions of content, dates, access statistics, and other details of the collection. Unfortunately, many online collections and media sites do not make available the complete collection's metadata to the users as part of a site (although more museums now publish metadata for their collections separately on sites such as GitHub).

Popular media access technologies of the nineteenth and twentieth centuries, such as slide lanterns, film projectors, microform readers, Moviola and Steenbeck film editing devices, record players, and audio and videotape recorders, were designed to access a single media item at a time at a limited range of speeds. This went hand in hand with the organization of media distribution: record and video stores, libraries, television, and radio would also make available only a few items at a time. For instance, you could not watch more than a few TV channels at the same time or borrow more than a few videotapes from a library.

At the same time, hierarchical classification systems used in library catalogs made it difficult to browse a collection or navigate it in an order not supported by catalogs. When you walked from shelf to shelf, you were typically following a classification system based on subjects, with books organized by author names inside each category.

Together, these distribution and classification systems encouraged twentieth-century media researchers to decide beforehand what media items to see, hear, or read. A researcher usually started with some subject in mind—films by a particular author, works by a particular photographer, or categories such as "1950s experimental American films" and "early twentieth-century Paris postcards." It was impossible to imagine navigating through all films ever made or all postcards ever printed. (One of the first media projects that organizes its narrative around navigation of a media archive is Jean-Luc Godard's *Histoire(s) du cinéma* made during 1989–1999. It combines samples from hundreds of films.) The popular social science method for working with larger media sets—content analysis, that is, the content of each media collection item being tagged by several people using a predefined vocabulary of terms[8]—also requires that a researcher decide beforehand what information would be relevant to tag. Similarly, if you use crowdsourcing services such as Amazon Mechanical Turk or Figure Eight in which workers tag each image, you also need to define these tags beforehand. And finally, supervised machine learning in which a computer is first trained to classify media objects into multiple categories and then given a new dataset to classify has the same limitation: we need to first define these categories.

In other words, as opposed to exploring a media collection without any preconceived expectations or hypotheses—just to "see what's there"—a researcher has to postulate what is there—that is, what are the important types of information worth seeking out.

Unfortunately, the current standard in media access—*computer search*—does not take us out of this paradigm. A search interface is a blank frame waiting for you to type something. Before you click on the search button, you have to decide what keywords or phrases to search for. So, though search brings a dramatic increase in speed of access, its deep assumption is that you know beforehand something about the collection worth exploring further.

Search and presentations of its results as they are implemented today can be traced back to the late 1940s and the beginnings of the *information retrieval* research paradigm.[9]

As I mentioned in chapter 3, this term was introduced by Calvin Mooers in 1950. In his original paper, he says that "information retrieval is the process of finding stored information when the approximate subject is known." He then conceptualizes user interaction with the system in this way:

> Information retrieval is a service carried out for the benefit of the "User" of the information. The process of retrieval begins with a vague statement by the User outlining the subject content of the needed information. The statement must be vague, since if the User knew exactly what he wanted, he wouldn't be in trouble, and he would probably know where to find the answer. The process of retrieval ends. If successful, with the discovery and presentation to the User of *an exhaustive list of information* meeting his subject prescription. With such a list, the relevant documents can be brought out and examined.[10]

It is remarkable how precisely this describes today's search interfaces—including the ones used by media collections sites, museums, and libraries. We start by searching for some subject, and the computer finds all relevant results and presents them as a list. We can then click on a particular result and get more information.

Mooers does not tell us how to design the presentation of "an exhaustive list of information" if it is very long or consists of media items. Most likely the second case was outside computer scientists' thinking at that time. But we can already find examples of thinking about how to organize the presentation of long lists of text information. In a 1951 paper, Mooers refers to "a nearly dozen different notched card and sorting machine information retrieval systems," with some already in operation for over three years, and notes that "one of them has an accumulation of 30,000 cards."[11] He also describes an example of the use of one such system in which the results are shown with approximately a dozen cards. But the possibility of much longer results is already present in his original 1950 paper, wherein he writes: "Information retrieval falls into two levels. In the ordinary company, or for the individual, the aim of information retrieval must be to organize any selected items of high utility information—those items can be reasonably anticipated to be needed in the future. The comprehensive organization of *all world's information and knowledge* is quite another aim, and for this second aim the rules are very different."[12]

The comprehensive organization of all the world's information and knowledge became practically conceivable only when people started to publish information and knowledge in digital forms on the World Wide Web (1991–). However, just as search limits how you can access a large body of information, the hypertext paradigm that defines the web only allows navigation through it according to links defined by others, as opposed to by moving in any direction. This is consistent with the original vision of hypertext as articulated by Vannevar Bush in 1945 in his famous article "As We May

Think":[13] a way for a researcher to create "trails" though massive scientific information and for others to be able to follow those traces later.[14] (The navigation interfaces
of social networks such as Instagram are more flexible: you can search for accounts,
places, and tags, click on a tag below a photo to see all photos with this tag, see the
accounts similar to that one you are looking at, and also use the recommendations
screen.[15])

Looking at the largest public online institutional media collections, such as Europeana (europeana.org), the Internet Archive (archive.org), and Wikimedia Commons
(commons.wikimedia.org), I feel that the interfaces they offer combine the nineteenth-
century technology of hierarchical categories and the mid-twentieth-century technology of information retrieval. The main interface offered is to search using metadata
such as names, titles, dates, medium, video length, and so on. Sometimes collections
also have subject tags. You also may be offered a browsing mode in which you move
through parts of a collection in a systematic way enforced by metadata.

In all cases, the categories, metadata, and tags were originally entered by the archi-
vists who manage the collections. This process imposes particular orders on the data.
As a result, when a user accesses an institutional media collection via its website,
she can only move along a fixed number of trajectories defined by the taxonomy of
the collection and types of metadata. (Note that the particular websites I listed have
been and remain pioneers in getting massive numbers of digitized media artifacts and
records online, so if they do not offer alternative interfaces, we may not expect that
others will.)

In contrast to such interfaces, when you observe a physical scene directly with your
eyes, you can look anywhere in any order. This allows you to quickly notice a variety
of patterns, structures, and relations. Imagine, for example, turning the corner on a
city street and taking in the view of the open square, with passersby, cafes, cars, trees,
store windows, and all other elements. You can quickly detect and follow a multitude
of dynamically changing patterns based on visual and semantic information: cars moving in parallel lines, houses painted in similar colors, people who move along their own
trajectories and people talking to each other, unusual faces, shop windows that stand
out from the rest, and so on. (Perceiving patterns in a city is an important theme in
films such as Vertov's *A Man with a Movie Camera* and Jacques Tati's *Playtime*.)

We need similar techniques to allow us to observe vast media universes and quickly
detect all interesting patterns. These techniques have to operate with speeds many
times faster than the normally intended playback speeds (in the case of time-based
media). Or, to use an example for still images, I should be able to see many patterns in
one million images in the same amount of time it takes me to see it in a single image.

These techniques have to compress massive media universes into smaller observable media landscapes compatible with human information processing rates. At the same time, they have to keep enough of the details from the original images, videos, audio recordings, or interactive experiences to enable the study of subtle patterns in the data.

The Interface

The limitations of the typical interfaces for online media collections also apply to interfaces of software for media viewing, cataloging, and editing. These applications allow users to browse and search image and video collections and display image sets as a slideshow. However, as research tools, their usefulness is quite limited. Desktop applications such as Adobe Lightroom Classic CC and mobile apps and media sharing services such as Instagram, 500px, or Photobucket can only show images in a few fixed formats—typically a single column, two-dimensional grid, or slideshow, and, in some cases, a map view (photos superimposed on the world map).[16] These formats became standard in the 2000s when people used desktop interfaces. With the switch to mobile toward the end of the decade, a single vertical row of images became the most popular because of the small size of a mobile screen, but others also remain.

To display my own photos in a particular order, I have to invest time in adding new metadata to all of them. (In only the first ten weeks of 2019, I captured twenty thousand photos on my Huawei Mate 20 Pro phone, so actually tagging them manually would take a really long time.) However, this is not possible on an institutional collection website. I also cannot automatically organize a collection of images by particular visual properties or by semantic relationships. Nor can I compare collections, which each may have hundreds of thousands of images, or use various data visualization techniques to explore patterns across image sets.

Starting around 2014, leading mobile photo apps such as Google Photos begun to automatically categorize user photos into semantic categories using computer vision and machine learning technologies. Flickr also started adding machine-generated semantic tags to its photos. Image search engines ranging from Google Image Search to more specialized ones available on stock photo websites offer search by color and certain other visual and semantic features. For example, popular stock image company Shutterstock (shutterstock.com) allows you to search photos by selecting the number of people, one or more of fourteen ethnicity types, age range, and gender.

Institutional collections will likely add such functions in the future. (As of 2016, Cooper Hewitt Design Museum and the Victoria and Albert Museum of decorative arts and design websites were offering search by color.) However, if interface navigation methods overall remain the same as they are today, their tools would not allow serendipitous explorations of media collections or making research links as in Vannevar Bush's 1945 speculative design.

Graphing and visualization tools that are available in Power BI, Google Docs, Excel, Tableau, Plotly, R, Python, ggplot2, and other graphing, spreadsheet, and statistical software and programming libraries do offer a range of data visualization techniques. However, these tools have their own limitations. As I showed in the previous chapter, a key principle that underlies the creation of information visualizations is the representation of data using points, bars, lines, curves, and similar graphical primitives. This principle has remained unchanged from the early statistical graphics of the early nineteenth century to the contemporary interactive visualization software designed to work with much larger datasets. Although such representations make clear the relationships in a dataset, they also hide the objects behind the data from the user. This is perfectly acceptable for many types of data, but in the case of images and videos this becomes a serious problem. For instance, a 2-D scatter plot that shows a distribution of grades in a class with each student represented as a point serves its purpose, but the same type of plot representing the stylistic patterns over the course of an artist's career via points has more limited use if we cannot see the images of the artworks.

In chapter 8, I introduced the concept of media visualization and discussed a few well-known artistic visualization projects that, in my view, use this approach. The work of these artists inspired me to adapt the same approach for cultural analytics research. However, whereas each artistic project I described in that chapter found a unique technique suitable to the artistic idea and media being visualized (frames from movies, short phrases from online forums, or editions of Darwin's most famous book), my goal was to employ only a few techniques that are effective and at the same time simple enough to be used by people who are not professional media artists or visualization designers. In other words, I wanted to "standardize" the media visualization approach, create open-source tools, and show how they can be used with many types of visual media.

Since 2008, in our lab we have explored the possibilities of a few such techniques by progressively applying them to different types of visual media. These techniques are suitable for exploring collections of visual media ranging from a few dozen to millions of items, and the user does not need to learn computer programming to use them. Both I and many others have successfully used them in teaching. In my own classes, students in digital art, media arts, design, and history of art have used our tools for class assignments and independent projects.

Media visualizations can be also implemented as interactive tools and applications. For example, a user can choose between seeing all objects in a collection, or exploring only its parts that fit particular parameters. She can also choose which parameters control sorting of images shown on a display, get more details about a particular image, switch between showing data as full images or as points, and perform other operations. All these operations were implemented in our 2009 HiperView application running on high-resolution tiled displays. For examples of other interactive operations, see our Selfiexploratory application in the *Selfiecity* and *On Broadway* project.[17] (Plate 5 shows a screenshot from Selfiexploratory; plate 11 shows a screenshot from the *On Broadway* interface.)

Typical data visualization involves first translating the world into numbers and then visualizing relations between these numbers. In contrast, media visualization involves translating a set of images into a new image that can reveal patterns in the set. In short, *pictures are translated into pictures.*

Media visualization can be formally defined as *creating new visual representations from the visual objects in a collection or from parts of these objects.* In the case of a collection containing single images, media visualization means displaying all images, or their parts, organized in a variety of configurations according to their metadata (dates, places, authors), content properties (e.g., presence of faces), and/or visual properties (e.g., dominant colors, amount of texture, number of shapes).

If we want to visualize a video collection, it is usually more convenient to select some frames that capture the properties and the patterns of a video and visualize them. This selection can be done automatically using a variety of criteria—for example, significant changes in color, movement, camera position, staging, and other aspects of cinematography; changes in content, such as the first frame of every new shot or the start of a scene or music or dialog; new topics in characters' conversations; and so on. The media visualization shown in figure 10.2 uses one frame from every shot in Dziga Vertov's 1928 film *The Eleventh Year* arranged in the order of the shots in the film (left to right and top to bottom).

Image Processing and Computer Vision

Media visualizations can be created using existing collection metadata or can use the results from *digital image processing applied to a collection of images or videos.*[18] Digital image processing is conceptually similar to the computational analysis of texts adopted in the digital humanities by the end of the 2000s.[19] Such analysis involves automatically calculating various statistics about the content of each text object in a collection, such as word usage frequencies, their lengths and positions, sentence lengths, noun and verb usage frequencies, and so on. These statistics (which, as noted earlier, are called *features* in data science) are then used to study the patterns in a single text, relationships between texts, literary genres, evolution of styles of individual writers or literary genres, and the like. Other information that can be algorithmically calculated on a group of texts includes topics (a set of words expressing some theme present in the text), short summaries, semantic similarities and differences that are visualized as distances between texts in 2-D space, measures of variability, and many other measurements. (In computer science, computational text analysis is a part of the field called natural language processing [NLP].) One popular online tool for the quantitative analysis, comparison, and visualization of texts aimed at humanists is Voyant; reading its documentation will give you a good idea of many standard text analysis techniques.[20]

Similar to text features used in NLP, computational analysis of images and videos also involves first calculating statistics about various visual properties. The design of such features is a part of the field of computer vision. I already talked about features in the "Semantic Gap" section earlier; now we'll look at them again for the purpose of making media visualizations. Features summarize details of images or videos and represent them as one, a few, or a series of numbers. Examples include average brightness, saturation and hue, their histograms, number of distinct shapes, number of edges and their orientations, most frequent colors, characteristics of textures, and positions of cuts in a video, among others. If such a statistic summarizes some details over a whole image, it is called a *global feature*. If the statistic summarizes details over a part of an image, it is called a *local feature*. For instance, Adobe Photoshop can measure the following grayscale image statistics: minimum, maximum, mean, media, and histogram. You can measure these statistics for the whole image or for selected image parts. If you divide an image into a rectangular grid and measure local features for each part of the grid, together the local features provide more details than global features.

As the speed of computers gradually increased, digital image processing moved from simpler global to more complex local features during the 1990s. In the 2000s, even more complex features such as SIFT and HOG became possible; in the 2010s, convolutional neural networks that learn what features to derive and organize them in hierarchical layers of increasing abstraction became popular.[21] Such complex or automatically derived features are better for certain popular image processing tasks such as image classification, but as we have discovered in many projects in our lab, *simple global features are often better for exploring patterns in collections of cultural images, and seeing their evolution over time* (see plates 3–4 and 6–10). These simple features are *interpretable*; that is, they *refer to visual dimensions for which we have concepts in language*. Thus, we can understand the meaning of features such as "the most frequent colors," "the average grayscale level," or "the number of distinct shapes."

These features can be then used for investigations similar to those of texts—for example, the analysis of visual and content differences between news photographs in different magazines or between news photographs in different countries, the changes in visual style over the career of a photographer, or the evolution of news photography in general over the twentieth century. Our work in the lab was driven by an insight that we can also use image features in a more basic way: for the initial exploration of any large image collection. In other words, they work well for exploratory media analysis.

The field of computer vision states that its main goal is automatic image under-standing. What is meant by such "understanding" changes over time as new research questions and tasks draw the attention of scientists and find applications in industry. Today such tasks include detecting the presence of bodies and faces, various object types, scene types, image styles, and abstract concepts.[22] There are also many more specific applications such as recognizing types of clothing, types of food, brand logos, celebrities, and the presence and level of nudity; detecting smiles (used in cameras); classifying medical images; and so on.[23] For example, in April 2019, Clarifai, one of the leading companies offering computer vision services, had a system trained to recognize eleven thousand types of objects and concepts. The following are the terms it returned when I chose one of the demo images—a professional photo of skyscrapers against the skyline, shot from the ground looking up:

> Window, urban, business, sky, reflection, cityscape, skyline, tallest, modern, futuristic, tower, mirror, perspective, glass items, city, architecture, skyscraper, building, downtown, office, win-dow, urban, business.

If digital image processing can be compared to the first stage of information processing in a human visual system, computer vision is thought to be equivalent to a later stage, in which we recognize faces, objects, scenes, and concepts. Thus, computer vision takes various features extracted at the image processing stage and further processes them to accomplish tasks such as detecting the presence of thousands of different object types, detecting faces and measuring emotions they express, identifying where a photograph has been taken (outdoor, indoor, etc.), identifying the types of activities people in a photo are engaged in, and performing other tasks, similar to what human vision does in our everyday life.

Here is an example of how a single app may employ computer vision in a number of ways. The app is TikTok, used for sharing short videos: "TikTok decides what videos to show by tapping into data, starting with your location. Then, as you start watching, it analyzes the faces, voices, music, or objects in videos you watch the longest. Liking, sharing, or commenting improves TikTok's algorithm further. Within a day, the app can get to know you so well it feels like it's reading your mind. . . . It also started using facial-recognition software to identify youthful faces, expelling underage creators, and preventing younger viewers from seeing mature content."[24]

Using Image Features for Exploratory Media Analysis

Computer vision techniques are also useful for exploration of large visual media collections. For instance, in 2015 we compared the frequencies of popular subjects in images shared on Twitter in twenty US cities using a sample of one million images.[25] In another project also from 2015, we used a neural network to detect the presence of one thousand types of objects and activities in one hundred thousand Instagram images shared in five global cities.[26]

The Yale Digital Humanities Lab created interactive tool for exploring a collection of twenty-seven thousand historical photographs.[27] The tool also uses a neural network trained to recognize many subjects in photographs, but in a different way. Such networks automatically extract high-level features from images, which then can be used to organize the images by visual similarity. To use the tool, you select one photograph, and computer shows you eight photographs from the collection that the algorithm thinks are the most similar. Another Yale lab project called PixPlot visualized these twenty-seven thousand photographs together, organizing them by similarity.

The successful application of neural networks for the detection of image content in the 2010s has been one of the biggest AI success stories of the decade, but how well does it work in practice? When we used a state-of-the-art computer vision service from Google (e.g., the Google Vision API) in summer 2016 to identify content in fifty thousand Instagram photos shared in St. Petersburg, Russia, the service returned 3,882 unique tags. Most images were assigned multiple tags, with some receiving as many as thirty. Overall, 261,290 tags were assigned to these images. The results also include the probability that each tag is assigned correctly (1 indicates full certainty). Here is an example of the tags the system returned for a single photo:

{'emotion': 0.675, 'sketch': 0.737, 'art': 0.833, 'selfie': 0.527, 'laughter': 0.617, 'photography': 0.859, 'illustration': 0.591, 'tooth': 0.640, 'modern art': 0.615, 'facial expression': 0.889, 'portrait': 0.794, 'painting': 0.843, 'drawing': 0.531}

The information presented in this way is a typical output of computer vision software today. Now imagine such information returned for billions of social media images.

Simply counting the frequencies of all tags or looking at all images that share a particular tag ("portrait," "laughter," etc.) misses all the interesting details such results provide. This is why as computer vision develops and we can automatically detect types of content, human activities, emotions, and other aspects, using such results for cultural analytics brings new challenges as opposed to simply making it simpler.

Within computer science, there is now a whole research area focused on developing methods for exploring massive image and video collections. These methods use data science techniques to cluster images, to visualize them together in one large image using automatically extracted visual features, to automatically learn image contents using networks, and so on. The scientists also have developed many prototype interfaces that offer various layout options and support navigation across massive collections.[28] However, only some authors of these interfaces publish their code online, and even when it is published, you need to have sufficient technical knowledge to use it. And typically, the code has only been tested on sample datasets described in a published paper.

But most importantly, in computer science, articles and conference papers are usually supposed to present new algorithms or refinements of existing algorithms rather than applications. So the majority of papers in an image collection exploration area (just as in other areas of computer science related to cultural analytics) describe such algorithms and demonstrate their application to one or a few datasets. The researchers do not go on to apply their algorithms to other cultural media collections to generate interesting cultural insights; that would not constitute real "research" in computer science. Thus we often do not know how new algorithms (or new techniques that use machine learning) would perform in the wild—if applied to real museum collections, portfolios of designers, social media images shared on a particular platform, and so on.

One important exception to this trend is a Replica project by Benoît Seguin. Developed as his PhD thesis in the Digital Humanities Lab at the Swiss Federal Institute of Technology in Lausanne, the project offers an interactive web interface for searching large art historical collections.[29] The collection used in this project is over 300,000 digitized art images from Foundation Giorgio Cini. The interface allows the user to search for similar images using a single image as an input, to select a detail in one image and search for similar regions in other images in a collection, and to select a number of images as a search query if a single image can't adequately convey a desired concept. The results can also be displayed in ways that go beyond standard layouts of image search engines. Instead of a grid, Replica can organize images as a "map" according to their content and visual similarity. Such a layout also allows users to mark new connections between any two images or their parts, and this information enriches the system.

As Seguin describes it, "Users can freely drag and zoom on the map visualization interface to explore the space of visual similarity as defined by the learned visual descriptors. They can also select elements and create connections between them directly from this view."[30]

While Replica has powerful capabilities, building it required both significant resources and time. Using it with a new collection may again require significant time to adjust the code and do human annotations on connections within this collection. Similarly, our interactive interfaces in *Selfiecity* and *On Broadway* were also developed only for particular image collections. In contrast, simple media visualization techniques we have been using in our lab allow initial exploration of any media collection, and they do not require the use of digital image processing or computer vision. In the next chapter, I present some of our techniques and illustrate them with examples drawn from our work with different types of visual media. The techniques are quite basic from a computer science point of view, and this is intentional: they are intended for people who may have a variety of nontechnical backgrounds. We developed open-source software, fully documented the code, and it has been used by many researchers and students in classes in digital humanities, cultural analytics, digital art, media arts, and other subjects. In the lab, we used our software for explorations of over forty different image and video collections covering a number of fields. The examples include 776 paintings by Vincent van Gogh; every cover of *Time* magazine published between 1923 and 2009 (4,553 images); one million manga pages; twenty-one thousand photographs from the MoMA photo collection; one million artworks shared on the leading user-generated art network, deviantart.com, from 2001–2010; a hundred hours of gameplay videos; 130 hours of President Obama's weekly video addresses (2009–2011); films by Dziga Vertov; and all the pages of the *Popular Science* and *Science* magazines from the first decades of their publication (1872–; 1880–).

Rather than keep developing new techniques or implement more complex ones, we wanted to see how far we can push the simplest techniques. We also wanted to see if they will allow us to notice new patterns in familiar cultural artifacts such as the paintings of Piet Mondrian and Mark Rothko and to come up with new interpretations based on these patterns. Such very familiar cultural images provide a good test of the usefulness of cultural analytics methods because art historians and museum curators have seemingly already written anything you can say about them. As we discovered, even when we are dealing with a couple hundred images, particular visualization techniques can reveal patterns, small differences, and gradual changes over time we cannot notice with our bare eyes. But when we have hundreds of thousands or hundreds of millions of images, we do not have a choice. We have to use computers to simply "look" at such datasets. Media visualization (or other computational methods) becomes a must, no longer just an option.

Seeing versus Analyzing

As I noted, media visualization can be understood as the opposite of statistical graphs and information visualization. But it can also be contrasted with the *content analysis* widely used in communication and media studies fields. This term refers to manual coding of a media collection, typically to describe its semantics. (Since the late 2000s, crowdsourcing, exemplified by Amazon Mechanical Turk, Figure Eight, and other services, started to be frequently used to create manual annotations of large datasets of social media images, to find objects or logos in photos, and to perform other tasks.)

In contrast to content analysis, the media visualization techniques we are using do not require the time-consuming creation of new metadata about media collections. And, in contrast to automatic computational methods, they also do not require specialized technical knowledge and can be used by anybody with only a basic familiarity with desktop digital media tools (think Apple Photos and basic Microsoft Excel).

While media analytics fully automates analysis and decision-making because of the amount and velocity of data that needs to be processed, media visualization for us is about manual explorations of new *data representations* generated iteratively in response to previous insights and new questions. In other words, it involves careful looking and comparisons—not between only a few images or video clips, but between any number of items presented in a visualization and between multiple visualizations. And while standard media visualization often allow us to quickly see the overall "shapes" of a collection, often I also work with the same collections for years, inventing new ways to visualize them that bring out new patterns.

Finally, there is yet another and most crucial difference between media visualization on the one hand and content analysis and media analytics on the other. After researchers manually code some information in images or automatically extract image features using algorithms (see chapter 10), often they are no longer looking at the original images. Instead, they are only analyzing information about them: metadata, tags, features. When we do this, we are dealing with nonvisual semiotic codes—text and numbers. (Text can include tags manually assigned by researchers, hashtags assigned by people who shared these images online, usernames, departments in museums that house the artworks shown in images, and so on. The numbers are extracted features). These texts and numbers have some relations to original images, but they are not the originals. Such representations limit anything we can find about these images in the course of further data analysis. For example, if our features have not captured details of composition, we will not analyze these details. Or, if the tags describe image content but not the type of space shown, we will not consider the range of spaces in a collection.

In contrast, media visualizations show us the original images. We stay in the visual domain. This allows us to use the full capacities of our perception and cognition to compare these images and notice all kinds of patterns and details that manual text tags or numerical features may not capture.

Often researchers think of visualization as only useful for initial exploration of data to generate hypotheses or to present the results obtained by analyzing data computationally. However, if our data is visual media, media visualization can be used as a research method that can often achieve as much as the standard quantitative analysis pipeline, or lead us to unique results that this analysis will miss.

Media visualization is a deeply qualitative rather than quantitative approach. It allows us to work with big data without counting something first or translating it into very different semiotic signs, such as text and numbers.

But how is this possible? Media visualization exploits the fact that real-world image collections always contain some metadata. This metadata can be used to sort images and group them in various categories. For example, in the case of digital video, the ordering of individual frames is built into the format itself. Depending on the genre, other higher-level sequences can be also present: shots and scenes in a narrative film, the order of subjects presented in a news program, the weekly episodes of a TV drama. In the case of single images, we also usually have at least some information: dates and times of creation, modification, or sharing; creators' names; titles, hashtags, or short descriptions; metadata captured by the camera; and so on.

We can exploit this already existing information in two complementary ways. On the one hand, we can visualize all images in a collection together in the order provided by metadata. For example, in our visualization of 4,535 *Time* magazine covers of all issues published from 1923 to 2009, the images are organized by publication date, going from left to right and top to bottom (see plate 12). On the other hand, to reveal patterns that such an organization may hide, we can also organize the images via new sequences and layouts. In doing this, we deliberately go against the conventional understanding of cultural image sets, which metadata often reify. I call such conceptual operation *remapping*. By changing the accepted ways of sequencing media artifacts and organizing them in categories, we create alternative "maps" of our familiar media universes and landscapes.

Media visualization techniques can be also situated along a second conceptual dimension depending on whether they use all media in a collection or only a sample. We may sample in *time* (i.e., use only some of the available images) or in *space* (i.e., use only parts of the images). An example of the first technique is my visualization of Dziga Vertov's *The Eleventh Year*, which uses one frame from every shot (see figure 10.2). The example of the second technique is a "slice" of 4,535 covers of *Time* magazine that uses only a single-pixel-width vertical line from each cover (see plate 13).

The third conceptual dimension that helps us sort possible media visualization techniques is the types and sources of information they use. As I already explained, media visualization exploits the presence of at least minimal metadata in a media collection, so it does not require the addition of new metadata about the individual media items. However, if we decide to add such metadata—for example, content tags we create via manual content analysis, labels for groups of similar images generated via automatic cluster analysis, automatically detected semantic concepts (such as objects, types of scenes, or photographic techniques used), face detection data, or visual features extracted with digital image processing—all this information can also be used in visualization.

In fact, media visualization offers a new way to work with such information. For example, consider information about content we added manually to our *Time* covers dataset, such as whether each cover features portraits of particular individuals, or whether it illustrates some concept or issue. I can use standard graphing techniques such as a line graph to display how the proportions of covers in these two categories change over time of publication (see figure 10.1). But I can also create a media visualization that shows all cover images and uses color borders or some other technique to label categories. Since such a visualization shows the content of all images, potentially it will let us notice many more patterns than a graph that shows the same information but without any images.

In the rest of this chapter, I discuss these distinctions in more detail, illustrating them with visualizations created in our lab. I will start with the simplest technique: using all images in a collection and organizing them in a sequence defined by existing metadata. Next, I will cover temporal and spatial sampling techniques. The final section discusses and illustrates the operation of remapping.

Image Montage

Conceptually and technically, the simplest technique is to show all images in a collection or a sample in a single visualization. I call this media visualization technique an *image montage*. We can order images by existing metadata or by a visual feature extracted from all images using image processing. For example, the image montage of *Time* covers organizes them by order of publication (plate 12).

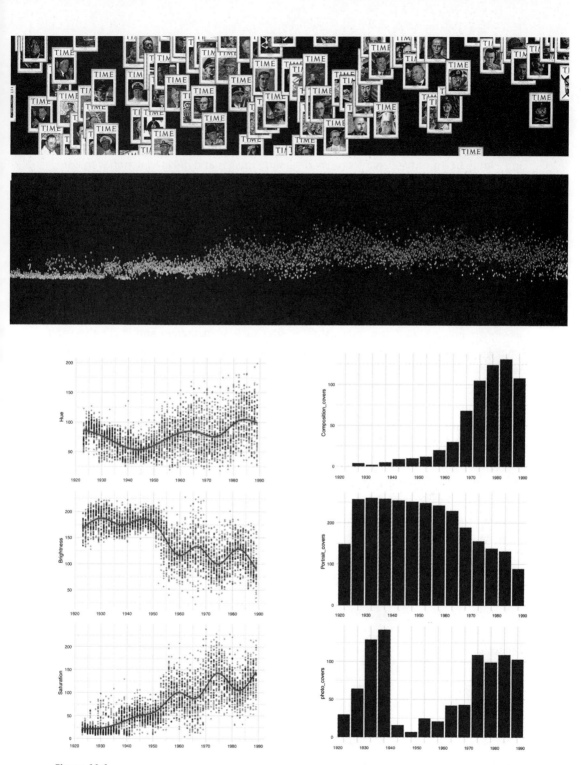

Figure 10.1
Selected changes in the design and content of 4,535 *Time* magazine covers, 1923–2009. X-axis represents time; y-axis represents the proportion of covers with particular characteristic in a given year.

This technique can be seen as an extension of the most basic intellectual operations of media studies and humanities—comparing a set of related items. In 2000, John Unsworth proposed that there are seven *scholarly primitives* common to all scholarship: discovering, annotating, comparing, referring, sampling, illustrating, and representing.[1] An image montage enables *comparing* many images and *discovering* trends in content and visual form.

Twentieth-century technologies only allowed for comparison among a small number of artifacts at the same time; for example, the standard lecturing method in art history (introduced around 1900) was to use two slide projectors to show and discuss two images side by side. Contemporary software running on computer devices now allows simultaneous display of thousands of images. As discussed earlier, all commonly used photo organizers and editors, including macOS Finder, Preview and Photos, and Adobe Bridge, can show images in a grid format. Similarly, image search engines such as Google image search and media sharing sites such as Instagram and Flickr also use image grids. However, typically they do not allow users to sort images in arbitrary ways or fully control the presentation layout. And though they can often show images automatically divided into a few categories—such as favorites, selfies, panoramas, and screenshots in the Photos app on an iPhone—the user often cannot create her own categories and use them to organize collection display.

To use image grids for comparison and discovery, we need to be able to sort images using metadata fields or extracted features, create our own categories, and control all details of the presentation. Such controls over elements of a visualization are standard in data visualization software, but not in media organizing applications. At the end of 2008, I realized that the open-source image analysis software ImageJ, popular in a number of scientific fields, could be adapted to visualize image collections as grids and provide control I wanted. (You can also use Processing, Python, Java, or other programming languages to make such visualizations or to program interactive apps.) ImageJ calls its command to make image grids *make montage*.[2] So after we started to use ImageJ in our lab, we began to refer to such media visualization as *montages*. In 2009 I wrote a program in the ImageJ scripting language to add additional controls not available in the standard commands. The largest montage we made in 2010 contains a sequence of 22,500 frames sampled from 62.5 hours playing the *Kingdom Hearts* video game from beginning to end (see plate 14).

The quantitative increase in the number of images that can be visually compared using the image montage technique leads to a qualitative change in the type of observations you can make. Being able to display thousands of images simultaneously allows us to see patterns in composition, color, content, and other characteristics. If we sort the images by creation or publication dates, we can see if any of these characteristics change over time and if the changes are gradual or sudden. We can notice the images that stand out from the rest (i.e., outliers). We can also discover groups of images that share some characteristics in common (i.e., clusters). If we find some patterns during exploratory media analysis and we want to quantify any of them, in many cases we can extract the appropriate features and then analyze them using standard statistical and data visualization techniques. This approach where visual exploration of a media collection comes first before generating hypotheses extends Turkey's paradigm of exploratory data analysis to media data.[3]

To be effective, even this simple media visualization technique may require some transformation of all the media being visualized. For example, to be able to observe similarities, differences, and patterns in large image collections, it is crucial to make all images the same size. In some cases, it is best to place images side by side without any gaps; in other cases, we need to add some empty spaces in between and change the background color. And rather than being satisfied with a single image montage, it is better to make a few of them, sorting the images in different ways.

One member of our lab, Damon Crockett, wrote software in Python that speeds such explorations. You can use this software to create six different media visualization layouts: rectilinear and circular montages, Cartesian and polar image histograms, and Cartesian and polar image plots.[4] All visualizations and the code that generates them are presented in a single Jupiter Notebook document that can be edited, expanded, and shared with others. The software can also extract features from images and process them using clustering and dimension reduction techniques. The results of this analysis can be then used to organize images according to their visual characteristics. Another interactive media visualization software we developed for large tiled displays allows for very quick generation of montages sorted in different ways. We also wrote scripts for ImageJ and ImageMagic that render new montage layouts for particular datasets.

Figure 7.3 shows one such layout we developed to visualize twenty-one thousand historical photographs in the MoMA's photography collection. Each row shows photographs from the collection for a given year, from 1844 to 1989 (top to bottom). The visualization reveals how the collection represents some historical periods much better than other periods. So rather than thinking of an image montage as a single technique, think of it as a more general strategy for exploratory media analysis that supports many different montage variations—and you can invent new ones to fit your project needs.

The following example illustrates the kinds of patterns a basic montage can help to see. This example is a visualization of 4,535 *Time* magazine covers for all issues from 1923 to 2009 (see plate 12). A large percentage of the covers included red borders. We cropped these borders and scaled all images to the same size. Here are the patterns I found by studying this visualization:

Medium: In the 1920s and 1930s, *Time* covers mostly use photography. After 1941, the magazine switches to paintings. In the later decades, photography gradually comes to dominate again. In the 1990s, we see the emergence of the contemporary software-based visual language, which combines manipulated photography, graphic, and typographic elements.

Color versus black and white: The shift from early black-and-white covers to full-color covers happens gradually, with both types coexisting for many years. Because full-color printing was quite expensive, in the beginning we see occasional covers that that use only a single color for a side area. Eventually all covers start to be printed in color.

Hue: Distinct "color periods" appear in bands over time: green, yellow/brown, red/blue, yellow/brown again, yellow, and a lighter yellow/blue in the 2000s.

Brightness: The changes in brightness between 1923 and 2009 (the mean of all pixels' grayscale values for each cover) follow a similar cyclical pattern.

Contrast and saturation: Both gradually increase over time. However, since the end of the 1990s, this trend is reversed: recent covers have lower contrast and lower saturation.

Content: Initially most covers are portraits of individuals set against neutral backgrounds. Over time, portrait backgrounds change to feature compositions representing concepts. Later, these two different strategies come to coexist: portraits return to neutral backgrounds, while concepts are now represented by compositions that may include both objects and people—but not particular individuals.

Metapattern: The visualization also reveals an important metapattern: almost all changes are gradual. Each of the new communication strategies emerges slowly over a number of months, years or even decades.

This image montage takes advantage of the serial and periodic nature of a magazine publication. Because the issues are published every week, we have an equal number of of *Time* covers' visual images per year over eighty-six years. And because all covers have the same size and proportions, we can clearly see which visual characteristic change, when the changes start, and if they are rapid or slow.

Human vision is very good at noticing patters that involve repetition and deviations from this repetition. In the case of *Time* covers, we can, for example, notice occasional color covers that stand out against the black-and-white covers in the 1920s. We are also good at picking up gradual changes and seeing 2-D configurations when everything else is kept equal. The first ability enables bar plots and line graphs, and the second enables scatter plots. For example, if all bars have the same width and color, then the brain can focus on their respective lengths, detecting even small differences. In the case of the *Time* visualization, all cover images have exactly the same size and proportions, similar to bars in a bar chart. And this allows us to notice a number of temporal patterns across these images.

In both the natural and human-created worlds, *particular semantics are often correlated with particular visual characteristics*. The sky in the summer tends to be blue in color, and trees are green; clouds do not have sharp boundaries, but pebbles on the beach do; airplanes all have a similar shape, and cars have four wheels; most Instagram photos tagged with #selfie indeed show one or more people. These correlations mean that when our brain notices visual patterns in a media visualization, often these patterns correspond to particular content. For example, in the *Time* covers montage, we see a large area in yellow-orange colors in the upper part (if you divide the montage into five parts from the top, this will be the second part). Zooming in, we learn that this area corresponds to the 1940s and war years, and these are all hand-drawn portraits of military leaders and others associated with the war. This gives the overall yellow-orange look to this whole period.

However, seeing certain content patterns in the image montage of *Time* covers is more difficult. Once we reach the 1950s, the semantic and visual content of the covers in this and following decades is just too varied. The visual cortex of the brain cannot quickly compute how often each subject appears over time, the ratio of symmetrical versus asymmetrical compositions, the ratio of men versus women, patterns in head sizes and angles, and so on. To investigate such characteristics, we need to either automatically detect subjects, the positions of people and objects, and visual characteristics of covers using computer vision, or tag them manually and then analyze and visualize this new metadata.

We have manually tagged every *Time* cover using fourteen different categories to indicate if a cover is a portrait of a particular person or an illustration of some concept; if it is a drawing or a photograph or if a portrait is that of a man or a woman; the ethnicity suggested by the skin color of a person; and so on. Plotting the frequencies of these tags over time shows a number of important patterns we would not see in an image montage. (A few of these plots are shown in figure 10.1.) A number of trends start in the early 1950s and grow stronger over the following decades. Their speed of growth is similar. They include an increase in the proportion of concept illustrations versus portraits; use of photos versus drawings; an increase in the number of topics shown; and a decrease in the number of covers that show a male portrait (or full-figure view). It is tempting to think these all are expressions of a larger megatrend that contains trends that all support each other: development of a consumer and youth culture, growth of travel and improvements in color photography all happening in the 1950s. Also, in the 1960s, *Time* and many other publications around the world start covering more subjects—travel, science, lifestyles, sports, and more. This may be the main reason that covers from 1960 onward have such visual variety in contrast to earlier decades.

Although media visualizations certainly cannot reveal every pattern contained in an image collection, they can often show some patterns, as the example of *Time* covers image montage demonstrates. In general, we found that media visualizations are very useful if all images in a collection have some common characteristics. For example, *Time* covers all come from a single publication, have the same proportions, and feature the word *time* in approximately the same position in the top area. Other image collections that work well for media visualizations are a group of images in a single medium that have a time dimension: paintings created over time by one artist or by members of an artistic movement, key frames from a movie or a video, or pages from a number of magazine issues published consequently.

One example of such image collections are photos shared on social media over a period of time. I have used this method to visualize photos shared on Instagram in the center of Kiev during five days of 2014 Ukrainian Revolution (see our project *The Exceptional and the Everyday: 144 hours in Kiev*; the-everyday.net). Here I will discuss another example: two image montages from our 2013 *Phototrails* project led by Nadav Hochman (phototrails.info). They are shown in plate 15. Each montage is made of fifty thousand images shared on Instagram in a central area of a particular city over a few days in the spring of 2012. The top montage uses images shared in New York, and bottom montage uses images shared in Tokyo. These images represent a random sample from all publicly shared images with geoinformation we collected from a 5 × 5 km area. In New York case, this area covers Manhattan from its south end to Central Park. In the montage, the images are organized by sharing date and time (top to bottom and left to right).

The photographs were captured and shared by thousands of people, as opposed to a single artist or a single publication. They did not coordinate what and when to photograph. But when we place these images together along the time dimension, the result is a new kind of "city film." This film has systematic patterns, but also lots of variability. In other words, it visualizes well how a a city (or society in general) functions: individuals have free will and can determine their own actions, and at the same time they are likely to follow certain regular routines, creating "social facts."

For example, the New York and Tokyo montages show alternating lighter and darker vertical areas, and this pattern repeats horizontally. The lighter parts correspond to daytime, while darker parts correspond to nighttime. But this pattern does not repeat mechanically: each day and each night and their transitions are all different, as people share more or fewer images. At the time of our data collection, people were sharing more images in New York than in Tokyo: we see approximately three twenty-four-hour cycles in the upper montage versus four such cycles in the bottom montage. Each montage has variety of colors, but in Tokyo certain colors are more prominent. These are the yellow and brown of traditional food dishes. Finally, the Tokyo montage is more uniform than the New York City montage: the photos that are next to each other are often more similar in Tokyo than in New York. This difference in visual diversity of images does a good job of capturing the difference in cultural diversity between two giant cities: for example, while Tokyo saw approximately fifteen million foreign tourists in 2018, New York saw sixty-five million.

This example demonstrates how important it is to experiment with organizing images in a media visualization in different ways. Compare the image montage in plate 15 with the radial image plot in plate 16. The latter sorts the same fifty thousand Instagram images shared in Manhattan by average brightness and hue values, which control images distances from the center and their angles. While our image montage is in effect a 1-D visualization, since images are only sorted by their timestamp, it is more informative than the 2-D radial image plot that uses two extracted features.

The image montage technique has been pioneered in digital art projects such as Brendan Dawes's *Cinema Redux* (2004) and Jonathan Harris's *The Whale Hunt* (2007). To create their montages, artists wrote custom code; in each case, the code was used with particular datasets and not released publicly. In 2009, I wrote and published the code to create image montages with the open-source, free ImageJ software. The code was later expanded and refined by our lab members (github.com/culturevis/imagemontage).

When I started creating image montage visualizations in 2008, there were only a few examples of this technique used by digital artists. But a few years later, Apple added dynamic montage-like display modes into its Photo app in iOS. You can view photos by years, collections, and moments, and the app automatically arranges them in grids, making individual photos bigger or smaller depending on how many it needs to show.[5] If you are using an iPhone or Apple laptop that comes with the Photos software that offers the same display modes, you can see them for yourself.

Although the montage method is the simplest conceptually and technically, it is quite challenging to characterize it theoretically. Given that information visualization normally takes data that is not visual and represents it in a visual domain, is it appropriate to think of a montage as a visualization method? To create a montage, we start in the visual domain and we end up in the same domain; that is, we start with individual images, put them together, and then zoom out to see them all at once.

I believe that calling this method *visualization* is justified if instead of focusing on the transformation of data in information visualization (from numbers and categories to images), we focus on its other key operation: arranging the elements of visualization in such a way as to allow the user to easily notice the patterns that are hard to observe otherwise. From this perspective, a montage is a legitimate visualization technique. For instance, the current interface of Google Books can only show 10 covers of any magazine on one page, so it is hard to observe the longer historical patterns. However, if we gather all the covers of a magazine and arrange them in a particular way, these patterns are now easy to see. Specifically, we scale all covers to exactly the same size and display them in a rectangular grid in publication date order as we did in *Time* covers montage. In other words, just as in the bar chart example I evoked, we make everything the same so the eye can focus on comparing what is different—the content of covers, their layouts, colors, and other visual characteristics.

Sampling versus Summarization

The next two techniques I will present add another conceptual step. Instead of displaying all the images in a collection, we can *sample* them using some procedure to select only some images and/or their parts. (For examples, see figure 10.2 and plate 13.)

In statistics, a *sample* is a part of data that is representative of the whole, and I am using this term in the same way here. However, if our whole is a large collection of images or videos, *representative* can be defined in many ways. One type of sample may be best in revealing some characteristics and patterns, while another may reveal different patterns. Therefore, there is not one correct way to sample a media collection. We should try different sampling strategies and visualize these samples not because we want to come up with one "correct" strategy, but because we want to enrich our understanding of a collection and create its alternative visual representations. In other words, we want to create not a single map, but many different ones.

We can contrast such an approach with one adopted in the area of computer science called *automatic video summarization*. Here the goal is to produce the "best" compact summary of a given video that satisfies the following principles:

> The video summary must contain high priority entities and events from the video. For example, a summary of a soccer game must show goals, spectacular goal attempts, as well as any

other notable events such as the ejection of a player from the game, any fistfights or scuffles and so on. In addition, the summary itself should exhibit reasonable degrees of continuity—the summary must not look like a bunch of video segments blindly concatenated together. A third criterion is that the summary should be free of repetition—this can be difficult to achieve. For example, it is common in soccer videos for the same goal to be replayed several times. It is not that easy to automatically detect that the same event is being shown over and over again. These three tenets, named the CPR (Continuity, Priority and no Repetition) form the basic core of all strong video summarization methods.[6]

Video summarization is used in the interfaces of some online media collections; for instance, the Internet Archive includes regularly sampled frames for some of the videos in its collection. There are also mobile apps that produce short video summaries.

The algorithms that can quickly process videos and produce their visual summaries are certainly useful for practical applications. But if we want to explore a media collection to find different patterns and to question our standard understanding of the material, is video summarization the right approach? This approach samples videos to summarize them, but why would we want to use sampling for media exploratory analysis? After all, we have entered the "big data" research paradigm, and our computers can render visualizations showing millions of images. So why would we want instead to only use a small part of the whole? Why do we want to engage again in *reduction* after we critiqued and promoted media visualization as an alternative?

The reason for video sampling is to highlight the unique elements of the whole and leave out repetitive parts. This allows the brain to compare these unique elements without being distracted by the repetitive elements, which, to use the language of Shannon's mathematical theory of communication, do not carry any new information. However, we do not have to follow the goal of video summarization to always include "high priority" events. Importance is defined by convention, and we may want to question such conventions. In fact, we should always generate a few different media visualizations that sample the collection is alternative ways and highlight different kinds of events and patterns.

The rich traditions of video and media art offer many examples of such alternative sampling of original media that not only reveal meanings intended by the media producers but also read this media against the grain, expose its ideologies, and construct new audiovisual experiences from sampled material. Equally rich and inspiring is the history of sampling in music. These traditions are the opposites of video summarization research aiming to create a single best solution that is "true" to the original. The beauty of cultural analytics is that it does not have to choose between the objective approach of computer scientists and the transformative approach of artists.

The companies that use this computer science research create practical applications for mass audiences, and they adapt the commonsense but (in reality) only one possible interpretation of media and the world. When they automate our interactions with media, such as summarizing video contents or promoting social media photos in recommendations that we are likely to like, what is being automated is the mainstream "average" taste and mainstream and seemingly normal understanding of reality.

In the 1970s, members of the Birmingham School of Cultural Studies argued that receiving "objective" (i.e., intended) messages encoded in mass communication is not the only correct outcome. In his well-known 1973 article "Encoding and Decoding in the Television Discourse," Stuart Hall proposed that the subject decoding a mass media message can follow three strategies: hegemonic, negotiated, and oppositional.[7] In the first case, the subject decodes the message as it was intended—that is, the way it was encoded. (*Hegemonic* refers to "definitions of situations and events which are 'in dominance.'"[8]) In the second case, the subject understands the intended message but then modifies it to fit her/his situation. Finally, in the third case the subject rejects the intended code. Here is one such example Hall provides: "This is the case of the viewer who listens to a debate on the need to limit wages but 'reads' every mention of the 'national interest' as 'class interest.'"[9]

From this perspective, the subject taken for granted by most computer science publications dealing with media is the one that follows a hegemonic strategy of decoding. This is the subject of a consumer society that accepts it and only looks for help to make life more efficient and satisfying, without questioning this society. So many areas in computer science want to help—by improving image search engines, by providing better movies and book recommendations, by making UIs more efficient. At the same time, they see their functions as serving industry needs, which means, for example, making more people click on online and app ads. In other words, lots of research in computer science is aligned with the hegemonic system. One indirect support for such an interpretation is a phrase that was popular in the 2010s: "The best minds of my generation are thinking about how to make people click ads."[10] Of course, in reality things are not so black and white. Talking to many computer scientists made it clear to me that what they really care about is interesting research and working on hard problems, but regardless everybody has to justify their research in publications by referring to industry needs and people's needs.

This means that, for example, video summarization as it is presented in computer science publications is an instance of such hegemonic decoding. When researchers say that "a summary of a soccer game must show goals, spectacular goal attempts, as well as any other notable events," such a summarization follows the intended messages of sports as they exist today (live global broadcasting and selling of ads that require the sports to have frequent "spectacular" moments).

For cultural analytics, many other parts of a media collection or a video and its overall patterns are often more interesting. Figure 10.3 is one example of an oppositional media visualization I created. By sampling a movie in an unconventional way, it reveals the largely static character of a film by a director famous for his dynamism. (This example will be discussed in more detail later in the chapter).

Temporal Sampling

Because time-based visual media exists in space (images are 2-D representations) and in time (a sequence of images like *Time* covers, frames of a video, states of an interactive interface), we can sample either in space or time, or use both types of sampling together. *Temporal sampling* means selecting a subset of images from a larger image sequence. We assume that this sequence is defined by existing metadata, such as frame numbers in a video, sharing dates of images on a social media site, or page numbers in a comic book. We keep the original sequence, but instead of showing every image or video frame, we show only some of them.

Temporal sampling is particularly useful in representing cultural artifacts, processes, and experiences that unfold over significant periods of time—such as playing a video game. Completing a single-player game may take dozens or even hundreds of hours. In the case of massively multiplayer online role-playing games (MMORPGs), users may be playing for years. (A 2005 study by Nick Yee found that MMORPG players spend an average of twenty-one hours per week in the game world.[11]) In the following example, two visualizations created by William Huber in our lab together represent one hundred hours of game play.

The games in question are *Kingdom Hearts* (2002) and *Kingdom Hearts II* (2005). Each game was played by one player from beginning to end over a number of sessions. The *Kingdom Hearts* gameplay was 62.5 hours in twenty-nine sessions over twenty days. The *Kingdom Hearts II* gameplay was thirty-seven hours in sixteen sessions over eighteen days. The video captured from all game sessions of each game were assembled into a single sequence. The sequences were sampled at six frames per second. This resulted in 225,000 frames for *Kingdom Hearts* and 133,000 frames for *Kingdom Hearts II*. The visualizations use every tenth frame from the complete frame sets. Frames are organized in a grid in order of game play (left to right, top to bottom). Plate 14 shows one of the two visualizations, for the original *Kingdom Hearts* gameplay.

Kingdom Hearts is a franchise of video games and other media properties created in 2002 via a collaboration between Tokyo-based videogame publisher Square (now Square Enix) and the Walt Disney Company. The franchise includes original characters created by Square traveling through worlds representing Disney-owned media properties (*Tarzan, Alice in Wonderland, The Nightmare before Christmas*, etc.). Each world has distinct characters derived from the respective Disney-produced film. It also features distinct color palettes and rendering styles, which are related to visual styles of the corresponding Disney film. Visualizations reveal the structure of the gameplay, which cycles between progressing through the story and visiting various Disney worlds.

For an example of using temporal sampling for the visualization of films, see figure 10.2. The visualization of Vertov's *The Eleventh Year* shown in this figure relies on a semantically and visually important segmentation of the film—the shots sequence. The film is fifty-two minutes long and contains 654 shots. Instead of mechanically sampling the film at a fixed rate (e.g., one frame for every second), we sample the film at shot boundaries. Each shot is represented by its second frame, but middle or last frames can be also used. The frames are organized left to right and top to bottom following the shot order in the film. We can think of this visualization as a reverse-engineered imaginary storyboard of the film—a reconstructed plan of its cinematography, editing, and content. You can use free shot detection software shotdetect and our ImageMontage program to make such visualizations for any film. (For more examples of image montages and other visualizations of films, video, and TV programs, see our projects *Visualizing Vertov, Media Species, ObamaVideo, PoliticalVideoAds.viz*, and *Remix.viz*, and Adelheid Heftberger's book *Digital Humanities and Film Studies: Visualising Dziga Vertov's Work*.)

Spatial Sampling

Spatial sampling involves selecting *parts* of images according to a chosen procedure. For example, our visualization of *Time* covers used spatial sampling because we cropped some of the images to get rid of the repeating red borders that the magazine employed for decades. Because of their saturated color, these borders attract the attention of a viewer, making it harder to see patterns in the rest of the covers. Therefore, we removed these red parts from all images prior to rendering the final visualization. However, as the next example demonstrates, often more dramatic sampling, which leaves only a small part of an image, can be quite effective in revealing additional patterns that a full image montage may not show as well. In keeping with the standard name for such visualizations used in medical and biological research and in the ImageJ software, we refer to them as *slices*.[12]

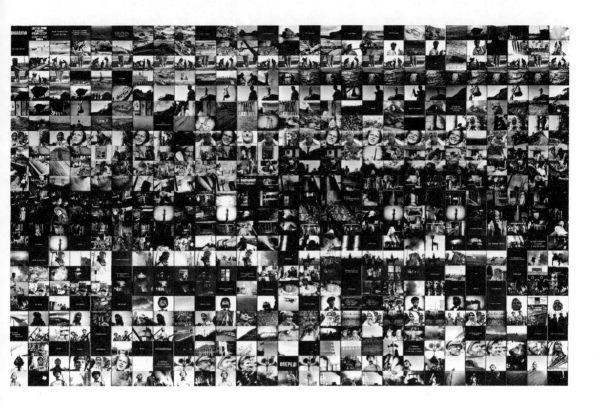

Figure 10.2
Visualization of *The Eleventh Year* (Dziga Vertov, fifty-two minutes, 1928). Every one of the 654 shots in the film is represented by its second frame. Frames are organized from left to right and top to bottom following the order of the shots in the film. A close-up of a single row of frames is shown separately below.

In biology, neuroscience, and medical sciences, researchers use slicing techniques to study and visualize brain activity. For example, current research to produce very detailed maps of the brain uses microthin slices created 100 μm apart.[13] MRI and fMRI technologies also image the brain by recording information in slices. Subsequently, software such as ImageJ is used to assemble individual slices together and study them.[14] In fact, ImageJ and its predecessor Image were originally developed at the U.S. National Institutes of Health (NIH) for working with images obtained using light microscopes, and the software has been particularly popular in biomedical image processing. These origins are clearly visible in ImageJ's UI: it calls individual images *slices*, and a sequence of these slices is called a *stack*.[15] When I started to explore the program, I came across one of the commands designed to work with slices: orthogonal views. The User Guide described the command as follows: "if a stack displays sagittal sections, coronal (YZ projection image) and transverse (XZ projection image) will be displayed through the data-set."[16] I realized that these are terms from medical science, but instead of looking them up, I just applied this command to my own sequence of images (all frames from a short music video). The resulting visualizations turned out to be very revealing, and we started referring to them as slices. The slicing operation extracts a narrow column from the center of each image in a sequence and assembles them together. You can control the width of a column. This is conceptually similar to an image montage, but instead of assembling full images, here each image is first sampled.

The visualization in plate 13 demonstrates the use of slices using images of 4,535 covers of *Time*. Each cover has been sampled to leave a one-pixel-wide vertical slice from its center. These slices are positioned one after another in order of publication (1923–2009, left to right). This visualization makes easily visible some patterns that are harder to see in an image montage of full covers. The magazine name keeps changing its vertical position and design over the decades: first it's black and relatively large, then it becomes smaller, later it almost disappears, and later again it becomes more visible printed in red. The use of photography in the first decade after beginning of the publication gives way to a period of the painted portraits during the years of the World War II (the uniform orange area). While most patterns change gradually, one important change takes place quickly over just a few months in 1952. Before an image occupied only a part of the cover; now it fills the whole cover. We see how this change happens in two stages: first an image is extended to the top edge of a cover, and after a few months it is also extended to the bottom edge.

What are the relations between the techniques for visual media sampling as illustrated here and the theory and practice of sampling in statistics and the social sciences?[17] Statistics is concerned with selecting a sample in such a way as to yield some reliable knowledge about the larger population. Because it was often not practical to collect data about the whole population, the idea of sampling was the foundation of twentieth-century applications of statistics. Today, in the era of big data, in retrospect it may look strange that throughout the twentieth century countless studies and practical policies were based on very small samples of human populations. And the use of small samples is still standard today in many areas such as population surveys. (For a detailed discussion of the limitations of sampling when used for the study of society and culture, see chapter 5.)

The design of experiments, including types and sizes of samples, has been an important area of modern statistics development. The theory and methods of sampling were elaborated by Charles Peirce, Ronald Fisher, and others between 1870 and 1930. Statisticians developed a variety of methods that allow them to draw conclusions about a larger population using carefully designed experiments and small samples.

When using media visualization, we often face the same limitations. A ninety-minute-long feature film sampled at twenty-four frames per second is 129,600 frames. A video recording of a gameplay that lasts fifty hours sampled at the same rate is 1,728,000 frames. This is why in our visualizations of *Kingdom Hearts* we sampled the complete gameplay videos to show only a selection of frames.

Ideally, if the ImageJ software was capable of creating a montage using all the video frames, we would not have to do this. However, as the *Time* covers slice visualization and the image montage of Vertov's film demonstrate, sometimes dramatically limiting part of the data shown is more effective in revealing certain patterns than using all the data. While we could have noticed changes in cover layout over time in the full-images montage, a slice montage is much clearer. We see irregular placement and the changing size of the word *time*, and the switch to full images covering the whole cover in the early 1950s. We also see that the visual variability of the covers sequence is much lower until around 1960. After that, variability increases, and it becomes hard to predict the colors and content of the next cover based on the previous ones.

Remapping

Any representation can be understood as a result of a mapping operation between two entities. In terms of semiology developed by Ferdinand de Saussure, the mapping is from a signified to a signifier. In terms of Charles Peirce's semiotics, the mapping is from object to sign. The taxonomy of signs defined by Peirce—icon, index, symbol, and diagram—defines different types of mapping between an object and its representation.

Mathematically, *mapping* is a function that creates a correspondence between elements in two domains. For a familiar example of such mappings, consider geometric projection techniques that are used to create two-dimensional images of three-dimensional scenes, such as isometric projection and perspective projection. Another example is two-dimensional maps that represent physical spaces.

Twentieth-century cultural theory often stressed that all cultural representations are partial maps because they can only show some aspects of the objects. A cultural representation is always selective, and what gets represented is often determined by power interests or ideologies, as well as the media technology used. However, this assumption needs to be rethought today, given the dozens of technologies developed in the last decades for capturing data about physical objects and biological bodies and the ability to process massive amounts of data to extract features and other information. Google, for instance, crawls the web continuously to update its search database, which contained one trillion links by 2008.[18]

Modern media technologies—photography, film, audio records, fax and copy machines, audio and video magnetic recording, media editing software, the web—led to a new practice of cultural mapping: using an existing media artifact and creating new meaning or a new aesthetic effect by sampling and rearranging parts of this artifact. While this strategy was already used in the second part of the nineteenth century (e.g., with photomontages), it became more central to modern media arts in the 1910s and 1920s, and even more important since the second part of the 1950s. Its different manifestations include pop art, compilation films, appropriation art, remixes, and a significant part of media art—from Bruce Conner's very first compilation film *A Movie* (1958) to Dara Birnbaum's *Technology/Transformation: Wonder Woman* (1979), Douglas Gordon's *24 Hour Psycho* (1993), Joachim Sauter and Dirk Lüsebrink's *The Invisible Shapes of Things Past* (1995), Mark Napier's *Shredder* (1998), Jennifer and Kevin McCoy's *Every Shot/Every Episode* (2001), *Cinema Redux* by Brendan Dawes (2004), Natalie Bookchin's *Mass Ornament* (2009), Christian Marclay's *The Clock* (2011), and many others. While earlier remappings were done manually and had a small number of elements, use of computers allowed artists to automatically create new media representations containing thousands of elements.

If the original media artifact, such as a news photograph, a feature film, or a website, can be understood as a map of some "reality," an art project that rearranges the elements of this artifact can be understood as a remapping. These projects derive their meanings and aesthetic effects from systematically rearranging the samples of original media in new configurations. In retrospect, many of these art projects can also be understood as media visualizations. They examine ideological patterns in mass media, experiment with new ways to navigate and interact with media, defamiliarize our media perceptions, or create new dynamic media landscapes.

For instance, visual artist and video director Marco Brambilla produced a series of stunning videos for the elevators of The Standard Hotel in New York's Chelsea area (they were installed in 2008). One such video, *Civilization (Megaplex)*, uses over four hundred video clips drawn from historical films that are composited in an elaborate, overlapping, dynamic "map."[19] As you take the elevator to the top floor, the video progresses from images of hell to images of heaven. In other videos in this series, the artist and his production company similarly combine hundreds of movie clips that represent iconic moments in twentieth-century visual culture. The characters and scenes appear as miniatures each following its own movement. Together they form a media history galaxy unfolding before our eyes. The animations build numerous links among faces, bodies, set designs, and periods accumulate as we watch, making the overall map thicker with references and denser visually.

The methods of media visualization described in this chapter use some of the techniques already explored earlier by artists. However, the practices of photomontages, film editing, sampling, remixing, and digital arts are likely to contain many other strategies that can be appropriated for media visualization. Just as with the sampling concept, the relationship between these artistic practices of media remapping and the use of media visualization as a research method for media studies is a rich topic for further reflection. As a way to begin, we can consider important differences between these two paradigms.

Artistic projects typically sample media artifacts, select parts, and then deliberately assemble these parts in a *new order*. For example, in a classical work of video art titled *Technology/Transformation: Wonder Woman* (1979), Dara Birnbaum sampled the television series *Wonder Woman* to isolate a number of moments, such as the transformation of the woman into a superhero. These short clips were then repeated many times to create a new narrative. The order of the clips did not follow their order in the original television episodes.

In cultural analytics, we are interested in revealing the patterns across a complete media artifact or a series of artifacts. Therefore, regardless of whether we are using all media objects (such as in the *Time* covers montage or *Kingdom Hearts* montages) or their samples (the *Time* covers slices), we typically start by arranging them *in the same order* as in the original work.

Additionally, rather than selecting samples intuitively or intentionally to present our new interpretation of the cultural media or expressing our opinion, we start with a more systematic sampling method—for instance, selecting the first frame of every shot in a film or every frame when some parameter in a video changes significantly (a new person enters the shot; a change in color palette; a change in shot composition; etc.).

However, we also intentionally experiment with various sampling strategies and also different spatial arrangements of the media objects in a visualization. Such deliberate remappings are closer to the practice of rearrangements of media materials by designers and artists. (Their rearrangements may be sometimes quite "violent" in terms of how they treat media samples. I am thinking of photomontages of the 1920s and 1930s by Hannah Hoch, László Moholy-Nagy, and John Heartfield, montages by surrealist Gherasim Luca, and works by 1960s pop artists.) However, typically our goal is revealing the patterns that are already present, as opposed to making new statements about the world using media samples.

Whether this goal is realizable is a different question. It is certainly possible that our remappings are reinterpretations of the media works that force viewers to notice some patterns at the expense of others. In other words, even the seemingly most "natural" and "objective" sampling method or visualization layout is already a strong interpretation of the material—a reading that is negotiated or oppositional, rather than hegemonic.

As an example of our use of a remapping technique, figure 10.3 shows parts of the visualization I created that compares the first and last frame of every shot in Vertov's *The Eleventh Year*. The complete visualization is 133,204 × 600 pixels; in order to make the frames visible in the figure, I have zoomed into one small part, shown at zoom levels.

Vertov is a neologism invented by the director, who adopted it as his last name early in his career. It comes from the Russian verb *vertet*, which means "to rotate." Vertov may refer to the basic motion involved in filming in the 1920s—rotating the handle of a camera—as well as to the dynamism of film language developed by Vertov. Along with a number of other Russian and European artists, designers, and photographers working in that decade, Vertov wanted to defamiliarize the familiar reality by using dynamic diagonal compositions and shooting from unusual points of view.

However, our visualization suggests a very different picture of Vertov. Almost every shot of *The Eleventh Year* starts and ends with practically the same composition and subject. In other words, the shots are largely static. Going back to the actual film and studying these shots further, we find that some of them are indeed completely static—such as the close-ups of people's faces looking in various directions without moving. Other shots employ a static camera that frames some movement—such as working machines, or workers at work—but the movement is localized completely inside the frame; that is, the objects and human figures do not move outside or across frame

Figure 10.3

Close-ups of a small part of the visualization of all 654 shots in *The Eleventh Year* (Vertov, 1928). Each shot is represented by its first frame (top row) and last frame (bottom row). The shots are organized from left to right following their order in the film.

boundaries. Of course, a number of shots in Vertov's most famous film, *Man with a Movie Camera* (1929), were specifically designed to be dynamic: shooting from a moving car meant that the subjects were constantly crossing the camera view. But even in this most experimental film by Vertov, such shots constitute a very small part of a film.

In this chapter, I described visual techniques for exploring large media collections. These techniques follow the same general idea: use the content of the collection— all images, their subsets (temporal sampling), or their parts (spatial sampling)—and present it in various spatial configurations to make visible the patterns and the overall "shape" of a collection. To contrast this approach to the more familiar practice of information visualization, I call it *media visualization*.

I included examples that show how media visualization can be used with already existing metadata such as magazine issues dates or film frame numbers. However, if researchers add new information to the collection, this new information also can be used to create media visualizations. For example, images can be plotted using manually coded or automatically detected content characteristics, or visual features extracted via digital image processing. In the case of videos, we also can use automatically extracted or coded information about editing techniques, framing, presence of human figures and other objects, amount of movement in each shot, and so on. Thus, to compare the first and last frames of every shot in Vertov's film, I used shotdetect software that finds boundaries between the shots.

Conceptually, media visualization is based on three operations: zooming out to see the whole collection (image montage), temporal and spatial sampling, and remapping (rearranging the samples of media in new configurations). Achieving meaningful results with remapping techniques often involves experimentation and time. The first two methods usually produce informative results more quickly. Therefore, every time we assemble or download a new media dataset, we first explore it using image montages and slices of all items.

Consider this definition of *browse* from Wiktionary: "to scan, to casually look through in order to find items of interest, especially without knowledge of what to look for beforehand."[20] Also relevant is one of the meanings of the word *exploration*: "to travel somewhere in search of discovery."[21] How can we discover interesting things in massive media collections? In other words, how can we browse through them efficiently and effectively, without prior knowledge of what we want to find? Media visualization techniques give us some ways of doing this.

Conclusion: Can We Think without Categories?

Since the turn of the twenty-first century, global digital culture has entered a new stage. Computational analysis of cultural digital artifacts, their online "lives," and people's interactions with these artifacts and each other have redefined dynamics and mechanisms of culture. This analysis is now used by numerous players—the companies that run social networks, NGOs planning their outreach, tens of millions of small businesses around the world advertising online, and hundreds of millions of people who plan, create, and manage their self-presentation on the web. At the same, fashion companies, book and music publishers, television and film producers, food and beverage companies, hotel chains, airlines, and other big companies in culture and lifestyles industries use big data that is relevant to them and data science to design, test, and market their offerings, and to predict the demand.

Some of the same computational methods and their underlying concepts also make possible new exciting research about cultures and societies in fields that include computer science, data science, computational social science, digital humanities, urban studies, media studies, data visualization, data design, data art, and so on. Cultural analytics is one such field that emerged in the second part of the 2000s. The goal of this book was to present my own cultural analytics journey and what I have learned since starting this research in 2007. The book took you through the sequence of steps involved in representing and exploring cultural phenomena as data. My goal was to examine the concepts involved in each step, questioning normal ways of doing things and pointing out possibilities not yet explored.

The book's particular perspective reflects the three domains in which I have been working for a long time—media theory, digital art, and data science. Its media theory contributions include analysis of some of the key concepts and practices of data science and a new stage in the development of modern technological media that I call *media analytics*. This stage is characterized by algorithmic large-scale analysis of media and user interactions and the use of the results in algorithmic decision-making such as contextual advertising, recommendations, search, and other kinds of information retrieval, filtering of search results and user posts, content categorization of user photos, document classification, plagiarism detection, video fingerprinting, automatic news production, and more. And we are still only at the beginning of this stage. Given the trajectory of gradual automation of more and more functions in modern society using algorithms, I expect that production and customization of many forms of commercial culture will also gradually become more automated. Thus, in the future already developed digital distribution platforms and media analytics will be joined by the third part: *algorithmic media generation*. Experimental artists, designers, composers, poets, and filmmakers have been using algorithms to generate work since the early 1960s, but in the future this is likely to become the norm across culture industry. We can see this at work already today in automatically generated news stories, online content written about topics suggested by algorithms, commercially distributed music generated with AI, movie acquisition and release decisions, production of television shows and TV broadcasts during sport events in which multiple robotic cameras automatically follow and zoom into dynamic human performances and video games. (My 2018 book *AI Aesthetics* discusses cultural uses of AI in more detail.[1])

Until the beginning of the twenty-first century, key cultural techniques we used to *represent and reason* about the world and other humans included natural languages, capturing reality as media information (photos, videos, and audio recordings), map making, logic, calculus, and digital computers. The core concepts of the *data society* we covered are now as important. They form the data society's mind—the particular ways of encountering, understanding, and acting on the world and the humans in it. And this is why even if you have no intention of doing practical cultural analytics research yourself, you still need to become familiar with these new data-centered cultural techniques.[2]

Contemporary data science includes hundreds of algorithms and dozens of methods for working with data. They belong to a number of larger areas defined by different types of operations—data preparation, exploratory data analysis (including visualization), descriptive statistics, unsupervised machine learning (clustering, dimension reduction, etc.), statistical models, supervised machine learning (with its main applications—classification and regression), time series analysis, network analysis, and others. Some of these areas had already started to develop in the first decades of the twentieth century; others became popular only recently because their algorithms and methods require faster computers or rely on very large datasets.

Among these areas, two in particular are so important today that we can think of them as *types of data society's cognition*: unsupervised machine learning and supervised machine learning. In our work, we focus on the first as opposed to the second because we want to see the structures of cultural fields and their "landscapes" and find groupings and connections that can be revealed by starting with objects' features—rather than impose existing categories and classification systems on cultural data. But you should become familiar with both approaches because both can be used creatively. Certainly, both descriptive statistics and visualization should be also in your toolbox. Among all other areas, network analysis and time series analysis are particularly relevant for exploring culture, in my view. And you should learn methods specific to the particular media type you are interested in—natural language processing, computer vison, music information retrieval, or spatial analysis (used for analysis of texts, images and videos, music and sound, and space).

Do We Want to "Explain" Culture?

Approaching cultural processes and artifacts as data can lead us to ask the kinds of questions about culture that people who professionally write about it, curate it, and manage it do not normally ask today—because such questions would go against the accepted understanding of culture, creativity, aesthetics, and taste in the humanities, popular media, or the art world. For example, would collectors and museums pay millions for the works of contemporary artists if data analysis shows that they are completely unoriginal despite their high financial valuations? Or what if data analysis reveals that trends in the art world can be predicted as accurately as trends in fashion?

The most well-known and influential quantitative analysis of cultural data within social sciences remains Pierre Bourdieu's *Distinction* (1979). As I already mentioned, the data used in this analysis comes from the surveys of the French public. For analysis and visualization of this data, Bourdieu used the recently developed method of *correspondence analysis*. It is similar to PCA but works for discrete categories, showing their relations in graphical form. For Bourdieu, this form of data analysis visualization went along with his theoretical concepts about society and culture, and that's why it plays a central role in this book. *Distinction* is Bourdieu's most well-known book, and in 2012 Bourdieu was the second-most quoted academic author in the world, just behind Michel Foucault.[3]

Bourdieu did not use the most common method in quantitative social science: "explaining" some observed phenomena, represented by dependent variables, by predicting their values using other phenomena, represented by independent variables, via a mathematical model. However, given the variety and the scale of cultural data available today, maybe now such a method can produce interesting results?

What would happen if we also took other standard methods of quantitative social science and used them to "explain" the seemingly elusive, subjective, and irrational world of culture? For example, we can use factor analysis to analyze the choices and preferences of local audiences around the world for music videos from many countries to understand the dimensions people use to compare musicians and songs. Or we can use regression analysis and a combination of demographic, social, and economic variables to model choices made by *cultural omnivores*—people who like cultural offerings associated with both elite and popular taste.[4] (For the first quantitative study of cultural taste that uses large social media data, see the 2016 paper "Understanding Musical Diversity via Online Social Media.")[5]

In quantitative sociology of culture and marketing and advertising research, investigators ask similar questions all the time in relation to consumer goods and cultural artifacts. And computer scientists do this as well when they analyze social media and web data. But this does not happen in the humanities. In fact, if you are in the arts or humanities, such ideas may make you feel really uncomfortable. And this is precisely why we should explore them.

The point of any application of quantitative or computational methods to analysis of culture is not whether it ends up being successful or not, unless you are in the media analytics business. It can force us to look at the subject matter in new ways, to become explicit about our assumptions, and to precisely define our concepts and the dimensions we want to study.

So at least as a thought experiment, let's think about applying a quantitative social science paradigm to culture. Quantitative social science aims to provide explanations of social phenomena, expressed as mathematical relations among small numbers of variables (what influences what and by how much). Once such models are created, they are often used for prediction. The common statistical methods for such explanations are regression models, versions of factor analysis, or fitting a probability distribution to the data. The latter means determining if observed data can be described using a simple mathematic model: Gaussian distribution, log-normal distribution, the Paretto distribution, and so on. For example, in quantitative film studies, a number of researchers found that shot frequencies in the twentieth-century Hollywood films follow a log-normal distribution.[6]

Are we interested in trying to predict future of culture with mathematic models? Do we need to explain culture through external economic and social variables? Do we really need to find that an author's biography, for example, accounts for 30 percent of the variability in her works? Or that age, location, and gender variables account for, let's say, 20 percent of variability in Instagram posts? And even if we find that a combination of some variables can predict the content and style of Instagram posts of some users with 95 percent accuracy, probably what is really important in this cultural sphere is the 5 percent we cannot predict.

Applied to real-life data, regression models typically can only predict some of the data, not all of it. The part that is not predicted is often treated as "noise" because it does not fit the mathematical model. In fact, in the standard presentation of regression analysis, the term that is added to the model to represent the unpredicted data is called an *error term*, or *noise*. The assumption is that the noise is due to some possibly random variation, which adds disturbance to the process we are observing and modeling. However, in cultural processes, the parts that statistical models would not be able to predict is what is most interesting. We call something original if it can't be predicted.

Can we pay equal attention to the norms and the exceptions? Our common histories of culture often focused too much on the original elements and the new inventions. This focus on the avant-garde in human history comes at the expense of the norm, the typical, the conventional. Use of bigger cultural data and quantitative methods are well suited for the study of these norms. As Moretti wrote about this already in 1998 in relation to literature: "A history of literature as a history of norms, then: a less innocent, much 'flatter' configuration than the one we are used to; repetitive, slow—boring, even. But this is exactly what most of life is like, and instead of redeeming literature from its prosaic features we should learn to recognize them and understand what they mean."[7] I fully agree—but I also hope that cultural analytics can do more than this. Ideally, it should look both at the boring and the exiting, the norms and the inventions. And this may require a fundamental rethinking of statistical and other data science methods if they can only account for the regular parts of cultural history.

Is the Goal of Cultural Analytics to Study Patterns? (Yes and No)

While humanities often focus on individual human creations, they are also concerned with larger cultural patterns. Some of the terms that twentieth-century humanities used to refer to such patterns are *techniques, conventions, structures, types, themes, topics,* and *motifs*. These patterns were discussed as common features of works or authors who belonged to particular *genres, cultural movements, historical periods, national cultural traditions,* or *subcultures*.

Cultural analytics, as I see it, is situated within the same paradigm, but it works with bigger and more representative samples, expands the number of dimensions for study, and uses computer techniques to measure and quantify these dimensions. Most importantly, rather than starting with already accepted cultural categories, it analyzes "raw" cultural data to find patterns, connections, and clusters that often do not correspond to these categories.

Cultural analytics thus also can be defined as *the quantitative study of cultural patterns on different scales*. But we need to keep in mind that any cultural pattern we may detect and describe captures similarities among a number of artifacts on only some dimensions, ignoring their other differences. When we start considering these differences, what looked like a single group of similar artifacts reveals the presence of multiple and distinct smaller groups. A single pattern breaks down into many patterns. Thus, any cultural analytics results are always relative to what dimensions we choose to compare and which ones we choose, for the time being, to ignore.

In summary, although we want to discover repeating patterns on different scales in cultural data, we should always remember that they account for only *some* aspects of the artifacts and their reception.

In the previous section, I briefly explored the implications of looking at culture the way twentieth-century social scientists looked at society. Do we actually want to do this? Cultural analytics does not want to "explain" most or even some data using a simple mathematical model and treat the rest as an error or as noise just because our mathematical model cannot account for it. And we do not want to assume that cultural variation is a deviation from a mean. We also do not want to assume that large proportions of works in a particular medium or genre follow a single or only a few patterns, such as the hero's journey, the golden ratio, or binary oppositions, or that every culture goes through the same three or five stages of development as was claimed by some art historians in the nineteenth century.

I believe that we should study cultural diversity without assuming that it is caused by variations from certain types or structures. This is very different from the modern thinking of quantitative social science and the statistical paradigm it adapted. As I explained in this book, the historical development of statistics in the eighteenth and nineteenth centuries leads that field to consider observed data in terms of deviations from the mean.

Does this mean that we are only interested in the differences and that we want to avoid any kind of reduction at all cost? To postulate the existence of cultural patterns is to accept that we are doing at least some reduction when we think and analyze data. Without this, we cannot compare anything, unless we are dealing with extreme cultural minimalism or seriality, such as the artworks by Sol LeWitt who makes everything else equal and only varies a single variable.

My answer is presented in the next two paragraphs, and for me, these are the most important paragraphs in the whole book. In them, I describe cultural analytics as it developed until now, and I sketch a more difficult task ahead.

Unless it is a 100 percent copy of another cultural artifact or produced mechanically or algorithmically to be identical with others, every expression and interaction is unique. In some cases, this uniqueness is not important in analysis, and in other cases it is. For example, certain facial features we extracted from a dataset of Instagram self-portraits revealed interesting differences in how people represent themselves in this medium in particular cities and time periods we analyzed. But the reason we do not get tired looking at endless faces, bodies, and landscapes when we browse Instagram is that each of them is unique.

The ultimate goal of cultural analytics can be to map and understand in detail the diversity of contemporary professional and user-generated artifacts created globally— that is, to *focus on what is different among numerous artifacts and not only on what they share*. In the nineteenth and twentieth centuries, the lack of appropriate technologies to store, organize, and compare large cultural datasets contributed to the popularity of reductive cultural theories. Today I can use any computer to map and visualize thousands of differences among tens of millions of objects. We do not have an excuse any more to only focus on what cultural artifacts or behaviors share, which is what we do when we categorize them, or perceive them as instances of general types. So though we may have to start by extracting patterns first just to draw our initial maps of contemporary cultural production and dynamics, given their scale, eventually these patterns may recede into the background or even completely dissolve as we focus only on the differences among individual objects.

How to Think without Categories

In my experience, these ideals are easier to state than to put in practice. The human brain and languages are categorizing machines. Our cognition constantly processes sensory information and categorizes it. A pattern we observe is like constructing a new category: a recognition that some things or some aspects of these things have something in common. So how can we learn to think about culture without categories?

How do we move away from the assumption of the humanities (which until now "owned" thinking and writing about culture) that their goal of research is discovery and interpretation of general cultural types, be they "modernism," "narrative structures," or "selfies"? How do we instead learn to see cultures in more detail, without immediately looking for, and noticing, only types, structures, or patterns?

In this book, I described one possible strategy for doing this, which borrows ideas from data science. First, we need sufficiently large cultural data samples. Next, we extract sufficiently large numbers of features that capture characteristics of the artifacts, their reception and use by audiences, and their circulation. (We also need to think more systematically about how to represent cultural processes and interactions—especially since today we use interactive digital cultural media as opposed to historical static artifacts.) Once we have such datasets, we can explore them using data science methods—while also keeping in mind that the features can't capture everything, so our human abilities to see and reason about similarities and differences and our knowledge of cultural histories and theories are still crucial.

In part III, I discussed some exploratory methods we have been using for visual media datasets. But now I want to suggest an alternative and more general way to think about what it means to observe cultures. It expands further the idea expressed earlier that one possible goal of cultural analytics is to focus on what is different among numerous cultural artifacts, as opposed to what they have in common, like we did in the nineteenth and twentieth centuries.

Most generally, I suggest that to observe and analyze culture means to be able to map and measure five fundamental characteristics. The first four are diversity, uniqueness, dynamics (temporal changes), and structure. The last term here means clusters, networks, and other types of relations between many objects—that is, structure as it is understood in exploratory data analysis and unsupervised machine learning, as opposed to in 1960s structuralism. In situations in which artifacts were created using a prescriptive aesthetic or template—for example, Instagram filters provided by the app or the Instagram themes described and illustrated in thousands of advice posts—we can also consider a fifth characteristic: variability. For example, if we analyze a sample of Instagram images, we can first detect the presence of all themes suggested in many posts and then look at deviations from these themes and also at images that do not follow any of them. But we do not want to assume that the deviation from the type (or from a mean or another statistic we can compute for our dataset) is a necessary measurement for all cultural situations.

The development and testing of *measures of cultural variability, diversity, temporal change, influence, uniqueness, and structure* appropriate for many kinds of cultural artifacts and experiences is a massive theoretical and practical task. Certainly, cultural analytics is not going to quickly solve this challenge by itself. There are many such measures or concepts that can be turned into such measures developed in statistics, information theory, computer science, ecology, demography, machine learning, and other fields—for example, diversity indexes in biology, the Gini coefficient in economics, the index of dissimilarity in demographics, and the divergence measure and shared information distance in information theory. Seeing what measures work better with different types of cultural data and refining those is an important direction for cultural analytics as I see it.

As an example of this research, in the *Visual Earth* project we used the Gini index for measurement of *social media inequality*—that is, unequal spatial distribution of volumes of social media posts in a particular geographic area or between areas. We used a dataset of 7,442,454 public and geocoded Instagram images shared in Manhattan over five months (March–July) in 2014, and also selected demographics data for 287 Census tracts in Manhattan. (The inequality of Instagram sharing in Manhattan turned out to be bigger than inequalities in levels of income, rent, and unemployment.[8])

For inspiration for thinking about quantitative analysis of diversity, variability, uniqueness, structure, and temporal change, we can turn to the pioneering work of Russian quantitative humanities scholar Boris Jarkho from the 1920s and the 1930s. A presentation at the 2018 Digital Humanities conference to which I contributed summarized features of his approach: "variety, mutability and continuity as the methodology's foundations; discovering typical patterns in literary works using comparison and statistics; finding changes in patterns across time and genres; biology and systems approaches as benchmarks for future literary studies."[9] As Jarkho wrote,

> Theoretically, literature can be perceived as a structure, not as a combination but as a system of proportions and relations between its properties. The system is perceived to be in a continuous movement, with properties (features) moving along the curves of various types, sometimes independently of each other, sometimes in pairs or sets of features. This, in turn, results in understanding the organic dynamics (change) in literature, with a variety of qualitative, quantitative and hierarchical concepts to follow. . . . The specifics of these concepts is, first, that they are very close to how contemporary science understands the concepts of life (organic world) and second, that most of these properties can be measured.

Jarkho's vision of cultural dynamics as temporal curves showing changes in features is very relevant today, but one of his ideas—literature as a single system—may be more problematic for us. But it is crucial to remember that he was theorizing the development of literature in previous centuries, when the numbers of professional creators in each cultural field active in a particular country in a given period were relatively small, so for these creators and their critics their professional world could have indeed appeared as a single system. When we consider certain cultural fields today with a small number of agents such as big social networks companies and other massive online platforms, their behaviors may also look like a system (e.g., they closely monitor each other, and periodically include new features added by one company in their own platforms). But in other contemporary fields with millions of participants, such as music, fashion, filmmaking, or design, nobody can hear, read, view, or interact with all works being created, and even large-scale computational analysis (i.e., cultural analytics) can't reveal all patterns.

Learning to See at a New Scale

To *explore* is to *compare*. And to *compare*, we need first to *see*. To see contemporary culture at its new scale, we can use data science methods and larger datasets. But even if a given historical or contemporary cultural field or phenomenon does not have such scale, data-driven analysis helps us question our inherited intuitions, assumptions, and categories.

Until the twenty-first century, we typically compared small numbers of artifacts, and the use of our human cognitive capacities unaided by machines was considered to be sufficient. But today we need to be able to compare millions or billions of cultural artifacts being created. User-generated content, professional shared content, and online interactions (between users, between users and software, and between users and artifacts) are examples of large-scale cultural data, but some digitized collections of historical artifacts can be also large, running into tens of millions of items (e.g., the Internet Archive collections,[10] the Europeana collections, or Russian proza.ru and stihi.ru). So even if we use sampling to select small parts of such cultural universes for analysis, we have no choice but to use computational methods.

If we do not learn to see at sufficient resolution what people today create and how they behave culturally, any theories or interpretations we may propose based on our intuitions and received knowledge are likely to be misguided. This was the case when we analyzed data on 16 million Instagram images shared in 17 global cities in 2012-2015, one million manga pages, five thousand paintings of Impressionist artists, and other cultural datasets. In each case, my assumptions about what I am going to see based on intuitions and accepted knowledge were overturned.

This computational *cultural vision* can be understood as an extension of the most basic method of the humanities—comparing cultural artifacts, periods, authors, genres, movements, themes, techniques, and topics. So though it may be radical in terms of its scale—how much you can see in one glance, so to speak—it continues the humanities' most basic and oldest way of thinking.

I want you to think of cultural analytics as a toolkit of ideas, methods, and techniques to experiment, explore, discover, and communicate your discoveries. This book's purpose was to discuss why we need this toolkit today, to present the core concepts and a few methods we found most useful in our explorations. Now it is up to you to expand this toolkit and make your own discoveries.

Notes

Introduction

1. Dell H. Hymes, "Introduction," in *The Use of Computers in Anthropology*, ed. Dell H. Hymes (The Hague: Mouton, 1965), 29–30. Emphasis in original.

2. United States Securities and Exchange Commission, Form S-1 Registration Statement for Pinterest, Inc., March 22, 2019, https://www.sec.gov/Archives/edgar/data/1506293/000119312519083544/d674330ds1.htm.

3. "About," *Meetup*, accessed August 12, 2019, https://www.meetup.com/about/.

4. This feature was first introduced in Apple's iPhone 7 in 2016. However, even earlier some mobile apps and services, such as Google Photos, were already offering object detection in photos on mobile phones.

5. Cultural Analytics Lab, "About," accessed February 28, 2020, http://lab.culturalanalytics.info/p/about.html.

6. *Cultural Analytics: Computational Approaches to the Study of Culture*, symposium at the University of Chicago, Chicago, May 22–23, 2019, http://neubauercollegium.uchicago.edu/events/uc/cultural_analytics/; *Cultural Analytics 2017*, symposium at Notre Dame University Notre Dame, May 26–27, 2017, https://sites.google.com/nd.edu/ca2017.

7. "Culture Analytics program," Institute for Pure and Applied Mathematics (IPAM), UCLA, March 7–June 10, 2016, http://www.ipam.ucla.edu/programs/long-programs/culture-analytics/.

8. "About," *Journal of Cultural Analytics*, accessed July 23, 2019, http://culturalanalytics.org/about/.

9. "Articles," *Journal of Cultural Analytics*, accessed October 1, 2019, https://culturalanalytics.org/category/articles/.

10. Digital Humanities 2019 Conference, Utrecht, Netherlands, July 9–12, 2019, https://dh2019.adho.org.

11. Erik Malcolm Champion, "Digital Humanities Is Text Heavy, Visualization Light, and Simulation Poor," *Digital Scholarship in the Humanities* 32, s1 (2017): 25–32.

12. Miriam Redi, Frank Z. Liu, and Neil O'Hare, "Bridging the Aesthetic Gap: The Wild Beauty of Web Imagery," in *Proceedings of the 2017 ACM International Conference on Multimedia Retrieval,* (New York: ACM, 2017), 242–250.

13. Clarifai reported being able to detect eleven thousand types of objects reliably in 2017. See Clarifai, "Models," accessed October 13, 2017, https://www.clarifai.com/models.

14. Douglas Engelbart, "Augmenting Human Intellect: A Conceptual Framework," SRI Project no. 3578, October 1962, http://dougengelbart.org/content/view/138.

15. David Moats and Nick Seaver, "'You Social Scientists Love Mind Games': Experimenting in the 'Divide' between Data Science and Critical Algorithm Studies," *Big Data & Society* 6, no. 1, (2019), https://doi.org/10.1177/2053951719833404; Andrew Iliadis and Federica Russo, "Critical Data Studies: An Introduction," *Big Data & Society* 3, no. 2 (2016), https://doi.org/10.1177/2053951716674238.

16. Jean-Baptiste Michel et al., "Quantitative Analysis of Culture Using Millions of Digitized Books," *Science* 331, no. 6014 (2011): 176–182, https://doi.org/10.1126/science.1199644.

17. Adelheid Heftberger, *Digital Humanities and Film Studies: Visualising Dziga Vertov's Work* (Basel: Springer, 2018).

18. Karin van Es and Mirko Tobias Schäfer, eds., *The Datafied Society. Studying Culture through Data* (Amsterdam: Amsterdam University Press, 2017), https://oapen.org/search?identifier=624771.

19. Eli Pariser, *The Filter Bubble: What the Internet Is Hiding from You* (New York: Penguin Press, 2011).

20. Chris Anderson, "The Long Tail," *Wired*, October 1, 2004, https://www.wired.com/2004/10/tail/; Erik Brynjolfsson, Yu Jeffrey Hu, and Michael D. Smith, "The Longer Tail: The Changing Shape of Amazon's Sales Distribution Curve," September 22, 2010, https://papers.ssrn.com/sol3/papers.cfm?abstract_id=1679991.

21. "On Broadway," 2014; http://on-broadway.nyc/; "Inequaligram," 2016, http://inequaligram.net/.

22. "How I Edit My Instagram" (search results), *YouTube,* accessed January 15, 2016, https://www.youtube.com/results?search_query=%22how+i+edit+my+instagram%22.

23. Lev Manovich, *Software Takes Command*, rev. ed. (London: Bloomsbury Academic, 2013). An earlier version was released under a Creative Commons license in 2007, 15; italics in original.

24. Lev Manovich, *AI Aesthetics* (Moscow: Strelka Press, 2018).

25. Lev Manovich, "Teaching," accessed September 20, 2019, http://manovich.net/index.php/teaching.

1   From New Media to More Media

1. Gustav Theodor Fechner, *Elements of Psychophysics* (New York: Holt, Rinehart & Winston, 1966); L. L. Thurstone, "The Vectors of Mind," *Psychological Review* 41 (1934): 1–32; Jacob Levy Moreno, *Who Shall Survive? A New Approach to the Problem of Human Interrelations* (Washington, DC: Nervous and Mental Disease Publ. Co, 1934).

2. The later version of this text was published as Lev Manovich, "Cultural Analytics: Visualizing Cultural Patterns in the Era of 'More Media,'" *Domus* 923 (March 2009), http://manovich.net/index.php/projects/cultural-analytics-visualizing-cultural-patterns.

3. International Conference on Weblogs and Social Media (ICWSM) 2017, "Previous Conferences," accessed October 11, 2017, https://icwsm.org/2019/contact/previous-conferences/.

4. International Conference on Weblogs and Social Media (ICWSM) 2019, accessed October 11, 2017, https://icwsm.org/2007/.

5. "How Many Online Forums Are in Existence?," *Quora*, accessed October 11, 2017, https://www.quora.com/How-many-online-forums-are-in-existence.

6. "How Many People Use Quora?," *Quora*, accessed October 11, 2017, https://www.quora.com/How-many-people-use-Quora-7?redirected_qid=12824.

7. "Academia: About," accessed February 7, 2020, https://www.academia.edu/about.

8. WGSN, "Fashion," accessed October 11, 2017, https://www.wgsn.com/en/products/fashion/.

9. WGSN, "About WGSN," accessed October 11, 2017, https://www.wgsn.com/en/wgsn/#!/page/our-services.

10. Fern Seto, "How Does Trend Forecasting Really Work?," Highsnobiety, April 5, 2017, https://www.highsnobiety.com/2017/04/05/trend-forecasting-how-to/.

11. Uma Karmarkar and Hilke Plassmann, "Consumer Neuroscience: Past, Present, and Future," *Organizational Research Methods* 22, no. 1 (2019): 174–195.

12. Behance, "Year in Review—2015," accessed July 5, 2016, http://www.behance.net/yearinreview.

13. Jesse Alpert and Nissan Hajaj, "We Knew the Web Was Big . . . ," *Google Official Blog*, July 25, 2008, http://googleblog.blogspot.com/2008/07/we-knew-web-was-big.html.

14. Wikipedia, "YouTube," accessed August 1, 2008, http://en.wikipedia.org/wiki/YouTube.

15. Heather Champ, "3 Billion!," *Flickr Blog*, November 3, 2008, http://blog.flickr.net/en/2008/11/03/3-billion/.

16. John F. Gantz et al., The Diverse and Exploding Digital Universe: An Updated Forecast of Worldwide Information Growth through 2011 (Framingham, MA: International Data Corporation, March 2008), https://www.atour.com/media/images/service/IDC-EMC-The-Diverse-and-Exploding-Digital-Universe-2008.pdf.

17. The number of design portfolios submitted by users to Coroflot.com grew from 90,657 on May 7, 2008, to 120,659 on December 24, 2008.

18. "A Brief History of Google Analytics, Part One," *Digital State*, May 1, 2014, http://digitalstatemarketing.com/articles/brief-history-google-analytics-part-one.

19. Lev Manovich, "Cultural Analytics Visualizations on Ultra High Resolution Displays," *Software Studies Initiative* (blog), December 24, 2008, http://lab.softwarestudies.com/2008/12/cultural-analytics-hiperspace-and.html.

20. "UC San Diego Unveils World's Highest-Resolution Scientific Display System," California Institute for Telecommunications and Information Technology, July 9, 2008, http://www.calit2.net/newsroom/release.php?id=1332.

21. Gapminder, "Gapminder Tools," accessed September 18, 2019, http://www.gapminder.org/world/.

22. Brandon Keim, "Map of Science Looks Like Milky Way," *Wired*, March 11, 2009, https://www.wired.com/2009/03/mapofscience/.

23. Sprout Social, accessed July 29, 2016, http://sproutsocial.com/.

24. Mention, accessed July 29, 2016, https://mention.com/en/.

25. Brandwatch, "Historical Data," accessed July 29, 2016, https://www.brandwatch.com/historical-data/.

26. DataSift, accessed October 14, 2017, http://datasift.com/.

27. *Operationalization* is the practice in natural and social sciences of defining concepts through measurement operations. For example, in psychology, emotion can be measured in a number of ways, such as by facial expression, body movements, choice of vocabulary, and tone of voice.

28. Lynn Gamwell, *Mathematics and Art: A Cultural History* (Princeton, NJ: Princeton University Press, 2015), 169–170.

29. Hymes, *The Use of Computers in Anthropology*, 29–30.

30. Martin Wattenberg, "The Shape of Song," 2001, http://www.bewitched.com/song.html; "History Flow," 2003, http://www.bewitched.com/historyflow.html.

31. Peter Eleey, "Mark Hansen and Ben Rubin," *Frieze*, May 6, 2003, https://frieze.com/article/mark-hansen-and-ben-rubin.

32. Jason Salavon, *The Top Grossing Film of All Time, 1 x 1*, 2000, digital C-print mounted to plexiglass, 47" × 72", http://www.salavon.com/work/TopGrossingFilmAllTime/.

33. George Legrady, Making Visible the Invisible, 2005–2014, six LCD screens on glass wall, 45" × 24", Seattle Central Library, Seattle, http://www.mat.ucsb.edu/g.legrady/glWeb/Projects/spl/spl.html.

34. Susan Hockey, "The History of Humanities Computing," in *A Companion to Digital Humanities*, ed. Susan Schreibman, Ray Siemens, and John Unsworth (Oxford: Blackwell, 2004), 3–19.

2   The Science of Culture?

1. Friedrich von Hayek, "Prize Lecture" (Nobel Prize lecture, December 11, 1974), https://www
.nobelprize.org/nobel_prizes/economic-sciences/laureates/1974/hayek-lecture.html.

2. *The 22nd ACM Conference on Computer-Supported Cooperative Work and Social Computing*, Austin, Texas, November 9–13, 2019.

3. Joan Serrà et al., "Measuring the Evolution of Contemporary Western Popular Music," *Scientific Reports* 2, no. 521 (2012), https://doi.org/10.1038/srep00521; Maximilian Schich, Chaoming Song, Yong-Yeol Ahn, Alexander Mirsky, Mauro Martino, Albert-László Barabási, and Dirk Helbing, "A Network Framework of Cultural History," *Science* 345, no. 6196 (2014): 558–562, https://doi.org/10.1126/science.1240064.

4. *PLOS ONE*, accessed September 18, 2019, http://journals.plos.org/plosone/.

5. Miriam Redi, Neil O'Hare, Rossano Schifanella, Michele Trevisiol, and Alejandro Jaimes, "6 Seconds of Sound and Vision: Creativity in Micro-videos," in *CVPR '14 Proceedings of the 2014 IEEE Conference on Computer Vision and Pattern Recognition* (Washington, DC: IEEE Computer Society, 2014), 4272–4279.

6. Yuheng Hu, Lydia Manikonda, and Subbarao Kambhampati, "What We Instagram: A First Analysis of Instagram Photo Content and User Types," in *Proceedings of Ninth International AAAI Conference on Web and Social Media* (Palo Alto, CA: AAAI Press, 2014), 595–598, https://www.aaai
.org/ocs/index.php/ICWSM/ICWSM14/paper/view/8118/8087.

7. Saeideh Bakhshi, David A. Shamma, Lyndon Kennedy, and Eric Gilbert, "Why We Filter Our Photos and How It Impacts Engagement," in *Proceedings of the 8th International Conference on Weblogs and Social Media* (Palo Alto, CA: AAAI Press, 2015), http://comp.social.gatech.edu/papers/
icwsm15.why.bakhshi.pdf.

8. Flávio Souza, Diego de Las Casas, Vinícius Flores, SunBum Youn, Meeyoung Cha, Daniele Quercia, and Virgílio Almeida, "Dawn of the Selfie Era: The Whos, Wheres, and Hows of Selfies on Instagram," paper presented at the ACM Conference on Online Social Networks 2015, Stanford University, Stanford, CA, October 19, 2015, https://arxiv.org/abs/1510.05700.

9. Kevin Matzen, Kavita Bala, and Noah Snavely, "StreetStyle: Exploring World-Wide Clothing Styles from Millions of Photos," June 6, 2017, https://arxiv.org/abs/1706.01869.

10. Babak Saleh et al., "Toward Automated Discovery of Artistic Influence," *Multimedia Tools and Applications* 75, no. 7 (2016): 3565–3591, https://doi.org/10.1007/s11042-014-2193-x.

11. Joan Serrà, Álvaro Corral, Marián Boguñá, Martín Haro, and Josep Ll. Arcos, "Measuring the Evolution of Contemporary Western Popular Music," *Scientific Reports* 2, no. 521 (2012), https://
doi.org/10.1038/srep00521.

12. James E. Cutting, Kaitlin L. Brunick, Jordan E. DeLong, Catalina Iricinschi, and Ayse Candan, "Quicker, Faster, Darker: Changes in Hollywood Film over 75 Years," *i-Perception* 2, no. 6 (2011): 569–576, https://doi.org/10.1068/i0441aap.

13. Susan Hockey, "The History of Humanities Computing." in *Companion to Digital Humanities*, ed. Susan Schreibman, Ray Siemens, and John Unsworth (Oxford: Blackwell, 2004), 3–19.

14. Ted Underwood, "A Genealogy of Distant Reading," *Digital Humanities Quarterly* 11, no. 2 (2017).

15. Rachel Sagner Buurma and Laura Heffernan, "Search and Replace: Josephine Miles and the Origins of Distant Reading," *Modernism/Modernity*, April 11, 1018, https://modernismmodernity .org/forums/posts/search-and-replace.

16. The Alliance of Digital Humanities Organizations (ADHO), "Conference," accessed September 18, 2019, http://adho.org/conference.

17. Ted Underwood, "Seven Ways Humanists Are Using Computers to Understand Text," *The Stone and the Shell* (blog), June 4, 2015, https://tedunderwood.com/2015/06/04/seven-ways-humanists -are-using-computers-to-understand-text/.

18. Ted Underwood, Michael L. Black, Loretta Auvil, and Boris Capitanu, "Mapping Mutable Genres in Structurally Complex Volumes," in *2013 IEEE Conference on Big Data* (Santa Clara, California), 95–103, http://arxiv.org/abs/1309.3323.

19. Underwood et al., "Mapping Mutable Genres."

20. Peter Klimek, Robert Kreuzbauer and Stefan Thurner, "Fashion and Art Cycles Are Driven by Counter-Dominance Signals of Elite Competition: Quantitative Evidence from Music Styles," *Journal of the Royal Society Interface* 16, no. 151, February 6, 2019, https://doi.org/10.1098/ rsif.2018.0731.

21. Natasha Singer, "In a Scoreboard of Words, a Cultural Guide," *New York Times*, December 7, 2013, https://www.nytimes.com/2013/12/08/technology/in-a-scoreboard-of-words-a-cultural -guide.html.

22. New York Public Library, "Visualize the Public Domain," accessed October 21, 2019, http:// publicdomain.nypl.org/pd-visualization.

23. New York Public Library, "Photographers' Identities Catalog," accessed October 21, 2019, http://pic.nypl.org.

24. Spotify, "Celebrating a Decade of Discovery on Spotify," October 18, 2018, https://newsroom .spotify.com/2018-10-10/celebrating-a-decade-of-discovery-on-spotify/.

25. Rossano Schifanella, Miriam Redi, and Luca Maria Aiello, "An Image Is Worth More than a Thousand Favorites: Surfacing the Hidden Beauty of Flickr Pictures," in *Proceedings of the 8th International Conference on Weblogs and Social Media* (Palo Alto, CA: AAAI Press, 2015), http:// arxiv.org/pdf/1505.03358.pdf.

26. Katharina Reinecke and Krzysztof Z. Gajos, "Quantifying Visual Preferences around the World," in *Proceedings of the 2014 ACM CHI Conference on Human Factors in Computing Systems* (New York: ACM, 2014), 11–20, http://www.eecs.harvard.edu/~kgajos/papers/2014/reinecke14visual.pdf; Yuheng Hu, Lydia Manikonda, and Subbarao Kambhampati, "What We Instagram."

27. Haewoon Kwak, Changhyun Lee, Hosung Park, and Sue Moon, "What Is Twitter, a Social Network or a News Media?," in *Proceedings of the 19th International World Wide Web (WWW) Conference* (New York: ACM, 2014), 591–600, http://www.eecs.wsu.edu/~assefaw/CptS580-06/papers/2010-www-twitter.pdf.

28. Google Scholar, "Haewoon Kwak," accessed February 20, 2010, https://scholar.google.com/citations?user=M6i3Be0AAAAJ&hl=en.

29. Paul F. Lazarsfeld and Frank N. Stanton, eds., *Radio Research, 1941* (New York: Duel, Sloan and Pearce, 1942).

30. See Pierre Bourdieu, *Distinction: A Social Critique of the Judgement of Taste*, trans. Richard Nice (London: Routledge & Kegan Paul, 1979).

31. Maeve Duggan, Nicole B. Ellison, Cliff Lampe, Amanda Lenhart, and Mary Madden, "Demographics of Key Social Networking Platforms," Social Media Update 2014, Pew Research Center, January 9, 2015, http://www.pewinternet.org/2015/01/09/demographics-of-key-social-networking-platforms-2/.

32. Quoted in Philip Ball, *Critical Mass: How One Thing Leads to Another* (London: Arrow Books, 2004), 69–71.

33. Craig Smith, "By the Numbers: 400 Surprising Facebook Statistics (July 2016)," *Expandedramblings.com*, July 16, 2016, http://expandedramblings.com/index.php/by-the-numbers-17-amazing-facebook-stats/15/.

34. Christian Stefansen, "Google Flu Trends Gets a Brand New Engine," *Google AI Blog*, October 31, 2014, https://research.googleblog.com/2014/10/google-flu-trends-gets-brand-new-engine.html.

35. Michael Gavin, "Agent-Based Modeling and Historical Simulation," *Digital Humanities Quarterly* 8, no. 4 (2014); Graham Alexander Sack, "Character Networks for Narrative Generation: Structural Balance Theory and the Emergence of Proto-Narratives," in *Workshop on Computational Models of Narrative* (Dagstuhl, Germany: Schloss Dagstuhl-Leibniz-Zentrum fuer Informatik, 2013), 183–197.

36. Douglas Fox, "IBM Reveals the Biggest Artificial Brain of All Time," *Popular Mechanics*, December 18, 2009, http://www.popularmechanics.com/technology/a4948/4337190/.

37. Nigel Gilbert and Klaus G. Troitzsch, *Simulation for the Social Scientist,* 2nd ed. (Maidenhead, England: Open University Press, 2005): 3–4; italics in original.

38. For the example of how agent-based simulation can be used to study the evolution of human societies, see Peter Turchin, Thomas E. Currie, Edward A. L. Turner, and Sergey Gavrilets, "War,

Space, and the Evolution of Old World Complex Societies," in *Proceedings of the National Academy of Sciences of the United States of America* 110, no. 41 (2013): 16384–16389.

3   Culture Industry and Media Analytics

1. Max Horkheimer and Theodor W. Adorno, *Dialectic of Enlightenment*, trans. E. Jephcott (Stanford, CA: Stanford University Press, 2002). Original book was published in Germany in 1947.

2. Janet Wiener and Nathan Bronson, "Facebook's Top Open Data Problems," Facebook Research, October 22, 2014, https://research.fb.com/facebook-s-top-open-data-problems/.

3. Chartbeat, "About," accessed July 1, 2015, https://chartbeat.com/about.

4. Nathan Bierma, "Amazon's SIPs Let Readers Search and Dip into Books," *Chicago Tribune*, May 24, 2005, http://articles.chicagotribune.com/2005-05-24/features/0505240239_1_improbable -phrases-books-word-pairs.

5. Greg Linden, Brent Smith, and Jeremy York, "Amazon.com Recommendations: Item-to-Item Collaborative Filtering," *IEEE Internet Computing* 7, no. 1 (2003): 76–80.

6. Linden, Smith, and York, "Amazon.com Recommendations."

7. Gordon Donnelly, "75 Super-Useful Facebook Statistics for 2018," *WordStream* (blog), August 12, 2019, https://www.wordstream.com/blog/ws/2017/11/07/facebook-statistics.

8. J. Clement, "Most Famous Social Network Sites Worldwide as of July 2019, Ranked by Number of Active Users (in Millions)," Statista, accessed September 18, 2019, https://www.statista.com/ statistics/272014/global-social-networks-ranked-by-number-of-users/.

9. Axel Bruns, "Facebook Shuts the Gate after the Horse Has Bolted, and Hurts Real Research in the Process," *Medium*, April 25, 2018, https://medium.com/@Snurb/facebook-research-data -18662cf2cacb.

10. "2019 Conference on Digital Experimentation (CODE). About," *MIT Digital*, accessed September 18, 2019, http://ide.mit.edu/events/2017-conference-digital-experimentation-code.

11. Matt Asay, "Beyond Hadoop: The Streaming Future of Big Data," *InfoWorld* (blog), March 23, 2015, http://www.infoworld.com/article/2900504/big-data/beyond-hadoop-streaming-future-of -big-data.html.

12. Spotify, "Get Audio Features for a Track," Spotify for Developers, accessed October 12, 2019, https://developer.spotify.com/documentation/web-api/reference/tracks/get-audio-features/.

13. Google, "How Google Search Works," accessed October 21, 2019, https://www.google.com/ search/howsearchworks.

14. Alexis C. Madrigal, "How Netflix Reverse-Engineered Hollywood," *Atlantic*, January 2, 2014, http://www.theatlantic.com/technology/archive/2014/01/how-netflix-reverse-engineered -hollywood/282679/.

15. Stuart Dredge, "How Does Facebook Decide What to Show in My News Feed?," *Guardian*, June 30, 2014, https://www.theguardian.com/technology/2014/jun/30/facebook-news-feed-filters-emotion-study.

16. Françoise Beaufays, "The Neural Networks behind Google Voice Transcription," August 11, 2015, https://research.googleblog.com/2015/08/the-neural-networks-behind-google-voice.html.

17. Sundar Pichai, "TensorFlow: Smarter Machine Learning, for Everyone," November 9, 2015, https://googleblog.blogspot.com/2015/11/tensorflow-smarter-machine-learning-for.html.

18. Paul Sawers, "The Rise of OpenStreetMap: A Quest to Conquer Google's Mapping Empire," *TNW* (blog), February 28, 2014, http://thenextweb.com/insider/2014/02/28/openstreetmap/.

19. David Segal, "The Dirty Little Secrets of Search," *New York Times*, February 12, 2011, https://www.nytimes.com/2011/02/13/business/13search.html; Tom Vanderbilt, "The Science behind the Netflix Algorithms That Decide What You'll Watch Next," *Wired*, August 7, 2013, http://www.wired.com/2013/08/qq_netflix-algorithm/.

20. George Ritzer and Nathan Jurgenson, "Production, Consumption, Prosumption: The Nature of Capitalism in the Age of the Digital 'Prosumer,'" *Journal of Consumer Culture* 10 (1): 13–36. https://doi.org/10.1177/1469540509354673.

21. Mark Sanderson and W. Bruce Croft, "The History of Information Retrieval Research," *Proceedings of the IEEE* 100 (2012): 1444–1451, http://ciir-publications.cs.umass.edu/getpdf.php?id=1066.

22. Quoted in Eugene Garfield, "A Tribute to Calvin N. Mooers, a Pioneer of Information Retrieval," *Scientist* 11, no. 6 (March 17, 1997): 9, http://www.garfield.library.upenn.edu/commentaries/tsv11(06)p09y19970317.pdf.

23. This stage is analyzed in Lev Manovich, *Software Takes Command*, rev. ed. (London: Bloomsbury Academic, 2013).

24. Josh Constine, "How Instagram's Algorithm Works," *TechCrunch*, June 1, 2018, https://techcrunch.com/2018/06/01/how-instagram-feed-works/.

25. For other examples, see Celeste LeCompte, "Automation in the Newsroom," *Nieman Reports*, September 1, 2015, http://niemanreports.org/articles/automation-in-the-newsroom/; Shelley Podolny, "If an Algorithm Wrote This, How Would You Even Know?," *New York Times*, March 7, 2015, http://www.nytimes.com/2015/03/08/opinion/sunday/if-an-algorithm-wrote-this-how-would-you-even-know.html.

26. Mailchimp, "Use Send Time Optimization," October 5, 2017, https://kb.mailchimp.com/delivery/deliverability-research/use-send-time-optimization.

27. Twitter, "Follower Targeting on Twitter," accessed July 1, 2017, https://business.twitter.com/en/targeting/follower.html.

28. Felix Richter, "Digital Accounts for Nearly 70% of U.S. Music Revenues," Statista, September 30, 2014, https://www.statista.com/chart/2773/digital-music-in-the-united-states/.

29. According to the current default setting as of the time of writing, Facebook will show you only some of these posts, which it calls Top Stories, automatically selected by its algorithms. This setting can be changed by going to the News Feed tab and selecting Most Recent instead of Top Stories. See also Victor Luckerson, "Here's How Facebook's News Feed Actually Works," *Time*, July 9, 2015, http://time.com/3950525/facebook-news-feed-algorithm.

30. Corrado Mencar, "What Do You Mean by 'Interpretability' in Models?," ResearchGate, question posted July 7, 2013, https://www.researchgate.net/post/What_do_you_mean_by_interpretability_in_models.

31. Lev Manovich, "The Algorithms of Our Lives," *Chronicle of Higher Education*, December 16, 2013, http://chronicle.com/article/The-Algorithms-of-Our-Lives-/143557/.

32. Lev Manovich, *Software Takes Command*, rev. ed. (London: Bloomsbury Academic, 2013).

33. Wiener and Bronson, "Facebook's Top Open Data Problems."

34. Mikael Huss, "Data Size Estimates," *Follow the Data* (blog), June 24, 2014, https://followthedata.wordpress.com/2014/06/24/data-size-estimates/.

35. Alex Woodie, "The Rise of Predictive Modeling Factories," *Datanami* (blog), February 9, 2015, https://www.datanami.com/2015/02/09/rise-predictive-modeling-factories.

36. Gregory D. Abowd et al., "Towards a Better Understanding of Context and Context-Awareness," in *Handheld and Ubiquitous Computing 1999*, ed. H-W. Gellersen (Berlin and Heidelberg: Springer, 2001), ftp://ftp.cc.gatech.edu/pub/gvu/tr/1999/99-22.pdf.

37. David Carr, "Giving Viewers What They Want," *New York Times*, February 24, 2013, http://www.nytimes.com/2013/02/25/business/media/for-house-of-cards-using-big-data-to-guarantee-its-popularity.html.

38. Vanderbilt, "The Science behind the Netflix Algorithms."

39. Phil Simon, "Big Data Lessons from Netflix," *Wired*, March 2014, accessed February 28, 2020, https://www.wired.com/insights/2014/03/big-data-lessons-netflix/.

40. "Extracting Image Metadata at Scale," *Netflix Tech Blog*, March 21, 2016, https://netflixtechblog.com/extracting-image-metadata-at-scale-c89c60a2b9d2. .

41. Alex M., "Finding Beautiful Yelp Photos Using Deep Learning," *Yelp Engineering* (blog), November 29, 2016, https://engineeringblog.yelp.com/2016/11/finding-beautiful-yelp-photos-using-deep-learning.html.

42. Association for Psychological Science, "Political Polarization on Twitter Depends on the Issue," *ScienceDaily*, August 27, 2015, http://www.sciencedaily.com/releases/2015/08/150827083423.htm; Karen Kaplan, "Your Twitter Feed Says More about Your Political Views than You Think, Study Says," *Los Angeles Times*," September 18, 2015, http://www.latimes.com/science/la-sci-sn-twitter-political-conservative-republicans-20150917-story.html.

43. David A. Shamma, "One Hundred Million Creative Commons Flickr Images for Research," Yahoo Research, June 24, 2014, https://yahooresearch.tumblr.com/post/89783581601/one-hundred-million-creative-commons-flickr-images.

44. Miriam Redi, Damon Crockett, Lev Manovich, and Simon Osindero, "What Makes Photo Cultures Different?," in *Proceedings of the 24th ACM International Conference on Multimedia* (New York: ACM, 2016), 287–291, http://manovich.net/index.php/projects/what-makes-photo-cultures-different.

45. Cultural Analytics Lab, Phototrails, 2013, http://phototrails.info.

46. David Bordwell, Janet Staiger, Kristin Thompson, *The Classical Hollywood Cinema: Film Style and Mode of Production to 1960* (New York: Columbia University Press, 1985).

47. Max Horkheimer and Theodor W. Adorno, *Dialectic of Enlightenment*, trans. Edmund Jephcott (Stanford: Stanford University Press, 2002), 94.

48. Anant Gupta and Kuldeep Singh, "Location Based Personalized Restaurant Recommendation System for Mobile Environments," in *Proceedings of the International Conference on Advances in Computing, Communications and Informatics* (Mysore, India: Sri Jayachamarajendra College of Engineering, 2013), https://doi.org/10.1109/ICACCI.2013.6637223.

49. Renjie Zhou, Samamon Khemmarat, and Lixin Gao, "The Impact of YouTube Recommendation System on Video Views," in *Proceedings of the 2010 ACM Internet Measurement Conference* (New York: ACM, 2010), 404–410, http://conferences.sigcomm.org/imc/2010/papers/p404.pdf.

50. Nadav Hochman and Lev Manovich, "Zooming into an Instagram City: Reading the Local through Social Media," *First Monday* 18, no. 7 (July 1, 2013), http://firstmonday.org/ojs/index.php/fm/article/view/4711/3698.

51. Joan Serrà, Álvaro Corral, Marián Boguñá, Martín Haro, and Josep Ll. Arcos, "Measuring the Evolution of Contemporary Western Popular Music," *Scientific Reports* 2, no. 521 (2012), https://doi.org/10.1038/srep00521.

52. Matthias Mauch, Robert M. MacCallum, Mark Levy, and Armand M. Leroi, "The Evolution of Popular Music: USA 1960–2010," *Royal Society Open Science*, May 1, 2015, https://doi.org/10.1098/rsos.150081.

53. Academia.edu, accessed December 23, 2017, https://www.academia.edu/.

54. See also "List of Internet Phenomena," Wikipedia, accessed September 18, 2019, https://en.wikipedia.org/wiki/List_of_Internet_phenomena.

4 Types of Cultural Data

1. Samuel P. Fraiberger, Roberta Sinatra, Magnus Resch, Christoph Riedl, and Albert-László Barabási, "Quantifying Reputation and Success in Art," *Science* 362, no. 6416 (November 16, 2018): 825–829, https://science.sciencemag.org/content/362/6416/825.

2. "The 11th International AAAI Conference on Web and Social Media," accessed September 18, 2019, http://www.icwsm.org/2017/index.php.

3. Sandeep Junnarkar, "Bloggers Add Moving Images to Their Musings," *New York Times*, February 24, 2005, http://www.nytimes.com/2005/02/24/technology/circuits/bloggers-add-moving -images-to-their-musings.html; Nitecruzr, "Using Images in Your Posts," *The Real Blogger Status* (blog), October 6, 2006, http://blogging.nitecruzr.net/2006/10/using-images-in-your-posts .html.

4. Wikipedia, "DeviantArt," accessed August 2, 2016, http://en.wikipedia.org/wiki/DeviantArt.

5. DeviantArt, "About DeviantArt," accessed July 25, 2016, https://about.deviantart.com/.

6. Vimeo, "Motion Graphic Artists," accessed March 5, 2017, https://vimeo.com/groups/motion.

7. Daniela Ushizima et al., "Cultural Analytics of Large Datasets from Flickr," in *Proceedings of the Sixth International AAAI Conference on Weblogs and Social Media* (Palo Alto, CA: AAAI Press, 2015), http://manovich.net/index.php/projects/cultural-analytics-of-large-datasets-from-flickr.

8. Sirion Vittayakorn et al., "Runway to Realway: Visual Analysis of Fashion," in *Proceedings of 2015 IEEE Winter Conference on Applications of Computer Vision* (Waikoloa, HI: IEEE, 2015), 951–958.

9. Elena Garces et al., "A Similarity Measure for Illustration Style," *Journal ACM Transactions on Graphics* 33, no. 4 (July 2014). See also the Related Works section in this paper for more relevant research.

10. Yuji Yoshimura et al., "Deep Learning Architect: Classification for Architectural Design through the Eye of Artificial Intelligence," in *Computational Urban Planning and Management for Smart Cities*, ed. Stan Geertman et al. (Cham: Springer, 2019).

11. This topic is analyzed in detail in Lev Manovich, *Software Takes Command*, rev. ed. (London: Bloomsbury Academic, 2013).

12. In *Software Takes Command*, I argue that this constant evolution is the defining characteristic of computer media.

13. Schich et al., "A Network Framework of Cultural History."

14. Twitter Developer, "Tweet Objects," accessed March 12, 2017, https://dev.twitter.com/overview/ api/users.

15. US Department of Health and Human Services, "Considerations and Recommendations Concerning Internet Research and Human Subjects Research Regulations," for SACHRP, March 13, 2013, http://www.hhs.gov/ohrp/sites/default/files/ohrp/sachrp/mtgings/2013%20March%20 Mtg/internet_research.pdf.

16. Mike Schroepfer, "Research at Facebook," Facebook Newsroom, October 2, 2014, http:// newsroom.fb.com/news/2014/10/research-at-facebook/.

17. Social Media Research Group, *Using Social Media for Social Research: An Introduction,* May 2016, https://www.gov.uk/government/uploads/system/uploads/attachment_data/file/524750/GSR _Social_Media_Research_Guidance_-_Using_social_media_for_social_research.pdf.

18. Venturini Tommaso and Richard Rogers, "'API-Based Research' or How Can Digital Sociology and Digital Journalism Studies Learn from the Cambridge Analytica Affair," *Digital Journalism* 7, no. 4 (2019): 532–540.

19. Ars Electronica, "Interactive Art +," accessed October 1, 2019, https://ars.electronica.art/prix/ en/categories/interactive-art/.

20. Benjamin Tatler et al., "Yarbus, Eye Movements, and Vision," *Iperception* 1, no. 1 (2010): 7–27.

21. Alfred Yarbus, *Eye Movements and Vision* (New York: Plenum Press, 1967), 190.

22. Stanislav Sobolevsky et al., "Scaling of City Attractiveness for Foreign Visitors through Big Data of Human Economical and Social Media Activity," in *Proceedings of 2015 IEEE International Congress on Big Data* (Santa Clara, CA: IEEE, 2015), 600–607.

23. Senseable City Lab, accessed September 18, 2019, http://senseable.mit.edu/; Spin Unit, accessed September 18, 2019, http://www.spinunit.eu/; Habidatum, accessed September 18, 2019, https://habidatum.com/.

24. Todd Schneider, "A Tale of Twenty-Two Million Citi Bike Rides: Analyzing the NYC Bike Share System," *Todd W. Schneider* (blog), January 13, 2016, http://toddwschneider.com/posts/ a-tale-of-twenty-two-million-citi-bikes-analyzing-the-nyc-bike-share-system/.

25. Patrick Nelson, "Just One Autonomous Car Will Use 4,000 GB of Data/Day," *NetworkWorld,* December 7, 2016, https://www.networkworld.com/article/3147892/internet/one-autonomous-car -will-use-4000-gb-of-dataday.html.

26. Jordan Gilbertson and Andrew Salzberg, "Introducing Uber Movement," *Uber Newsroom,* January 9, 2017, https://newsroom.uber.com/introducing-uber-movement/.

27. William H. Whyte, *The Social Life of Small Urban Spaces* (New York: Project for Public Spaces, 1980).

28. This section summarizes arguments developed in more detail in Lev Manovich, *Software Takes Command,* rev. ed. (London: Bloomsbury Academic, 2013).

29. Meetup, "Meetup: About," accessed March 11, 2017, https://www.meetup.com/about/.

30. Eventbrite, "Eventbrite: About," accessed March 11, 2017, https://www.eventbrite.com/ about/.

31. J. Clement, "Number of Monthly Active Facebook Users Worldwide as of 4th Quarter 2019 (in Millions)," Statista, January 30, 2020, https://www.statista.com/statistics/264810/number-of -monthly-active-facebook-users-worldwide/; J. Clement, "Leading Countries Based on Number of Facebook Users as of July 2019 (in Millions)," Statista, February 14, 2020, https://www.statista .com/statistics/268136/top-15-countries-based-on-number-of-facebook-users/.

5   Cultural Sampling

1. Matthew Arnold, preface to *Culture and Anarchy* (1875), in *Arnold: Culture and Anarchy and Other Writings*, ed. Stefan Collini (Cambridge: Cambridge University Press, 1993).

2. Franco Moretti, "Conjectures on World Literature," *New Left Review* 1, no. 1 (January–February 2000): 54–68, http://newleftreview.org/II/1/franco-moretti-conjectures-on-world-literature.

3. Europeana, accessed August 3, 2018, http://www.europeana.eu/portal/en.

4. Internet Archive, accessed August 3, 2018, http://archive.org.

5. Google Arts & Culture, accessed July 26, 2016, http://www.google.com/culturalinstitute/beta/search/exhibit.

6. Lev Manovich, "How to Follow Global Digital Cultures, or Cultural Analytics for Beginners," in *Deep Search: The Politics of Search beyond Google*, ed. Konrad Becker and Felix Stalder (Innsbruck: Studien Verlag, 2009), 198–211, http://manovich.net/index.php/projects/how-to-follow-global-digital-cultures.

7. The very first large institutional collection that formed the core of Artstor was the slide library at the University of California, San Diego—the same university where I taught digital art and media theory since 1996. The library had over two hundred thousand slides, and they were all digitized and included in Artstor. In 2009, this was the largest single collection in Artstor. The slides were created either directly by art history faculty teaching in the Visual Arts Department or by art library staff via lists of images faculty provided. This collection is quite interesting because it reflects the biases of art history as it was taught over a few decades when color slides were the main media for teaching and studying art.

8. Manovich, "How to Follow Global Digital Cultures."

9. The New York Public Library Digital Collections, "Photographs of the Catskill Water Supply System in Process of Construction," accessed July 26, 2016, http://digitalcollections.nypl.org/collections/photographs-of-the-catskill-water-supply-system-in-process-of-construction.

10. The New York Public Library Digital Collections, "The Buttolph Collection of Menus," http://digitalcollections.nypl.org/collections/the-buttolph-collection-of-menus#/?tab=about.

11. The New York Public Library Digital Collections, "Catalogue of the Chiroptera by G.E. Dobson," accessed July 26, 2016, http://digitalcollections.nypl.org/collections/catalogue-of-the-chiroptera-by-ge-dobson.

12. Aleksandra Strzelichowska, "Maggy's Picks: New Content in Europeana," *Europeana Blog*, July 25, 2016, http://blog.europeana.eu/2016/07/maggys-picks-new-content-in-europeana/.

13. Lev Manovich, *Instagram and Contemporary Image* (self-published under Creative Commons License, 2017), http://manovich.net/index.php/projects/instagram-and-contemporary-image.

14. "Category: Geographic Region-Oriented Digital Libraries," Wikipedia, accessed September 18, 2019, https://en.wikipedia.org/wiki/Category:Geographic_region-oriented_digital_libraries; "List

of Digital Library Projects," Wikipedia, accessed September 18, 2019, https://en.wikipedia.org/wiki/List_of_digital_library_projects.

15. For an overview of different sampling methods, see Sam Cook, "Sampling Methods," Revise Sociology, May 4, 2011, https://revisesociology.wordpress.com/2011/05/04/5-sampling-methods. The longer list of methods is presented in Wikipedia, "Sampling (Statistics)," accessed August 2, 2018, https://en.wikipedia.org/wiki/Sampling_(statistics).

16. Nina Cesare, Christian Grant, Quynh Nguyen, Hedwig Lee, and Elaine O. Nsoesie, *How Well Can Machine Learning Predict Demographics of Social Media Users?*, ArXiv.org, February 6, 2017, https://arxiv.org/pdf/1702.01807.pdf.

17. Agustin Indaco and Lev Manovich, *Urban Social Media Inequality: Definition, Measurements, and Application*, ArXiv.org, July 7, 2016, https://arxiv.org/abs/1607.01845.

18. Manovich, *Instagram and Contemporary Image*.

19. Lydia Manikonda, Yuheng Hu, and Subbarao Kambhampati, *Analyzing User Activities, Demographics, Social Network Structure and User-Generated Content on Instagram*, Arxiv.org, October 29, 2014, http://arxiv.org/pdf/1410.8099v1.pdf.

20. National Gallery of Art, *The Art of the American Snapshot, 1888–1978: From the Collection of Robert E. Jackson*, accessed March 1, 2020, https://www.nga.gov/exhibitions/2007/snapshot.html.

21. Gallup, "Methodology Center," accessed August 2, 2016, http://www.gallup.com/178685/methodology-center.aspx.

22. Gallup, "How Does the Gallup U.S. Daily Work?," accessed August 2, 2016, http://www.gallup.com/185462/gallup-daily-work.aspx.

23. Rachel Donadio, "Revisiting the Canon Wars," *New York Times*, September 16, 2007, http://www.nytimes.com/2007/09/16/books/review/Donadio-t.html; Jan Gorak, *The Making of the Modern Canon: Genesis and Crisis of a Literary Idea* (London: Bloomsbury Academic, 2013).

24. Pew Research Center, "Internet User Demographics," accessed September 25, 2016, http://www.pewinternet.org/data-trend/teens/internet-user-demographics.

25. Brand Analytics, "Статистика по источникам," accessed September 20, 2016, https://br-analytics.ru/statistics/.

26. Statista, "Regional Distribution of Instagram Traffic in the Last Three Months as of April 2016, by Country," accessed September 20, 2016, https://www.statista.com/statistics/272933/distribution-of-instagram-traffic-by-country/.

27. Pierre Bourdieu, *Distinction: A Social Critique of the Judgement of Taste*, trans. Richard Nice (London: Routledge & Kegan Paul, 1979).

28. Frédéric Lebaron, "How Bourdieu 'Quantified' Bourdieu: The Geometric Modelling of Data," in *Quantifying Theory: Pierre Bourdieu*, ed. Karen Robson and Chris Sanders (Dordrecht: Springer, 2009), 11–29.

29. Christine A. Knoop, Valentin Wagner, Thomas Jacobsen, and Winfried Menninghaus, "Mapping the Aesthetic Space of Literature 'from Below,'" *Poetics* 56, no. 5 (June 2016): 35–49, https://doi.org/10.1016/j.poetic.2016.02.001.

30. Marc Verboord, Giselinde Kuipers, and Susanne Janssen, "Institutional Recognition in the Transnational Literary Field, 1955–2005," *Cultural Sociology* 9, no. 3 (September 2015): 447–465, https://doi.org/10.1177/1749975515576939.

31. Aurélie Van de Peer, "Re-artification in a World of De-artification: Materiality and Intellectualization in Fashion Media Discourse (1949–2010)," *Cultural Sociology* 8, no. 4 (December 2014): 443–461, https://doi.org/10.1177/1749975514539799.

32. James E. Cutting, *Impressionism and Its Canon* (Lanham, MD: University Press of America, 2006).

33. Jin Yea Jang et al., "Teens Engage More with Fewer Photos: Temporal and Comparative Analysis on Behaviors in Instagram," in *Proceedings of 2016 ACM Conference on Hypertext and Social Media* (New York: ACM, 2016), 71–81, https://doi.org/10.1145/2914586.2914602.

34. Manikonda, Hu, and Kambhampati, *Analyzing User Activities*.

35. Manikonda, Hu, and Kambhampati, *Analyzing User Activities*.

36. Émile Durkheim, *The Rules of Sociological Method* (New York: Free Press, [1895] 1982).

37. David Pierce, "Inside Spotify's Hunt for the Perfect Playlist," *Wired*, July 20, 2015, https://www.wired.com/2015/07/spotify-perfect-playlist/.

38. Franco Moretti, "Conjectures on World Literature."

39. "The Museum of Modern Art (MoMA) Exhibition and Staff Histories," GitHub, accessed September 18, 2019, https://github.com/MuseumofModernArt/exhibitions.

40. Cutting, *Impressionism and Its Canon*.

6   Metadata and Features

1. Ronald Fisher, *Statistical Methods for Research Workers* (Edinburgh: Oliver and Boyd, 1925), http://psychclassics.yorku.ca/Fisher/Methods/.

2. Theodore M. Porter, "Reforming Vision: The Engineer Le Play Learns to Observe Society Sagely," in *Histories of Scientific Observation*, ed. Lorraine Daston and Elizabeth Lunbeck (Chicago: University of Chicago Press, 2011), 281–302.

3. Michel Foucault, *Discipline and Punish: The Birth of the Prison*, trans. A. M. Sheridan Smith (New York: Pantheon Books, 1977), 129. Original book published in France in 1975.

4. Jean-Francois Lyotard, "The Field: Knowledge in Computerized Societies," in *The Postmodern Condition: Report on Knowledge* (Manchester, UK: Manchester University Press, 1984), 3–4. Original book published in France in 1979.

5. Museum of Modern Art, "Network Diagram of the Artists in Inventing Abstraction, 1910–1925," MoMA December 23, 2012–April 15, 2013, http://www.moma.org/interactives/exhibitions/2012/inventingabstraction/?page=connections.

6. Michel Foucault, *The Archaeology of Knowledge*, trans. A. M. Sheridan Smith (London: Routledge, 2002). Original book published in France in 1969.

7. "The Museum of Modern Art (MoMA) Collection," GitHub, accessed September 18, 2019, https://github.com/MuseumofModernArt/collection.

8. Alise Tifentale and Lev Manovich, "Selfiecity: Exploring Photography and Self-Fashioning in Social Media," in *Postdigital Aesthetics: Art, Computation and Design*, ed. David M. Berry and Michael Dieter (London: Palgrave Macmillan, 2015), 109–122, http://manovich.net/index.php/projects/selfiecity-exploring.

9. Saeideh Bakhshi, David Shamma, and Eric Gilbert, "Faces Engage Us: Photos with Faces Attract More Likes and Comments on Instagram," in *Proceedings of the SIGCHI Conference on Human Factors in Computing Systems* (New York: ACM, 2014), 965–974.

10. Lisa Gitelman and Virginia Jackson, "Introduction," in *"Raw Data" Is an Oxymoron*, ed. Lisa Gitelman (Cambridge: MIT Press, 2013), 3.

11. OpenStreetMap, "OpenStreetMap: About," accessed September 19, 2019, https://www.openstreetmap.org/about.

12. Pew Research Center, accessed September 19, 2019, http://www.pewinternet.org.

13. Gallup, "How Does the Gallup U.S. Daily Work?"

14. Victor Ginsburgh and Sheila Weyers, "Persistence and Fashion in Art: Italian Renaissance from Vasari to Berenson and Beyond," *Poetics* 34, no. 1 (2006): 24–44.

15. Fionn Murtagh, *Origins of Modern Data Analysis Linked to the Beginnings and Early Development of Computer Science and Information Engineering*, ArXiv.org, October 30, 2018, https://arxiv.org/pdf/0811.2519.pdf.

16. MongoDB, "Industries," accessed September 28, 2016, https://www.mongodb.com/industries.

17. For an example of the alternative history that argues that conventional history misses some crucial figures, see Paul F. Lazarsfeld, "Notes on the History of Quantification in Sociology—Trends, Sources and Problems," *Isis* 52, no. 2 (1961): 277–333, https://www.jstor.org/stable/228683.

18. Alain Desrosieres, *The Politics of Large Numbers* (Cambridge, MA: Harvard University Press, 2002).

19. For historical examples, see Michael Friendly and Daniel J. Denis, "Milestones in the History of Thematic Cartography, Statistical Graphics, and Data Visualization," 2001, accessed March 1, 2020, http://www.datavis.ca/milestones/index.php.

20. Michael Friendly and Daniel Denis, "The Early Origins and Development of the Scatterplot," *Journal of the History of the Behavioral Sciences* 41, no. 2 (2005): 103–130.

21. Quoted in Garabed Eknoyan, "Adolphe Quetelet (1796–1874)—the Average Man and Indices of Obesity," *Nephrology Dialysis Transplantation* 23, no. 1 (2008): 47–51, https://doi.org/10.1093/ndt/gfm517.

22. Lazarsfeld, "Notes on the History of Quantification in Sociology," 297.

23. Émile Durkheim, *Le Suicide. Étude de Sociologie* (Paris: F. Alcan, 1897).

24. For a contemporary presentation and practical tutorial, see Oleksandr Pavlyk, "Centennial of Markov Chains," *Wolfram Blog*, February 4, 2013, http://blog.wolfram.com/2013/02/04/centennial-of-markov-chains/.

25. Lazarsfeld, "Notes on the History of Quantification in Sociology," 310.

26. Charles E. Spearman, "'General Intelligence' Objectively Determined and Measured," *American Journal of Psychology* 15 (1904): 201–293.

27. Raymond B. Cattell, ed., *Handbook of Multivariate Experimental Psychology* (Chicago: Rand McNally, 1966).

28. L. L. Thurstone, "The Vectors of Mind," *Psychological Review* 41 (1934): 1–32.

29. Neil W. Henry, "Latent Structure Analysis at Fifty," in *Proceedings of the Survey Research Methods Section* (American Statistical Association, 1999), 587–592, http://www.asasrms.org/Proceedings/papers/1999_102.pdf.

30. T. W. Anderson, *An Introduction to Multivariate Statistical Analysis* (New York: Wiley, 1958).

31. Warren S. Torgerson, *Theory and Methods of Scaling* (New York: Wiley, 1958).

32. Michael Baxandall, *Painting and Experience in Fifteenth Century Italy: A Primer in the Social History of Pictorial Style* (Oxford: Clarendon Press, 1972); Victor Burgin, *The End of Art Theory: Criticism and Postmodernity* (Basingstoke: Macmillan, 1986).

33. For example, see the program for the 2016 Workshop on Human Interpretability in Machine Learning, New York, June 23, 2016, https://sites.google.com/site/2016whi/.

34. For example, see Matthew D. Zeiler and Rob Fergus, *Visualizing and Understanding Convolutional Networks*, ArXiv.org, November 28, 2013, http://arxiv.org/abs/1311.2901.

35. Phil Schiller, quoted in Tonya Riley, "Apple's iPhone 7 Camera Uses Machine Learning to Look for People," *Inverse*, September 7, 2016, https://www.inverse.com/article/20677-iphone-7-camera-isp-phone.

36. Glenn Fleishman, "Two Cameras in iPhone 7 Plus Allow Synthetic Zoom, Soft-Focus Backgrounds," *Macworld*, September 7, 2016, http://www.macworld.com/article/3117258/iphone-ipad/two-cameras-in-iphone-7-plus-allow-synthetic-zoom-soft-focus-backgrounds.html.

37. EyeEm, "EyeEm Team," accessed September 23, 2016, https://www.eyeem.com/u/team.

38. Olga Russakovsky et al., "ImageNet Large Scale Visual Recognition Challenge," *International Journal of Computer Vision* 115, no. 3 (2015): 211–252, https://doi.org/10.1007/s11263-015-0816-y.

39. See Russakovsky et al., "ImageNet Large Scale Visual Recognition Challenge." For the details of the results from all competing teams, see ImageNet, "Large Scale Visual Recognition Challenge 2015 (ILSVRC2015)," accessed March 1, 2020, http://www.image-net.org/challenges/LSVRC/2015/results.

40. Google Cloud Platform, "Cloud Vision API," accessed August 8, 2016, https://cloud.google.com/vision/.

41. Andrew Ng, Machine Learning Course, online course, week 6, accessed September 28, 2016, https://www.coursera.org/learn/machine-learning/home/week/6.

42. Kim Hye-Rin et al.,"Building Emotional Machines: Recognizing Image Emotions through Deep Neural Networks," *IEEE Transactions on Multimedia 20*, no. 11 (November 2018): 2980–2992.

43. David G. Lowe, "Object Recognition from Local Scale-Invariant Features," in *Proceedings of the Seventh IEEE International Conference on Computer Vision*, vol. 2 (Washington, DC: IEEE Computer Society, 1999), 1150–1157, https://doi.org/10.1109/ICCV.1999.790410. A good summary of the use of SIFT for object detection using the "bag of words" approach is provided in Gil Levi, "Bag of Words Models for Visual Categorization," *Gil's CV Blog*, August 23, 2013, https://gilscvblog.com/2013/08/23/bag-of-words-models-for-visual-categorization/.

44. Paul Viola and Michael Jones, "Rapid Object Detection Using a Boosted Cascade of Simple Features," in *Proceedings of the 2001 IEEE Computer Society Conference on Computer Vision and Pattern Recognition*, vol. 1 (Los Alamitos, CA: IEEE Computer Society, 2001), 511–518, https://doi.org/10.1109/CVPR.2001.990517.

45. A. Huertas and R. Nevatia, "Detecting Buildings in Aerial Images," *Computer Vision, Graphics, and Image Processing* 41, no. 2 (1988): 131–152.

46. Yann LeCun, Yoshua Bengio, and Geoffrey E. Hinton, "Deep Learning," *Nature* 521, no. 7553 (2015): 436–444, https://doi.org/10.1038/nature14539.

47. The paper that started the trend of using deep networks for image classification is Alex Krizhevsky, Ilya Sutskever, and Geoffrey E. Hinton, "ImageNet Classification with Deep Convolutional Neural Networks," *Advances in Neural Information Processing Systems 25* (New York: AMC, 2012), 1097–1105, http://papers.nips.cc/paper/4824-imagenet-classification-with-deep-convolutional-neural-networks.

48. Krizhevsky et al., "ImageNet Classification with Deep Convolutional Neural Networks."

49. The fact that certain data types are very popular has to do with the history of computer use in research and industry. Many algorithms were developed to analyze certain types, while other possible types did not receive the same attention. For each of the data types in my list, there are now

common methods of analysis, corresponding algorithms, and various data formats. For example, spatial data can be represented as coordinates, as shapefiles, or in other ways.

7 Language, Categories, and Senses

1. Peter M. Broadwell, David Mimno, and Timothy R. Tangherlini, "The Tell-Tale Hat: Surfacing the Uncertainty in Folklore Classification," *Journal of Cultural Analytics*, February 8, 2017, https://doi.org/10.31235/osf.io/a7dp8.

2. Ted Underwood, *Understanding Genre in a Collection of a Million Volumes*, Interim Performance Report Digital Humanities Start-Up Grant, Award HD5178713, December 29, 2014, https://figshare.com/articles/Understanding_Genre_in_a_Collection_of_a_Million_Volumes_Interim_Report/1281251.

3. "The Museum of Modern Art (MoMA) Exhibition and Staff Histories," GitHub, accessed September 18, 2019, https://github.com/MuseumofModernArt/exhibitions.

4. Wikipedia, "Statistical Data Type," accessed August 15, 2016, https://en.wikipedia.org/wiki/Statistical_data_type.

5. The literature on the introduction of metric time systems and their contribution to the rationalization of work and life is vast. See, for example, E. P. Thompson, "Time, Work-Discipline, and Industrial Capitalism," *Past & Present*, no. 38 (December 1967): 56–97; Jonathan Martineau, *Time, Capitalism, and Alienation: A Socio-Historical Inquiry into the Making of Modern Time* (Chicago: Haymarket Books, 2016).

6. Stanley S. Stevens, "On the Theory of Scales of Measurement," *Science* 103, no. 2684 (June 7, 1946): 677–680.

7. Affectiva, "Metrics," accessed September 18, 2019, https://developer.affectiva.com/metrics/.

8. Clement Greenberg, "Avant Garde and Kitsch," *Partisan Review* (1939): 34–49.

9. Roman Jakobson, "Verbal Communication," *Scientific American* 227 (1972): 72–80.

10. Marta J. Hardman, "Why We Should Say 'Women and Men' Until It Doesn't Matter Anymore," *Women and Language* 22, no. 1 (1999): 1–2.

11. Rensis Likert, "A Technique for the Measurement of Attitudes," *Archives of Psychology* 22 (1932–1933): 5–55, https://legacy.voteview.com/pdf/Likert_1932.pdf.

12. Maximilian Schich et al., "A Network Framework of Cultural History."

13. Lev Manovich, "There Is No Software," in *Nam June Paik Reader: Contributions to an Artistic Anthropology*, ed. Youngchul Lee and Henk Slager (Seoul: NJP Art Center, 2009), 26–29.

14. For a discussion of nineteenth-century debates about the meaning of the average and different types of averages, see Alain Desrosières, "Averages and the Realism of Aggregates," in *The Politics of Large Numbers: A History of Statistical Reasoning* (Cambridge, MA: Harvard University Press, 1998), 67–102.

15. On the change in phone designs from functional to highly aesthetic, see my 2007 article: Lev Manovich, "Information as an Aesthetic Event," *Receiver* 17, http://manovich.net/index.php/projects/information-as-an-aesthetic-event.

16. James Peckham, "Huawei P20 and P20 Pro Colors: What Shade Should You Buy?," *TechRadar*, March 27, 2018, https://www.techradar.com/news/huawei-p20-and-p20-pro-colors-what-shade-should-you-buy.

17. Huawei, "Huawei P20," accessed October 1, 2019, https://consumer.huawei.com/en/phones/p20/.

18. Paul Goldberger, "On Madison Avenue, Sometimes Less Is Less," *New York Times,* October 27, 1996, http://www.nytimes.com/1996/10/27/arts/on-madison-avenue-sometimes-less-is-less.html.

19. John Pawson, *Calvin Klein Collections Store*, Johnpawson.com, accessed June 1, 2017, http://www.johnpawson.com/works/calvin-klein-collections-store.

20. Walter Isaacson, "How Steve Jobs' Love of Simplicity Fueled a Design Revolution," *Smithsonian Magazine*, September 24, 2012, https://www.smithsonianmag.com/arts-culture/how-steve-jobs-love-of-simplicity-fueled-a-design-revolution-23868877/.

21. Ted Gibson and Bevil R. Conway, "The World Has Millions of Colors. Why Do We Only Name a Few?" *Smithsonian Magazine*, September 19, 2017, https://www.smithsonianmag.com/science-nature/why-different-languages-name-different-colors-180964945/.

22. Lev Nusberg, "Cybertheater," *Leonardo* 2 (1969): 61–62, https://monoskop.org/images/a/af/Nusberg_Lev_1969_Cybertheater.pdf.

23. Hadley Feingold, "Sculptural Fashion: Volume, Structure, and the Body," *Textile Arts Center* (blog), January 15, 2018, http://textileartscenter.com/blog/sculptural-fashion-volume-structure-and-the-body.

24. Tor D. Wager, Lauren Y. Atlas, Martin A. Lindquist, Mathieu Roy, Choong-Wan Woo, and Ethan Kross, "An fMRI-Based Neurologic Signature of Physical Pain," *New England Journal of Medicine* 368 (2013): 1388–1397.

25. Jeffrey Bardzell, "Interaction Criticism: An Introduction to the Practice," *Interacting with Computers* 23 (2011): 604–621.

26. Emotiv, "MyEmotiv," accessed September 18, 2019, https://www.emotiv.com/myemotiv/.

27. Affectiva, "Affectiva Automotive AI," accessed December 16, 2018, https://www.affectiva.com/product/affectiva-automotive-ai/.

28. Peter Weibel and Jeffrey Shaw, *Future Cinema: The Cinematic Imaginary after Film* (Cambridge, MA: MIT Press, 2003); Cristiane Paul, *Digital Art* (London: Thames and Hudson, 2003); Lucy Bullivant, *Responsive Environments: Architecture, Art and Design*, (London: Victoria and Albert Museum, 2006).

29. On progress in *neurocinema* (the field of measuring brain reactions to films), see Aalto University, "Nolan Film 'Memento' Reveals How the Brain Remembers and Interprets Events

from Clues," *Medical Press*, February 22, 2018, https://medicalxpress.com/news/2018-02-nolan-memento-reveals-brain-events.html.

30. Kevin Gray and Barry Gills, "South–South Cooperation and the Rise of the Global South," *Third World Quarterly* 37, no. 4 (2016): 557–574.

31. Martin Muller, "In Search of the Global East: Thinking between North and South," *Geopolitics*, October 2008, 1–22, https://doi.org/10.1080/14650045.2018.1477757.

32. Tuvikene, quoted in Wladimir Zbignev, "Theorizing Cities from/with a Global East," *Connections*, September 14, 2018, https://www.connections.clio-online.net/event/id/termine-38138.

33. Lev Manovich, *Software Takes Command*, rev. ed. (London: Bloomsbury Academic, 2013).

34. Wikipedia, "List of Subcultures," accessed August 12, 2016, https://en.wikipedia.org/wiki/List_of_subcultures.

35. Geoffrey C. Bowker and Susan L. Star, *Sorting Things Out: Classification and Its Consequences* (Cambridge, MA: MIT Press, 2000), https://www.ics.uci.edu/~gbowker/classification/. Emphasis in original.

36. Johan Bollen, Herbert Van de Sompel, Aric Hagberg, Luis Bettencourt, Ryan Chute, Marko A. Rodriguez, and Lyudmila Balakireva, "Clickstream Data Yields High-Resolution Maps of Science," *PLOS ONE* 4, no. 3 (2009), https://doi.org/10.1371/journal.pone.0004803; Katy Börner, Richard Klavans, Michael Patek, Angela M. Zoss, Joseph R. Biberstine, Robert P. Light, Vincent Larivière, and Kevin W. Boyack, "Design and Update of a Classification System: The UCSD Map of Science," *PLOS ONE* 7, no. 7 (2012), https://doi.org/10.1371/journal.pone.0039464.

37. Katy Börner at al, "Design and Update of a Classification System: The UCSD Map of Science."

38. Richard Klavans and Kevin Boyack, "Toward an Objective, Reliable and Accurate Method for Measuring Research Leadership," *Scientometrics* 82 (2010): 539–553.

39. Michel Foucault, *Les mots et les choses: Une archéologie des sciences humaines* (Paris: Éditions Gallimard, 1966).

40. Software Studies Initiative, "ImagePlot Visualisation Software," 2011, accessed March 1, 2020, http://lab.softwarestudies.com/p/imageplot.html.

41. Van Gogh Museum, "Meet Vincent," accessed July 31, 2016, vangoghmuseum.nl.

42. Van Gogh Museum, "Arles 1888–1889," accessed July 31, 2016, vangoghmuseum.nl.

43. Van Gogh Museum, "Arles 1888–1889," accessed July 31, 2016, vangoghmuseum.nl.

44. For additional examples, see Lev Manovich, *Style Space: How to Compare Image Sets and Follow Their Evolution*, 2011, accessed March 1, 2010, http://manovich.net/index.php/projects/style-space.

45. Franco Moretti, *Graphs, Maps, Trees: Abstract Models for a Literary History* (London: Verso, 2005). See also "Pamphlets," Stanford Literary Lab, accessed September 18, 2019, https://litlab.stanford.edu/pamphlets/.

46. Ted Underwood and Jordan Sellers, "The Emergence of Literary Diction," *Journal of Digital Humanities* 1, no. 2 (2012), http://journalofdigitalhumanities.org/1-2/the-emergence-of-literary -diction-by-ted-underwood-and-jordan-sellers/; Ted Underwood, Michael L. Black, Loretta Auvil, and Boris Capitanu, "Mapping Mutable Genres in Structurally Complex Volumes," arXiv.org, September 18, 2013, https://arxiv.org/abs/1309.3323; Ted Underwood, "The Life Cycles of Genres," *Cultural Analytics* 1 (May 23, 2016), http://culturalanalytics.org/2016/05/the-life-cycles-of-genres.

47. Lev Manovich, *One Million Manga Pages*, 2010 research report, March 1, 2020, http://lab .softwarestudies.com/2010/11/one-million-manga-pages.html.

48. Jeremy Douglass, William Huber, and Lev Manovich, "Understanding Scanlation: How to Read One Million Fan-Translated Manga Pages," *Image and Narrative* (Winter 2011), http:// manovich.net/index.php/projects/understanding-scanlation. For history of the OneManga site, see http://fanlore.org/wiki/OneManga, accessed October 26, 2016.

49. Nanjing University of the Arts, "Disciplines," accessed December 28, 2018, http://en.nua .edu.cn/2639/list.htm.

50. The New School, "Undergraduate Academics," accessed December 28, 2018, https://www .newschool.edu/academics/undergraduate/.

51. Mehrdad Yazdani, Jay Chow, and Lev Manovich, "Quantifying the Development of User-Generated Art during 2001–2010," *PLOS One*, August 7, 2017, http://journals.plos.org/plosone/ article?id=10.1371/journal.pone.0175350.

52. Eugene Garfield, "Citation Indexes for Science: A New Dimension in Documentation through Association of Ideas," *Science* 122, no. 3159 (1955): 108–111, https://doi.org/10.1126/ science.122.3159.108.

53. Tim Ingham, "World's Top 5 Music Publishers Now Control 11 Million Songs," *Music Business Worldwide*, May 25, 2015, https://www.musicbusinessworldwide.com/top-5-publishers-now -control-11m-songs/.

54. Kim Albrecht, "Cultural Development in Movie History," *Culturegraphy*, accessed September 18, 2019, https://www.culturegraphy.com/extras/findings/.

55. Kim Albrecht, "Cultural Development in Movie History."

56. Albrecht, "Cultural Development in Movie History."

57. Nadav Hochman and Lev Manovich, "A View from Above: Exploratory Visualizations of the Thomas Walther Collection," in *Object:Photo. Modern Photographs: The Thomas Walther Collection 1909–1949*, ed. Mitra Abbaspour, Lee Ann Daffner, and Maria Morris Hambourg (New York: Museum of Modern Art, 2014), 1–6, http://www.moma.org/interactives/objectphoto/assets/ essays/Manovich_Hochman.pdf.

58. Gallup, *Gallup Global Wellbeing: The Behavioral Economics of GDP Growth* (Washington, DC: Gallup, 2010), http://www.gallup.com/poll/126965/gallup-global-wellbeing.aspx.

59. Jean-Paul Benzécri, *L'Analyse des Données*, vol. 2, *L'Analyse des Correspondances* (Paris: Dunod, 1973). Correspondence analysis is available in various statistical software environments, including R.

60. Weibo, accessed August 12, 2016, http://d.weibo.com/.

61. Mitch Joel, "We Need a Better Definition of 'Native Advertising,'" *Harvard Business Review*, February 13, 2013, https://hbr.org/2013/02/we-need-a-better-definition-of.

62. Presentations during Advertising Week NYC 2016, New York, September 26–30, 2016.

63. Andrew Bosworth, "What's the History of the Awesome Button (that Eventually Became the Like Button) on Facebook?," Quora, October 17, 2014, https://www.quora.com/Whats-the-history-of-the-Awesome-Button-that-eventually-became-the-Like-button-on-Facebook.

64. Bart de Langhe, Philip M. Fernbach, and Donald R. Lichtenstein, "Navigating by the Stars: Investigating the Actual and Perceived Validity of Online User Rating," *Journal of Consumer Research* 42, no. 6 (2016): 817–833.

8 Information Visualization

1. William Playfair, *An Inquiry into the Permanent Causes of the Decline and Fall of Powerful and Wealthy Nations: Illustrated by Four Engraved Charts* (London: Printed for Greenland and Norris, 1805).

2. Robert Venturi, Denise Scott Brown, and Steven Izenour, *Learning from Las Vegas: The Forgotten Symbolism of Architectural Form* (Cambridge, MA: MIT Press, 1977). Emphasis in original.

3. Bruno Latour, "Tarde's Idea of Quantification," in *The Social after Gabriel Tarde: Debates and Assessments*, ed. Mattei Candea (London: Routledge, 2010), 116.

4. Eric Rodenbeck, keynote lecture at O'Reilly Emerging Technology 2008 conference, March 4, 2008.

5. "Interview: Fernanda Viégas and Martin Wattenberg from Flowing Media," *Information Aesthetics*, May 7, 2010, https://flowingdata.com/2010/05/13/interview-fernanda-vigas-and-martin-wattenberg/.

6. Google, "Public Data," accessed September 18, 2019, http://www.google.com/publicdata/directory.

7. Daniel A. Keim, Florian Mansmann, Jörn Schneidewind, and Hartmut Ziegler, "Challenges in Visual Data Analysis," in *Proceedings of Information Visualization* (Piscataway, NJ: IEEE Computer Society, 2006), 9–16, 10, https://doi.org/10.1109/IV.2006.31.

8. Helen C. Purchase, Natalia Andrienko, T. J. Jankun-Kelly, and Matthew Ward, "Theoretical Foundations of Information Visualization," in *Information Visualization: Human-Centered Issues and Perspectives*, ed. Andreas Kerren, John T. Stasko, and Jean-Daniel Fekete (Berlin: Springer, 2008), 46–64.

9. Theusrus, "Mondrian: About," accessed September 18, 2019, http://www.theusrus.de/Mondrian/.

10. For example: "In contrast to scientific visualization, information visualization typically deals with nonnumeric, nonspatial, and high-dimensional data." Chaomei Chen, "Top 10 Unsolved Information Visualization Problems," *IEEE Computer Graphics and Applications* 25, no. 4 (2005): 12–16.

11. Fernanda B. Viégas, Martin Wattenberg, and Kushal Dave, "Studying Cooperation and Conflict between Authors with History Flow Visualizations," in *Proceedings of the SIGCHI Conference on Human Factors in Computing Systems*, April 2004, 575–582, https://doi.org/10.1145/985692.985765.

12. Aaron Koblin, *Flight Patterns*, accessed September 18, 2019, http://www.aaronkoblin.com/work/flightpatterns/.

13. Processing, accessed September 18, 2019, http://processing.org/.

14. Data-Driven Documents, accessed September 18, 2019, https://d3js.org/.

15. Hadley Wickham et al,, ggplot2 (software), accessed March 1, 2020, https://ggplot2.tidyverse.org/.

16. "Harry Beck's Tube Map," Transport for London, accessed September 18, 2019, https://tfl.gov.uk/corporate/about-tfl/culture-and-heritage/art-and-design/harry-becks-tube-map.

17. Edward Tufte, *The Visual Display of Quantitative Information* (Cheshire, CT: Graphics Press, 1983); *Envisioning Information* (Cheshire, CT: Graphics Press, 1990); *Visual Explanations: Images and Quantities, Evidence and Narrative* (Cheshire, CT: Graphics Press, 1997); *Beautiful Evidence* (Cheshire, CT: Graphics Press, 2006).

18. Several definitions of information visualization from the recent literature are available at "Information Visualization," InfoVis Wiki, accessed September 27, 2019, https://infovis-wiki.net/wiki/Information_Visualization.

19. Michael Friendly and Daniel J. Denis, "1800–1849: Beginnings of Modern Data Graphics," Milestones in the History of Thematic Cartography, Statistical Graphics, and Data Visualization, accessed March 1, 2020. http://www.datavis.ca/milestones/index.php?group=1800%2B.

20. Philip Ball, *Critical Mass* (London: Arrow Books, 2004), 64–65.

21. Michael Friendly and Daniel J. Denis, Milestones in the History of Thematic Cartography, Statistical Graphics, and Data Visualization, 2001, accessed March 1, 2020, http://www.datavis.ca/milestones/.

22. Historical data is from Friendly and Denis, Milestones in the History of Thematic Cartography, Statistical Graphics, and Data Visualization.

23. Ben Fry, *Distellamap*, August 2005, accessed March 1, 2020, http://benfry.com/distellamap/.

24. Marcos Weskamp, "The Movement," December 29, 2005, https://www.flickr.com/photos/pkeenan/79036462.

25. InfoVis Lab, "Research," accessed September 18, 2019, http://ivl.slis.indiana.edu/research/.

26. Edward Tufte, "Minard's Sources—from Virginia Tufte and Dawn Finley," Edwardtufte.com, August 7, 2002, http://www.edwardtufte.com/tufte/minard.

27. Visual Complexity, "The Evolution of The Origin of Species," accessed September 19, 2019, http://www.visualcomplexity.com/vc/project.cfm?id=696.

28. Google Trends, accessed September 19, 2019, http://www.google.com/trends.

29. One important case that does not fit my analysis is the use of different tones or colors to represent terrain elevation and relief in printed topographic maps already common in the eighteenth century. In these maps, tone or color codes quantitative data rather than categories.

30. Wikipedia, "Tag Cloud," accessed July 18, 2016, http://en.wikipedia.org/wiki/Tag_cloud.

31. As an example, open-source data visualization software Mondrian 1.0, running on my 2009 Apple PowerBook laptop with a 2.8 GHz processor and 4 GB of RAM, took approximately seven seconds to render a scatter plot containing one million points.

32. Many additional examples of direct visualization can be found in the field of motion graphics: film and TV titles and graphics, commercials, and music videos. In many motion graphics, text or images are animated to create dynamically changing, meaningful patterns made from these media objects.

33. Brendan Dawes, "Cinema Redux," 2004, accessed March 1, 2020, http://brendandawes.com/projects/cinemaredux.

34. Ben Fry, "Traces," 2009, accessed March 1, 2020, https://fathom.info/traces/.

35. I have created a few visualizations that show a whole book in a single image. See http://www.flickr.com/photos/culturevis/sets/72157615900916808/; http://www.flickr.com/photos/culturevis/sets/72157622994317650/. To display the whole text of Tolstoy's *Anna Karenina* in the smallest font that can be read, I had to make a 14,000 × 6,000 pixels image—well beyond current screen resolutions.

36. Roberta Smith, "Art in Review; Mark Hansen and Ben Rubin—'Listening Post,'" *New York Times*, February 21, 2003, https://www.nytimes.com/2003/02/21/arts/art-in-review-mark-hansen-and-ben-rubin-listening-post.html.

37. To see Manual Lima's taxonomy of network display methods, select "filter by method" from the "Filter by:" dropdown," accessed March 1, 2020, www.visualcomplexity.com/vc/.

38. Latour, "Tarde's Idea of Quantification."

39. Wikipedia, "Synechdoche," Wikipedia, accessed July 18, 2016, http://en.wikipedia.org/wiki/Synecdoche.

40. Stefanie Posavec, *Writing without Words*, 2008, accessed March 1, 2020, http://www.stefanieposavec.com/writing-without-words; Martin Wattenberg, The Shape of Song, 2001, accessed March 1, 2020, http://www.bewitched.com/song.html.

41. Lev Manovich, "Data Visualization as New Abstraction and Anti-Sublime," *SMAC! 3* (2002): n.p. (San Francisco, 2002), http://manovich.net/index.php/projects/data-visualisation-as-new-abstraction-and-anti-sublime.

42. David L. Small, *Rethinking the Book* (PhD thesis, MIT, January 1999), https://acg.media.mit.edu/projects/thesis/DSThesis.pdf.

43. Ben Fry, *Valence*, 2001, accessed March 1, 2020, http://benfry.com/valence/.

44. W. Bradford Paley, *TextArc*, 2002, accessed March 1, 2020, http://wbpaley.com/brad/projects.html.

45. Frank van Ham, Martin Wattenberg, and Fernanda B. Viégas, "Mapping Text with Phrase Nets," *IEEE Transactions on Visualization and Computer Graphics* 15, no. 6 (2009): 1169–1176, https://doi.org/10.1109/TVCG.2009.165.

46. Software Studies Initiative, "Image_Graphr Outputs," Flickr, accessed September 18, 2019, https://www.flickr.com/photos/culturevis/sets/72157617847338031/.

47. Wayne Rasband, ImageJ, accessed September 20, 2019, https://imagej.nih.gov/ij/.

48. Lev Manovich, "Cultural Analytics Visualizations on Ultra High Resolution Displays," Software Studies Initiative, December 24, 2008, http://lab.softwarestudies.com/2008/12/cultural-analytics-hiperspace-and.html.

49. Humanities+Digital Visual Interpretations Conference: Aesthetics, Methods, and Critiques of Information Visualization in the Humanities, Arts, and Social Sciences, conference at Massachusetts Institute of Technology, Cambridge, Massachusetts, May 22–22, 2010, https://www.iri.centrepompidou.fr/evenement/humanitiesdigital-visual-interpretations-conference-2010/.

50. It is possible, however, that our interactive interfaces with visualizations are effective precisely because they do provide certain reduction functions. I am thinking in particular about the zoom command. We zoom into direct visualizations such as *Time* covers to examine the details of particular covers. We zoom out to see the overall trends. When we do that, the images are gradually reduced in size, eventually becoming small color dots.

9   Exploratory Media Analysis

1. John W. Tukey, *Exploratory Data Analysis* (Reading, MA: Addison-Wesley, 1977).

2. "Chronicling America: Historic American Newspapers," Library of Congress, accessed July 7, 2019, http://chroniclingamerica.loc.gov/.

3. Internet Archive, accessed February 20, 2020, https://archive.org/.

4. "Art Now", Flickr group, accessed July 7, 2016, http://www.flickr.com/groups/37996597808@ N01/.

5. Coroflot, "About Us," accessed July 7, 2016, http://www.coroflot.com/about.

6. "Prints & Photographs Online Catalog," Library of Congress, accessed July 7, 2016. http:// www.loc.gov/pictures/.

7. Flickr, "The App Garden," accessed July 7, 2016, http://www.flickr.com/services/api/.

8. For more details, see Steve Stemler, "An Overview of Content Analysis," *Practical Assessment, Research & Evaluation* 7, no. 17 (2001), http://PAREonline.net/getvn.asp?v=7&n=17.

9. Calvin N. Mooers, *The Theory of Digital Handling of Non-Numerical Information and Its Implications to Machine Economics* (Boston: Zator Co., 1950).

10. Mooers, *The Theory of Digital Handling*, 1–2. Emphasis added.

11. Calvin N. Mooers, *Scientific Information Retrieval Systems for Machine Operation: Case Studies in Design* (Boston: Zator Co., 1951), 3.

12. Mooers, *The Theory of Digital Handling*, 2. Emphasis added.

13. Vannevar Bush, "As We May Think," *Atlantic Monthly*, July 1945, http://web.mit.edu/STS .035/www/PDFs/think.pdf.

14. Today, scientists do not keep up with research by moving from references in one article to other articles and sites; instead, they search giant databases and depositories of science publications and data, such as ACM, arXiv, IEEE, PubMed, ProQuest, Web of Science, ScienceDirect, and many others. And because science publishing is highly structured, with articles and conference papers including subject categories, keywords, overviews of related research with many citations, and ID numbers, all being generated automatically for each new publication, the database paradigm works quite well.

15. These features correspond to the Instagram UI as of March 2019. The interface can change in the future: new functions can be added and older ones altered.

16. This description applies to versions of these applications and apps as of March 2019.

17. Lev Manovich, Moritz Stefaner, Mehrdad Yazdani, Dominikus Baur, Daniel Goddemeyer, Alise Tifentale, Nadav Hochman, and Jay Chow, *Selfiecity,* a website and custom interactive app, 2014, and *Selfiecity London,* a website and custom interactive app, 2015, http://selfiecity.net/ and http://selfiecity.net/london/; Daniel Goddemeyer, Moritz Stefaner, Dominikus Baur, and Lev Manovich, *On Broadway,* interactive artwork for touch display, 2014, http://on-broadway.nyc.

18. Wikipedia, "Digital Image Processing," accessed June 6, 2016, http://en.wikipedia.org/wiki/ Digital_image_processing.

19. "Text Analysis," Tooling up for Digital Humanities, accessed July 27, 2016, http://toolingup .stanford.edu/?page_id=981.

20. Voyant, accessed September 20, 2019, https://voyant-tools.org; Matthew Jockers, *Text Analysis with R for Students of Literature* (Berlin: Springer, 2014).

21. For an explanation of image features learned by convolutional networks, see Matthew D. Zeiler and Rob Fergus, *Visualizing and Understanding Convolutional Networks*, ArXiv.org, November 12, 2013, https://arxiv.org/abs/1311.2901.

22. For discussion of computer vision adoption in photography services and phone cameras, see Lev Manovich, *AI Aesthetics* (Moscow: Strelka Press, 2018).

23. Clarifai, "Models," accessed September 20, 2019, https://clarifai.com/models.

24. David Ramli and Shelly Banjo, "The Kids Use TikTok Now Because Data-Mined Videos Are So Much Fun," *Bloomsburg BusinessWeek*, April 17, 2019, http://www.bloomberg.com/news/features/2019-04-18/tiktok-brings-chinese-style-censorship-to-america-s-tweens.

25. Mehrdad Yazdani and Lev Manovich, "Predicting Social Trends from Non-photographic Images on Twitter," in *Proceedings of the 2015 IEEE International Conference on Big Data* (Washington, DC: IEEE Computer Society, 2015), 1653–1660.

26. Miriam Redi, Damon Crockett, and Lev Manovich, "What Makes Photo Cultures Different?," in *Proceedings of the 24th ACM International Conference on Multimedia* (New York: ACM, 2016), 287–291.

27. Yale Digital Humanities Lab, "Neural Neighbors: Capturing Image Similarity," accessed October 1, 2019, https://dhlab.yale.edu/projects/neural-neighbors/.

28. Konstantinos Rematas, Basura Fernando, Frank Dellaert, and Tinne Tuytelaars, "Dataset Fingerprints: Exploring Image Collections through Data Mining," in *Proceedings of the IEEE Conference on Computer Vision and Pattern Recognition* (Washington, DC: IEEE Computer Society, 2015), 4867–4875.

29. Benoît Seguin, *Making Large Art Historical Photo Archives Searchable* (Lausanne: EPFL, 2018), https://infoscience.epfl.ch/record/261212?ln=en.

30. Seguin, *Making Large Art Historical Photo Archives Searchable*, 118.

10   Methods of Media Visualization

1. John Unsworth, "Scholarly Primitives: What Methods Do Humanities Researchers Have in Common, and How Might our Tools Reflect This?," Humanities Computing Symposium, May 13, 2000, King's College, London, accessed October 1, 2019, http://www.people.virginia.edu/~jmu2m/Kings.5-00/primitives.html.

2. Tiago Ferreira and Wayne Rasband, *ImageJ User Guide*, last updated October 2, 2012, https://imagej.nih.gov/ij/docs/guide/index.html.

3. John W. Tukey, *Exploratory Data Analysis* (Reading, MA: Addison-Wesley, 1977).

4. Damon Crockett, "ivpy," GitHub, accessed October 1, 2019, http://github.com/damoncrockett/ivpy.

5. Apple, "Photos," accessed July 17, 2016, http://www.apple.com/ios/photos/.

6. M. Albanese et al., "Video Summarization," in *Encyclopedia of Multimedia*, ed. B. Furht (Boston: Springer, 2006), https://doi.org/10.1007/0-387-30038-4.

7. Stuart Hall, *Encoding and Decoding in the Television Discourse* (Birmingham: Centre for Contemporary Cultural Studies, 1973).

8. Stuart Hall, "Encoding/Decoding," in *Culture, Media, Language: Working Papers in Cultural Studies, 1972–79*, ed. Stuart Hall (London: Hutchinson, 1980), 128–138.

9. Hall, "Encoding/Decoding."

10. Drake Baer, "Why Data God Jeffrey Hammerbacher Left Facebook to Found Cloudera," *Fast Company*, April 18, 2013, http://www.fastcompany.com/3008436/takeaway/why-data-god-jeffrey-hammerbacher-left-facebook-found-cloudera.

11. Nick Yee, "The Demographics, Motivations and Derived Experiences of Users of Massively Multi-User Online Graphical Environments," *Presence: Teleoperators and Virtual Environments* 15, no. 3 (2006): 309–329.

12. Ferreira and Rasband, *ImageJ User Guide*.

13. Jeffrey M. Perkel, "Life Science Technologies: This Is Your Brain: Mapping the Connectome," *Science* 339, no. 6117 (January 18, 2013): 350–352, https://doi.org/10.1126/science.339.6117.350.

14. Johannes Schindelin, Curtis T. Rueden, Mark C. Hiner, and Kevin W. Eliceiri, "The ImageJ Ecosystem: An Open Platform for Biomedical Image Analysis," *Molecular Reproduction and Development* 82, no. 7–8 (2015): 518–529, https://doi.org/10.1002/mrd.22489; Ferreira and Rasband, *ImageJ User Guide*.

15. Ferreira and Rasband, ch. 28, sec. 6 ("Stacks") in *ImageJ User Guide*.

16. Ferreira and Rasband, ch. 28, sec. 6 ("Stacks") in *ImageJ User Guide*.

17. For a very good discussion of general sampling concepts as they apply to digital humanities, see Anthony Kenny, *The Computation of Style: An Introduction to Statistics for Students of Literature and Humanities* (Oxford: Pergamon Press, 1982).

18. Jesse Alpert and Nissan Hajaj, "We Knew the Web Was Big . . . ," *Google Official Blog*, July 25, 2008, http://googleblog.blogspot.com/2008/07/we-knew-web-was-big.html.

19. Marco Brambilla, *Civilization (Megaplex)*, 2008, high-definition 3D video, https://www.marcobrambilla.com/civilization-megaplex.

20. Wiktionary, "Browse," accessed July 28, 2016, http://en.wiktionary.org/wiki/browse.

21. Wiktionary, "Explore," accessed July 28, 2016, http://en.wiktionary.org/wiki/explore.

Conclusion

1. Lev Manovich, *AI Aesthetics* (Moscow: Strelka Press, 2018).

2. The concept of "cultural techniques" has been mostly used in recent German media theory. See Geoffrey Winthrop-Young, Ilinca Irascu, and Jussi Parikka, eds., "Cultural Techniques," special issue, *Theory, Culture & Society* 30, no. 6 (November 2013).

3. Nicolas Truong and Nicolas Weill, "A Decade after His Death, French Sociologist Pierre Bourdieu Stands Tall," *Guardian*, February 21, 2012, https://www.theguardian.com/world/2012/feb/21/pierre-bourdieu-philosophy-most-quoted.

4. The term *cultural omnivore* was developed by American sociologist Richard Peterson. See Richard Peterson, "Understanding Audience Segmentation: From Elite and Mass to Omnivore and Univore," *Poetics* 21, no. 4 (1992): 243–258.

5. Minsu Park et al., "Understanding Musical Diversity via Online Social Media," in *Proceedings of the Ninth International AAAI Conference on Web and Social Media* (Oxford: AAAI Press, 2016), 308–317, http://www.aaai.org/ocs/index.php/ICWSM/ICWSM15/paper/view/10570.

6. See, for example, Jordan DeLong, "Horseshoes, Handgrenades, and Model Fitting: The Lognormal Distribution Is a Pretty Good Model for Shot-Length Distribution of Hollywood Films," *Digital Scholarship in the Humanities* 30, no. 1 (2015): 129–136.

7. Franco Moretti, *Atlas of the European Novel: 1800–1900* (London: Verso, 1998), 150.

8. Agustin Indaco and Lev Manovich, *Urban Social Media Inequality: Definition, Measurements, and Application*, arXiv.org, July 7, 2016, https://arxiv.org/abs/1607.01845.

9. Inna Kizhner et al., "The History and Context of the Digital Humanities in Russia," paper presented at the Digital Humanities 2018 conference, Mexico City, June 26–29, 2018, https://dh2018.adho.org/the-history-and-context-of-the-digital-humanities-in-russia.

10. Internet Archive, accessed September 10, 2019, https://archive.org.

Index

Page numbers followed by f refer to figures.